Alastair Aitken was born in Edinburgh and educated at Langley School in Norfolk. He has been an insurance claims broker in the City of London for over 35 years, and has always had a deep love for athletics. His first article on the subject was published when he was 18 years old. He ran in the first 19 London Marathons, and has been an accredited journalist at many major athletics meetings. His previous books on athletes and athletics, *More Than Winning* (1992) and *The Winning Edge* (1998), are also published by The Book Guild. He is married to Joanna, a theatre agent, and lives in South London. Aitken's son Andrew, who was a school and club runner, thought of the title *Athletics Enigmas*, as he did Alastair's previous two titles.

By the same author:

More Than Winning, The Book Guild 1992

The Winning Edge, The Book Guild 1998

ATHLETICS ENIGMAS

Alastair Aitken

The Book Guild Ltd
Sussex, England

First published in Great Britain in 2002 by
The Book Guild Ltd
25 High Street,
Lewes, East Sussex
BN7 2LU

Typesetting in Times by
Keyboard Services, Luton, Bedfordshire

Printed in Great Britain by
Athenaeum Press Ltd, Gateshead

A catalogue record for this book is available from
The British Library

ISBN 1 85776 603 2

*I dedicate this book to
Spartan and Mippy.*

CONTENTS

Gerrard Long, Jason Henderson, Steve Roe, Richard Priestly, Andy Catton, Robin Dickson, Tony & Mick Harran, Mick Mcleod, Bernie Ford, Brendan Foster, Tony Simmons, Mike Turner, Tony Milovsorov, Ricky Goad, Eamonn Martin, Alex Roe, Rachid Banouas, Scott Tompsett, Andy Morcombe, Hayley Yelling, Andy Hayward, Sharon Murphy, Ossie Arif, Lucy Elliott, Nick Bideau, Sonia O'Sullivan, Danielle Sanderson, John Sullivan, John Goodbody, Snowy Brooks, Ollie Flynn, James Mayo, Dave Cropper, Gary Oakes, Mike Bellingham, Al Oerter, Mel Watman, John Pennel, Ato Bolden, Nick Phipps, Stan Greenberg

(Payne), Bill Gentleman, Sylvester Stein, Howard Williams, Pete Mulholland, Gowrey Hodge (Retchakan), Jenny Mathews, Ian Chadband, Judy Oakes, Zara Hyde-Peters, Tom Petranoff, Jan Zelezny, Bill Collins, Al Oerter, Malcolm Fenton, Guido Mueller, John Gilmour, Charlie Dickinson, Les Presland, Ron Robertson, Tony Simmons, Ken Crooke, Dave Jones, Derek Thomas, Phil Lancaster, Alan Meddings, Charlie Williams, Ron Taylor, Bill Guy, Byron Gray, Evaun Williams, Bill Stoddart, John Henson, Walter Wilkinson, Sheila Carey, Rod Parker, Tom McNab, Maeve Kyle, Kate Hoey, Joe Caines, Anthony Whiteman, Steve Kemp, Steve Allen, Roger Mills, Pete Barber, Laurie Forster, Roger Honey, Tony Wells, Phillip Delbaugh, John Emmett Farrell, Earl Fee, Martin Duff, Jean Hulls, John Robinson, Pete Browne, Eric Smart, Jenny Gray, Judy Oakley, Clare Pauzers, Vince Hancock

Doogan, Tim Stobbs, Bill Foster, Seamus Kerr, Richard Nerurkar, Ray Auerback, Margaret Auerback, David Martin & Roger Gynn, Dave Taylor, Steve Smythe, Mark Steinle, Mark Watling, Mike Gratton, Stuart Major, Pat Collins, Dave Walsh, Jamie Lewis, Chris Holloway, Keith Anderson, Pat 'Paddy' Farrelly, Dave Cooper, Don Ritchie, Dave Beattie, Bruce Fordyce, Ian Champion, Ron Hopcroft, Peter Sugden, Andy Milroy, Carolyn Hunter-Rowe, Stephen Moore, Rae Bisscoff, Shaun Meiklejohn, Clyde Marwick, Sarel Ackerman, Danielle Sanderson, James Zarie, Derek Wood

1

Gordon Pirie in Retrospect

I devoted Chapter 5 of my first book 'More Than Winning' published 1992, to Douglas Alastair Gordon Pirie, who was born in Leeds on the 10th of February 1931 and died 7th of December 1991. The off the cuff interview I had with him was from 1hr 50 minutes of tape and done in 1989, as he drove me round the roads in Dorset. Despite having written another book since then called 'The Winning Edge' I have found that Pirie's comments seem to have created more interest in the athletics fraternity than anybody else's. Added to that fact Dick Booth wrote a very good book about Gordon Pirie called 'The Impossible Hero' published in 1999, but I still felt that nearly always Gordon preferred to be his own spokesman in no uncertain terms. So, with that in mind, I have decided to lengthen considerably the original chapter, with a lot of additional comment from the man himself.

Gordon's father Alick Pirie also ran for South London Harriers and was a Scottish International cross-country runner. His brothers Ian and Peter Pirie (National Youth Champion of 1947) were good runners and in fact Peter was the top senior when Gordon was the best junior at Purley County Grammar School. Gordon was married to former international sprinter Shirley Hampton and they had two daughters, Jing Guang and Sara. Among the guests at Gordon's wedding was an old friend of Gordon's the ex-hurdler Keith Whitaker, who is now the well respected President of the British Veterans Athletic Federation.

Enter Gordon: 'I won the Victor Ludorum at Purley County

School. I had the high jump record and played table tennis in club tournaments and won 11–0 in some games.

'When I look back now, I realise that what is going on now at the Olympic Games is anti-sport. Sport is fun. I was lucky I had some elements which enabled me to go and run in the Olympics. I was doing it for the hell of it. There are so many who are doing it for cash. People should want to do sport for fun as often as they can. It is really good fun when you have a relay race down with the guys in the club. We have a good laugh. We are all fired up and going like "hell", that is what sport is about. I think because of the money and regimentation that has changed. When the President of America stopped them going to the Moscow Olympics, all that generation could say was "We are ruined!" I say "Poor People!". If their whole life is centred round a pool for a few seconds – we are poor sissies. I think that is a load of rubbish! I saw a fellow yesterday doing his gardening in a wheelchair. How many would do that? You are either in the gutter like the football fan or you are doing something. It doesn't matter what you do as long as you do something.'

Walter Hesketh, the National Cross Country Champion of 1952

'Walter Hesketh beat me as a junior. He was very strong. When we ran the National in 1948 in Sheffield he won the youth race by quite a margin. He was already a mature man then, whereas I was a skinny little overgrown kid. I was a long way back. I did not get mature till five years later while he had at sixteen, like Jack Price and Eddy Ellis. There are a lot of runners like that who are very early to maturity.

'I won the Southern Junior by $2\frac{1}{2}$ minutes. I was running quite well there. I won the Surrey Senior and beat Charlie Walker by 2 minutes who was seventh in the Inter-Counties. I remember the best I ran abroad over the country was in Hannut.'

2

Gordon Pirie won the 'National' in 1953, 1954 and 1955

'In 1955 my club, South London Harriers, made history. We won every team race. Youth, Senior and Junior. You can't do that.

'We had a phenomenal group of runners. We were powered up. We got individual medals in all the races. What a senior team we had, with Ray Ashworth getting the Ottoway Cup for being the first non-scorer for the winning team in 32nd position. We had a phenomenal team of six. There is nothing like that any more. We had Roly Langridge who trained me. He was the Junior Champion.' (The winning team also included Roy Darchambaud, Ferdie Gilson and Laurie Reed. The latter will be remembered for his epic finish with Hugh Foord one year in the Senior Inter-Counties 6 miles. Ferdie Gilson was the President of South London Harriers in 2000–2002.)

'I did not continue forcing cross-country because I ran the National in 1955, a race where I had already 100 yards or more lead before running into the crowd. I met Jimmy Green much later on and he never told me that he never knew I ran into the crowd. In his resumé he had said that of all the runners Pirie was not running too well because he did not have any lead when he came round for the last lap. My answer to that was I had destroyed my lead by 100 yards and then I ran away from them by about 300 yards. When I ran away from them again I remember thinking "This is not interesting any more, I will do track running" because that had a more interesting challenge to it.'

In 1952 Gordon had the chance to run against his idol Zatopek

The Olympic Games were at Helsinki and Pirie ran in the 10,000 and then the 5000, both being dramatic for Pirie. It was after those games he was taken under the wing of coach Woldemar Gerschler and was helped with all Gerschler's many ideas but, one must remember, a radical thinker like Gordon

3

was still very much his own man when it came to training and racing.

The 10,000 result was 1. Emil Zatopek (Czechoslovakia) 29:17.0; 2. Alain Mimoun (France) 29:32.8; 3. Herbert Schade (Germany) 29:48.2 with brave Frank Sando, running most of the way with one shoe, fifth. And Pirie seventh in 30:09.5, but Gordon Pirie relates:

'In the Olympic 10,000 in Helsinki I went with Emil Zatopek and Alain Mimoun. There were just three of us left in the front at four miles, and then I was put in a coffin athletically and I don't know what I did to complete the race. If I had wanted to disregard Zatopek I could have been third in the race, but my attitude is that if I am going to run against somebody I am going to slug it out with them. Of course many people have said down the years, "You are crazy: you started too fast", but I said, "Later on I am going to run the whole race like that" – which I did when I beat Vladimir Kuts and the Hungarians.' (World record of 13:36.8 for 5000m against Vladimir Kuts – 19th of June 1956, and 3000m world record of 7:52.8 on 4th of September 1956 – beating Istvan Rozsavolgyi, Sandor Iharos and Laslo Tabori. One must not forget he also had a world record when beating the Polish 1958 European Champions Jerzy Chromik and Zdzislaw Kryzyszkowiak, 7:55.5 on 22nd June 1956.)

In the Olympic 5000m in 1952 the first five were 1. Zatopek (14:06.6), 2. Mimoun (14.07.4), 3. Schade (14:08.6), 4. Pirie (14:18.0), 5. Chataway (GB) (14:18.0).

'Zatopek was stronger,' Chataway remembered. 'I always kicked from the beginning of the back straight, so that was what I did. I overtook Zatopek right at the beginning of the back straight, and led the way up the straight and round the bend. I was pretty tired by then, and I hit my foot against the raised kerb on the inside of the track and fell. By the time I got up Mimoun and Shade had gone past me, but I certainly would not have won it. If I had left my kick to the home straight, which I probably ought to have done, and had I not fallen over, I would certainly have got third and might even have got second, I suppose. But I would not have beaten Zatopek.'

4

Gordon comes in, 'I did not know he had fallen, but when we were staggering across the middle to get our gear I saw he had this terrible graze. It was only then I found out he had tripped over. I was running in oblivion; all I saw was him in front of me and I just nipped him on the tape. That nearly caused me to give up athletics, because the British press never spoke to me but slammed me and criticised me as a bad sportsman for passing Chataway when he had tried so hard. I had tried hard too. Chataway himself and Geoff Dyson, the national coach, advised me not to take any notice of the press, and they soothed me down. To this day, I have not had justice from the press in this country.'

Gordon Pirie achieved a silver medal in the Olympics of 1956 in Melbourne in the 5000m in the year he achieved the world record of 13:36.8, but again (before the 5000m final) paid a heavy price, like he did with Zatopek in 1952, by sticking to Kuts in the Olympic 10,000m. Kuts kept surging and dropped Pirie, who eventually fell back to eighth place.

There were some descriptive press comments. Desmond Hackett in the *Daily Express* called Gordon Pirie 'The Bean Pole Prince of Pace' – 'Puff Puff Pirie'. I remember Neil Allen used to write knowledgeably about athletics in *The Times* which created much interest for the aficionados.

'Galloping Gordon' or 'Puff Puff Pirie' if you prefer that description, created fantastic excitement. I can remember seeing full houses for purely duel meets at the White City, something unimaginable these days, mostly created at the time by the man himself. There was the time Pirie was followed by that great character Frank Salvat (a one-eyed runner with a great sense of humour, who smoked cigars, and introduced me to a beer drinking club in Kensington). They destroyed two talented Frenchmen, Michel Bernard and Robert Bogey on the White City cinders, and at the same venue over 5000m in August 1957, Gordon Pirie followed by the 'favourite' Derek Ibbotson (who broke the mile world record in 1957) took the Soviet runners to the cleaners, and that included 1960 Olympic 10,000m champion Pytor Bolotnikov.

Gordon Pirie could also bring off the biggest surprises ever seen on these shores. On a Saturday at the British Whitsun Games he was not far off last in the 800 and mile, but came back on the Monday (28th of May, 1958) and clinched victory in the International 2 miles, beating the Hungarian Doctor Nicolas Szabo right on the tape, with Derek Ibbotson and Stan Eldon, a fine cross country runner, in his wake. One year Gordon got ranked among the world's best over 1500, 5000 and 10,000.

There is one race I would like to single out as the most exciting race I have seen because it had such an unexpected result. It was a mile race, despite the time not being near 4 minutes, which was something Pirie achieved (3:59.9). It was the first ever Emsley Carr Mile on the 18th of August, 1953, sponsored by the *News of the World*. As my Father Colonel David Aitken was a wartime friend of the manager of the White City Stadium, Captain Wally Eyres, my brother Ian and I, as lads, always had really good seats either in the restaurant overlooking the finish or in the best seats below it. That really started my love for athletics! My father was unlikely to be moved by most sporting events, having been toughened by being in active service in two World Wars and obtaining DFC (First World War), OBE, DSO, Croix de Guerre (with Palms), Légion d'Honneur and American Cross, but, after the race that Gordon Pirie will talk about, tears of sheer joy were falling down his face, as the capacity White City crowd roared Pirie home, the noise reverberating round the arena, as it only could at the White City Stadium. The race had comprised Wes Santee of the United States who was considered one the top milers in the world in 1953, Bill Nankeville, who was four times AAA Champion and father of comedian Bobby Davro, and the man who helped Roger Bannister to do his 4 minute mile in 1954, Chris Chataway. As a matter of fact at the time Pirie was considered more a 5 and 10k plus cross country man. Also in the race for Sir William Carr's trophy was Olaf Lawrenz of Germany and Ingvar Eriksson of Sweden, both rated in the top 20 1500m of all time, as printed on the 1st of September, 1955. Prior to the race four world mile record holders were driven round the cinders of the White City in a lap of honour. They were the current world record holder at the time

6

Gunder Haegg from Sweden (4:01.3 in 1945), Paavo Nurmi (Finland), Sydney Wooderson and Joe Binks.

Gordon explains, 'Nobody has seen my training books, but if they did they would say, "You are a complete lunatic. It is physically impossible to do that." So, when I went to a race I knew that going around the track, even for twenty-four laps, was a kind of a sprint – that "National" cross country was a sprint, because when you run five hours a day running an hour to forty-five minutes is a joke. You just go full out; as for the mile, it is a sprint, but the other factor in the mile was the intelligence to run the race properly. In the Emsley Carr Mile I knew, if we all sat around, there were some real good little sprinters off the bend, so I went, as you know, with 600 to go, and ran the 200 to the bell in 29 seconds. They all looked a bit green with me at the bell, but I had decided that was what I was going to do, and I had the machinery to do it. I would say, when Santee passed me in the back straight I was just about unconscious and my body had lost the race, but my mind kept my body going, and he faded and I took him. The speed we went round there was fantastic. We went at this phenomenal pace – my vision was lost in jumps. I was hanging on, then I realised I had got a gap and it stayed the same.' (1. Pirie 4:6.8; 2. Santee 4:7.2; 3. Nankeville 4:13.8.)

Pirie tied '13 all' with Chataway in winning races against each other and an even more significant fact was the 'Very Great' Emil Zatopek in his full career, tied '3 wins all' with Pirie. However, Gordon Pirie points out of Australian Herb Elliott, the Olympic 1500m Champion in Rome, 'With him you could go home, throw your spikes in the corner and say, "Forget it as he was the epitome of a competitor!".'

Should Gordon Pirie have been picked for the Olympic 1500 in 1956? Surely that race against Santee must have said something?

'I wanted to run the 1500 at the 1956 Games; my big fight was with the British Board, and Jack Crump in particular. Before Melbourne I ran against Klaus Richtzenhain of East Germany (who came second to Ron Delaney in the final with the outstanding Australian miler John Landy third), and I beat

7

him in a personal best of 3:42.5. He only beat me at the White City because I had a car smash before the race. (1. Richtzenhain 3:43.1, 2. Pirie 3:43.4 and 3. Chataway 3:46.4.) 'I reckon I was in with a chance to get in the top six, or even the top three in the 1500, and that was what I wanted to do.'

Gordon Pirie won the AAA's 6 miles at the White City in 1951, 1952, 1953 and again in 1960 in 28.0.96. Back in 1953 he had beaten Frank Aaron's AAA's Championship Best and set a new world record of 28:19.4 (by eleven seconds) on the Friday and then, the very next day, won the AAA's 3 mile Championship in 13:43.4, ten seconds inside the Championship Best. He won the 3 miles again in 1961 in 13:31.2. About the latter, in comes Gordon shooting from the hip!

'When I read "Tulloh dominated British 3 miling in 1960", rubbish! When I ran in 1961 he was a spectator applauding me running round and winning the race in the mud. He had dropped out as did Martin Hyman, Mike Bullivant and Ibbotson. I was running incredibly well that year. When we came to run that race it was ankle deep mud. I can remember running a 4.27 and a 4.23.'

Training

Gordon Pirie, besides being a very successful international orienteer, had been involved in advising so many of the UK's best like Jim Hogan, Peter Clark, Laurie Reed and Anne Smith and top New Zealanders like Anne Audain and Alison Roe, as well as sprinters and field events exponents. There was no doubt he had a knack of treating injuries too. It's simple. 'Where is the pain and where does it hurt?' he would say, then locate it and use his hands to manipulate it! He gave me two manipulations that improved an ankle injury I had had for several years, so I could run much more comfortably again. In his later years he had some sound advice on nutrition. It is interesting to look back on his training as he was such a prolific racer.

'I have done a phenomenal mileage, and the only thing I have learned from that is don't, because when you do your greatest mileage you have the worst results. At a conservative estimate I think I have done about 280,000 miles. When I ran in Scandinavia I ran for five hours a day, and when I read articles by the McWhirters at the time, of how Jim Peters did 15 to 18 miles a day, I realised I was doing twice as much when I won the National cross country of 1953, 1954 and 1955. In one year I ran over 12,000 miles. I have done more than 365 marathons. They are a load of sissies nowadays. A grown man in the prime of his life runs a marathon and tells me a month later that he has not recovered from it. I recovered the next day.

'Here I am training some guys, really fast runners, and they do 8×200 in 25.5. I used to do ten, twice a day in 24.0. When I was at my best I was incredible. I used to go and run thirty miles in training at Tooting Bec. One of the things I did in the 30 miles was to run 330 yards and jog the bend. A lot of good runners like Peter Driver, who won the Empire Games six miles in 1954, used to say, "Where is the interval?" and I used to say "This is it". They would say "This is too fast for the interval," and I used to say "Hell, there is no interval; you just take a bit of a breather here." I would do forty of them like that. In races I set out with the idea of getting hold of the other runners like a terrier with a bone. I would smash them, destroy them.

'I've run with Chataway, Brasher and those guys, and we would run ten quarters in 61, 62, 63, I found it so boring at that speed that I would pass them in the back straight and go out and run a 55–56 with a 25 second last 200m. It was like being in a dream world when I struck that form. I would run 8×880 in 1:58 with a short interval. When you are running like that, you can't lose a race, "Hard luck you guys, I am going to kick the arse off you, and you can't do anything with me."

'I remember one of my thirty mile sessions round the track at Tooting Bec. Bill Nankeville was there, and he came down to run a couple of miles and a couple of sprints. He shouted out to me "You will kill yourself, Pirie." I said, "No, I am going to kill you" – which I did in the Emsley Carr Mile!

'If you could see the training I did, you would say I was completely nuts. I would go to places like Catford track at 9.30 in the morning, do twenty minutes of hard weights, run an hour in the park then do something like 10×600 or 8×1000, and leave at 1.30. I did that sort of training every day. Today people are sissies and there is all this rubbish they write about recovering and taking it easy.

'I wish I knew when I was running what I know now. I did some terrible things in training, and I got away with murder. I used to do enormous training and then go out and run a world record straight on top of it, whereas now I know I need ten days to freshen up. I would have done some really good times then!

'If you do stretching exercises you will get injured. That was why Aouita was injured at the Olympic Games! Everyone I have treated for injuries, they all do stretching exercises. If you have a small child, who has never been brainwashed by advertising from the big shoe companies they will run properly. If you have advertising to convince you to cripple yourself, landing on your heels, buy orthopaedic boots which cause you to run incorrectly, you get injured then you are lost. It is no accident that the Africans are the best runners. They have run barefoot all their lives. Take them to America, like Zola Budd and put shoes on their feet – Zola Budd will be injured! Some running shoes I can only go shopping in and do gardening in them or I'll get injured.'

Gordon Pirie stops running as an International

'My wife had to practically starve because we did not have enough money for each of us. We had not got enough money for me to do my training. I had run against a guy who was state-aided, trains in the winter by the Caspian Sea. It was an enormous phenomenal miracle I beat Kuts on the unequalness of the situation. The reason I stopped running in the end was because I could not afford financially to do it any more. Shirley used to sit down and have half a meal and would not have a full meal because we did not have enough money to pay for it. I did not eat enough really. If I had more money I would have eaten more.'

Farthing Down

There was no doubt Gordon Pirie enjoyed running on Farthing Down near Coulsdon, Surrey, and being with his friends at South London Harriers. His ashes are sprinkled on the place he loved so much, but he was critical of what has been done to the countryside.

'I used to run up and down Farthing Down for hours and hours. Make my own footpaths around Happy Valley. Where I used to run three hours a day they call it "Elliott Hill". What an insult! I had been running there 365 days a year! People come up on a nice sunny day and say, "Do you come here often?" I say, "Every 'Bloody' day of the year – in the dark, snow and rain!"

'They have really ruined that area with the horse track and all that kind of thing. Like in America, and it has started in New Zealand. Every park is pegged out. People have to walk this way, follow the signs, read the signs, all "Organised people activities" like George Orwell's world. The Downs used to be a big open area. Now you "Put your cars here", "Horses to go there", "Dogs go here" and so on.

'When I go round England now I nominate areas, 100 dog park, 60 dog park, 1000 dog park – Nothing to do with people – organised for dogs.'

What did other athletes and coaches think of the 'Prince of Pace'?

Johnny Macnamara the London cross country champion of 1973: 'My friend from the Poly, Pat Wilkes, considers Pirie his hero. He trained with him. I think Pirie was dedicated wasn't he!'

Pete Mulholland, a long-standing member of Hercules & Wimbledon AC, who is an athletics journalist, and writes a lot in *Athletics Weekly*: 'Pirie had determination, single mindedness, guts and he was an innovator.'

Tom Richards who is an established Surrey official and son of Tom Richards, who was in Pirie's club and came second in

11

the Olympic marathon of 1948: 'If Pirie had not run in the 10,000 metres Olympic Final in Melbourne I think instead of coming second he could have beaten Vladimir Kuts in the 5000 metres and won the gold medal.'

Don Turner, a valuable athletics official, who was twice placed in the London to Brighton road race agrees with Peter Mulholland, 'Pirie tried new things rather than following people.'

Rod Turney, from Blackheath Harriers, a friend with whom I have raced on the track, road and country and gone for runs with since 1959, remembers getting a lift back with Gordon, from the Ladywell track, Catford. Rod had done his repetitions with Blackheath Harriers' Johnny Baldwin, Peter Bond and Derek Gregory. 'Gordon was always down there doing his intervals. He is one of the elite as far as great distance runners go. He really had quite a following.'

Peter Hamilton, who has been in Blackheath's top teams before and after turning veteran: 'Herb Elliott, Ron Clarke and Pirie were three I admired. Pirie died in a nursing home very close to where my parents live. My only regret is that I never went to talk to him. He was very happy to see people. *Running Wild* by Gordon Pirie was the first running book I ever read. I thought "What a superb bloke!".'

Robin Firth, like his father Mick Firth, knew Gordon Pirie well. The Firths' coach down at Crystal Palace now, Robin was once one of the better South London Harriers distance men, till he got injured in the 1990s. His father Mick Firth, a charming ex-president of the club, came third in the National Senior cross country and was on the winning club team many times with Gordon. Robin comments about Gordon, 'He was a very entertaining man. Gordon Pirie was South London Harriers and South London Harriers was Gordon Pirie. He had so much to offer and never got the recognition he deserved. He could have been an established coach or physio at the highest level but drifted in his life unfortunately.' (I back up those points by Robin. Having read *Athletics Weekly*'s News Editor Jason Henderson's article on Irish Triathlete Gerard Hartmann on 17th of January, 2001, and about his brand of physio that has become world renowned, I seriously feel Gordon Pirie could have been in that mould, if his life had been directed towards that aim earlier in life.

Barry Attwell was once a Southern 3000m track champion and later a National Veteran Cross Country Champion. Attwell recalls: 'My idol was Gordon Pirie. It was a pity he did not coach me.' Barry continued, 'I said to him when I was on 30 miles a week, that I couldn't run around Shepherds Bush where I lived because there are no hills.' Pirie replied, "Listen, you can run up and down this road 1000 times. Don't give me excuses." I needed someone like that to say "Do it or forget it". I wish he had coached me.'

Frank Sando, who was twice International World Cross Country Champion in the 1950s and a medallist on the track in the European and Commonwealth (Empire) Games, often competed against Gordon Pirie. He talked about the ones he thought were the best he ran against. 'Zatopek, Mimoun, Kuts and Gordon Pirie of course, as he did a lot for British athletics. He did not break his training for any race.'

George Rhodes who ran for North Staffs and Stone, won national recognition as a junior, senior and veteran, was an admirer of Len Eyre then Derek Ibbotson. Rhodes ran his first International 'world' cross country in 1955. It was a powerful England team that won – Frank Sando, Gordon Pirie, Hugh Food, Ken Norris, Bill Boak, Ken Caulder and his friend Eddy Hardy. 'Gordon Pirie was another of the greats; he showed us all just what the human body could stand up to. Zatopek was perhaps the greatest of all the post-war athletes but it was Gordon that we used to run against! I remember on the trip to San Sebastian for my first international I was sitting next to Gordon on the plane, feeling very much the new boy of the team. At one point I leaned over Gordon's shoulder and pointed out the window saying, "Oh look Gordon, there's the Pyrenees." "No, no," he replied, "these are the Pirie Knees," indicating his knee caps! Gordon was an absolute fanatic for training. I remember after his failure in Rome (5k non-qualifier 14:43.6–10k 10th 29:15.2), I asked him what he had done wrong. He simply replied "I was the best interval runner in the Games".'

Roy Fowler (whose sons became good club runners) was

third in the 1962 European 10,000 and won the International 'World' Cross Country Championship. In 1963: 'I think Gordon Pirie was a great runner and I think all the English athletes owe Gordon a thank you because he was the first Englishman, in my opinion, to prove that the foreigner could be beaten. Where in England, we used to sit back, reading the books on how to do it, the foreigner was getting out there and doing the training. He had the know-how and came to the White City and rubbed our noses in it, then along came Gordon Pirie with his fantastic training schedules punishing himself and also using his brain, and eventually got there and took them on. I think men like Pirie need to be admired.'

Bruce Tulloh, who was a leading runner for Portsmouth, like Martin Hyman, the Cook brothers, and Tim Johnston, won the European 5000m in 1962 and has advised or coached great athletes like Olympian Mike Boit of Kenya and Richard Nerurkar, who won the World Cup marathon in 1993. 'Zatopek was my main inspiration. Following his ideas and his book; a great man, a very nice chap. Gordon Pirie as well has done a great deal for British athletics – showed us the way to train. Most of us have benefited from his example.'

In Memoriam

Peter Hildreth, an outstanding hurdler, author and journalist, was on the team with Gordon in three Olympics and got on well with him. Peter gave an address at Gordon Pirie's funeral on the 12th of December 1991. I thought that would be an appropriate way to conclude this chapter on such a very special note:

'The poet John Dryden once wrote some words which might well have been echoed by the friend to whose memory we have come here today to pay our respects.

I am as free as nature first made man,
Ere the base laws of servitude began,
When wild in the woods the noble savage ran.

14

'Gordon – who chose the title "Running Wild" for his auto-biography – was indeed a man who found a way to be as free as nature. Perhaps it was his nature to be free. You could never imagine him spending a lifetime as a bank clerk, or even a paint salesman. He was not cut out for the humdrum nine-to-five routine that dogs the lives of so many of us. Secretly, some of us probably envied his ability to escape from it all and fashion his own life of liberty. How he did it was by no means a soft option. On his way to the levels of track prowess which quali-fied him to travel the world on meagre expenses as an amateur he had none of the feather bedding which helps the modern ath-lete to make his way. But make his way he did in what must be one of the hardest of all roads to sporting acclaim. In the end he said every sacrifice had been worth it, but admitted "I can't honestly advise youngsters to do what I have done." From the early days of training on Farthing Downs in Surrey en route to those amazing records at the White City, Bergen and Malmo there were many setbacks and few words of encouragement. Like the letter he received from Roger Bannister when bedrid-den with a broken foot. More constant in their attention were the doubters. Nearly forty years ago Joe Binks, that scion of the *News of the World*, thought Gordon wouldn't last a year in ath-letics. Gunder Haegg, the Swedish phenomenon, gave him a little longer. "Pirie," he predicted, "will be burned out in two years." He was to race on to achievements which today would have made him prosperous, if not wealthy. This is not perhaps the time to enlarge on those exploits which have been well cov-ered in the national press over the last few days. In those days the press gave him a hard time, but he returned their fire with gusto. He learned that to be a celebrity you need a hide, to use his own words "like a hippo". He was a man of decided opin-ions and when they were based on his own experience he was often close to the truth. He liked to demonstrate his theories in the clear light of immediacy. I remember once he and I motored down to Sussex from London to visit Derek Johnson (Olympic 800 silver in 1956) who was then in hospital. Gordon was at the wheel of an old VW beetle. "This car," he told me, "has absolutely superb suspension." I was prepared to take his word for it but he wanted to prove it and suddenly he swung the car off this quiet country road onto a very bumpy field. After a few hundred yards of fairly hair-raising cross-country travel we regained the road in perfect safety and no loss of momentum. I had to agree that he was right. His car did have good suspension.

'We all felt Gordon deserved a longer span than he enjoyed, but even the fittest can have an unlucky draw. His Australian friend, Hec Hogan, died of leukaemia only four years after sprinting in the 100m final at Melbourne. Gordon had a marvellous heart which must be one reason why he survived his last illness so long.

'As his daughter has told us, he was happiest in the great open air. Out on the fjords of Norway, living on wild berries and drinking water from the mountain streams. Or riding his motor scooter through the bush fires of Southern Australia. Or lumberjacking in New Zealand. Or at last here in the New Forest. He was reported, incidentally, to have a record for cutting down Christmas trees in Norway. I wonder if that one ever was ratified. I for one could believe it.

'He was an eccentric. Somebody once said that the English have a genius for producing eccentrics. People who add variety and enrich our national life. In our world of athletics, Gordon was a great and loveable eccentric. That, I think, is how we should like to remember him.'

2

3000 Metres Steeplechase

The event comprises 28 hurdles and seven water jumps to be negotiated in the course of the race. Sometime before that was ratified world wide as statutory for international competition, 2 miles for the steeplechase was the measurement used by seniors in the UK for their championships.

A comment was made in the 'Encyclopaedia of Sports & Pastimes', a Fleetway House production, where the records went up to and included results of 1934! 'Some inexperienced steeplechasers try to clear the water jump, but that practice cannot be recommended, as it entails a needless waste of energy.' That was disproved in 1968 in Mexico City, in the balmy high altitude, and marked the start of the Kenyan revolution. That followed on from the great Kip Keino's middle distance exploits, which at the time did not include the steeple-chase which he won in Munich in 1972.

Amos Biwott was the man who cleared the water jump completely in the Olympic heat and semi-final of the 1968 Games. The effect of that bold style of running set out a stall for the future of Kenyan steeplechasing, as, eventually, they dominated the event.

In the 2000 Sydney Olympics, Kenya had the first two past the post: Reuben Kosgei (8.21.43) and Wilson Boit Kipketer (8:21.77). Only three athletes in the 1990s ran inside eight minutes for the steeplechase and they were all Kenyans, Wilson Boit Kipketer, Moses Kiptanui and Bernard Barmasai. The latter set the world record of 7:55.72 in Koln in August 1997. (That time was not bettered till 24/8/2001 when Brahim Boulami from Morocco ran 7.55.28 in the Golden League meeting in Brussels.)

17

It was back in 1968 when Bob Sparkes, who eventually became President of the Association of Track and Field Statisticians, wrote in the *Athletics Arena Olympic Report* about Amos Biwott in heat 3: 'He drew roars of delight as he leapt high over the water, disdaining to wet his shoes, and thus encouraged repeated the performance on each lap, lapping up the applause like a circus acrobat.' In the final, just before the water jump on the last lap, Benjamin Kogo was leading, with George Young (the well known American coach) and Australian Kerry O'Brien battling it out just behind him. Sparkes wrote, 'But all unnoticed Biwott was closing up with tremendous strides, and was right behind Young and O'Brien as they took the last barrier. The unknown novice zoomed past them, then Kogo, to win an incredible race by a couple of strides with Young just edging out O'Brien for the bronze medal.' (1. Amos Biwott 8:51.0; 2. Benjamin Kogo 8:51.6; 3. George Young 8:51.8.)

Mel Watman, one of the world's most knowledgeable athletics writers of all time, points out in his *Encyclopaedia of Athletics* that the distance was internationally standardised in 1920. The Olympic event was over-distance in 1932 but the winner, Volmari Iso-Holo of Finland, won again in 1936 and was regarded as the father of modern steeplechasing.

When I interviewed stars of the 1950s and 1960s about the water jump, and why, in those days, it was almost impossible to take a very bold approach to the water jump, all was revealed.

One of the very best Cambridge University runners of the 1960s was Tim Johnston, who also was an Olympic marathon runner, an international 10,000m and cross country man, and later became a multi world veteran champion on the road. Tim Johnston ran the 3000m steeplechase in 8:50 in third place behind Maurice Herriott (8 times AAA Champion) and Ernie Pomfret in 1964. About those days, Tim recalls, 'Roelants and Herriott they were the best two. Roelants had the running ability and Herriott had an incredible hurdling ability, although he was not that good as a runner. I think steeplechasers have been helped more than anything by the synthetic tracks. Some of those water jumps that we had to go over were like places

18

where cows go down to drink in the river, and that must have made about two seconds a lap or more difference.'

In Tokyo Gaston Roelants, the first man ever to crack 8:30 for the 3000m steeplechase, talked to me about the 1964 Olympic final: 'At 11 o'clock the day before the final I hit the hurdle hard with my upper leg and was in bed for four hours, with two doctors applying ice packs. It was not till 3 p.m. I was able to put my foot on the ground again.' He continued, 'In the final I felt no pain at all, but just to make sure I hurdled very high and managed to clear them all. I always like to take the lead, so that I can see the distance between the hurdles. The first kilometre was a slow 2:52, so I just took off after that point.' (1. Gaston Roelants (Belgium) 8:30.8; 2. Maurice Herriott (GB) 8:32.4; 3. Ivan Belyayev (USSR) 8:33.8.)

John Disley was to me the most captivating steeplechaser to watch at the 'Old' White City and in fact he was undefeated in the world of international steeplechasing in 1955 and gained a bronze medal in the Olympics of 1952 [1. Horace Ashenfelter (USA) 8:45.4; 2. Vladimir Kazantsev (USSR) 8:51.5; 3. John Disley (GB) 8:51.8]. John Disley looked every bit an athlete, with his strong physique, helped by his love for mountaineering. He always appeared to have a smile on his face as he relished the challenges. Incidentally he was really instrumental in introducing orienteering to the UK and helped his Ranelagh Harrier friend Chris Brasher (the founder of the London Marathon), to get the 'London' started in 1981. John Disley's wife, Sylvia Cheeseman, was a former UK record holder for the 200m (24.5) and a relay bronze medallist in 1952. John Disley, like Eric Shirley, won three AAA's steeplechase titles, the first of those in 1952 over 2 miles.

'It was a bit more than the odd couple of hundred yards. There was one more water jump for a start. It would not matter much nowadays quite honestly because of tartan tracks. A tartan bottom to the water jump gives a bit of cushioning, but you may remember that at the White City when I was running there was a hedge that was three foot six inches high. Somewhere in the middle was the rail which your foot felt for, and if you were lucky and hit the rail, then you landed in a water jump which

19

had a concrete base, which was about a foot underneath the regulation slope height and on top of that concrete slope there were lumps of sod put there for the race which looked great when you examined it, but the first time the field ran through that they smashed through the sods as everybody lands more or less on the same place. You were falling a foot further down on to concrete, you really had to climb out of the water jumps, and you had a grass run-up at the White City for many years, even to the water jump. It was a different race; possibly it was a second and half to two seconds a lap harder to run the steeplechase those days than it is now.'

In 1956 in the Olympic steeplechase final there was a situation that has never happened since. All three representatives of the UK made the final. There was Chris Brasher, who hit form just at the right time, having won an international 2 miles (flat) race in Geelong, Australia, out of a strong international field, in a new All Australian record of 8:45.6. He attributed his good form to having had three weeks of acclimatisation, according to the *Daily Telegraph*. Brasher had been one of the pace setters for Roger Bannister's first ever 4-minute mile two years earlier. Eric Shirley, the Finchley Harrier, who has been an important official in Athletic Committees in recent years, was thought of as a great steeplechaser by John Disley. It was truly amazing that Eric Shirley made the Olympic team in the first place, when you consider he was an orphan living as a peasant in Ireland when he was young before being in abject poverty as a youth in Kilburn, London. Despite his early disadvantages he managed to make his way up to being a very good international athlete and, even as a veteran went on to win the over 65s 800m title in the British Veteran Championships.

Eric Shirley won his semi-final at Melbourne in 8:52.6 with Brasher fourth in 8:53.8. Sandor Rozsnyoi of Hungary had set a new world record in September of 8:35.6. He won the other semi-final in 8:46.6 which was the same time as John Disley in second spot.

After the final the winner Chris Brasher was disqualified because of a minor collision with another athlete in the race. That was overruled and Great Britain had a memorable gold medal which was achieved in an Olympic record. It was the first British track gold medal for 24 years. For the other two finalists their own story shows how unpredictable the sport of athletics can be. 1. Chris Brasher (GB) 8:41.2; 2. Sandor Rozsnyoi (Hungary) 8:43.6; 3. Ernst Larsen (Norway) 8:44.0; 4. Heinz Laufer (Germany) 8:44.4; 5. Semyon Rzhishchin (USSR) 8:44.6; 6. John Disley (GB) 8:44.6; 7. Neil Robbins (Australia) 8:50.00; 8. Eric Shirley (GB) 8:57.0; 9. C. 'Deacon' Jones (USA) 9:01.3.

John Disley: 'I had virus pneumonia six weeks before and Chris Brasher only beat me twice in something like 50 races we had together. I just was not fit actually. I was quite lucky to get to the final. Even if I had won in Melbourne, which would have been nice to do, at the back of my mind – and it could be in the back of Chris Brasher's mind too – is that the best steeplechaser in the world was the Hungarian, Rozsnyoi.'

Eric Shirley of Finchley Harriers (later to become Hillingdon) recollects of the 1956 Olympics: 'I know what happened now, it was diet. I was a poor boy from the back streets of Kilburn. My diet was bread, bread, pasta and pasta. When I got to Australia and you saw the steaks, salmon, fish, I put that in. I forgot all about the bread and pasta. The one thing I should not have done. That is one of the things that I did wrong, looking back on it now but there was no advice, no one to tell you, and I was out of my own environment. I won the semi-final, but the final was a blur. There was nothing there on the day. I saw Sonia O'Sullivan in the Olympics of 1996 and that was how I felt.'

Dave Chapman of Woodford Green AC, who has worked in the meat trade nearly all his life, was a talented junior runner before competing as a senior. He remembers finishing ahead of Eric Shirley, who was second in one race they ran together against France, and partnered Maurice Herriott in some of his early international matches. Chapman's best was 8:46.

'I did run with Maurice early on, but in Tokyo he got the silver in the Olympic steeplechase. He was a better competitor than I was. When I look back we all played at it with comparison to today's standards. We all trained relatively hard but we did not really regard other ancillary parts of the sport as important as they do these days. Things like diet.'

One of the world's greatest steeplechasers of all time was Bronislaw Malinowski from Poland. He was 4th in the Olympics of 1972; 2nd in 1976 and 1st in 1980 in Moscow. He also defeated the 1976 Champion Anders Garderud of Sweden, Michael Karst (W. Germany) and Franco Fava (Italy) in the European Games final of 1974 in Rome. Malinowski 'mixed it' at top level from 1500m to 10,000 (he did a 3:57.5 mile and 7:42.4 for 3000m on the flat) and was even second in the world cross country behind John Tracey in Ireland in 1979. Bronislaw Malinowski's best time for the 3000m steeplechase was 8:09.11 in 1976. Dennis Coates, who held the UK record at that time of 8:19.0 and was coached by Gordon Surtees, remarked, 'He had all round ability. He was willing to have a go at anything. He was no sitter.'

To finish this chapter I thought it might be useful to aspiring steeplechasers to know how Bronislaw Malinowski put in his initial groundwork that enabled him to progress to being a steeplechaser.

'My brother was a junior running for the Polish national team in the 1500m and it was because of him that I started. One day my brother just said, "Let's go out training", and that was how it all began. It was in that first training effort that something "clicked" inside me, and that made me continue running.

'I was born and lived just south of Gdansk (Danzig). When I started my training the first races I did were over 1000 and 1500m; the 1000m is very popular in Poland. At the time I was no longer in school but in technical college. My club from the very start was Olympia Grudziadz and right from the beginning of my athletics my coach has been Ryzsard Szezepanski. I was not given any specific training to begin with, just general development – gentle running, plenty of warm ups, even swinging from the trees, and started running when I was 18 and trained then every day on my own. My time to begin with was 3:58.0 for 1500m.

'When I began in the sixties, the first cuttings that I kept were of Ron Clarke.

'My first memorable race in my early career was the European Junior Championships in 1970 when I represented Poland in Paris, winning the 2000m steeplechase in a time of 5:35. That was really memorable for me, as it happened to be the very first Junior Championship in Europe. My success in Paris influenced me in my decision to concentrate on the steeplechase because up to then I was tackling a lot of events.'

The things he liked outside of athletics were, 'Women, good music in discotheques, good pictures, good soccer and other sports. My studies, which are taking me five years, are quite tough with bio-chemistry and other stuff. One very deep feeling – it's being rather sentimental – that I would love to run in Edinburgh where my mother comes from; and I would like to spend some time in England as I always admire the British runners.'

I talked with Bronislaw Malinowski accompanied by his great friend in England, Alex Mineyko, an effervescent character, who is a coach and ran for Middlesex as a young man. He was very saddened later to hear that 'Bronic' had died in a car crash, without realising his ambitions outside of athletics or being able to look back on his fantastic athletic achievements with pride.

3

Great Characters

The characters that are often remembered most are not just the ones who are inspirational at world level but those flamboyant or unusual personalities in the clubs. That is where stories are handed down through the years by generations of runners, with just a little understandable embellishment by the narrators. David Bedford and Gordon Pirie were two that stood out as characters from the south of England. From Yorkshire, the man dubbed by the Press as The 'Cheeky Chappie' Derek Ibbotson was another personality. New Zealanders Rod Dixon and Dick Quax are two more. Steve Prefontaine, Billy Mills and Haile Gebrselassie were depicted as interesting characters on film. In the case of Gebrselassie, after his first Olympic 10,000 metre win in Atlanta, *Runners World* magazine considered him the greatest distance runner of all time. Irishman Jim Hogan, an authority on race horses, slab laying and crazy paving, and the 1966 European Marathon Champion, was a forthright and amusing eccentric. He commented, 'If they saw you running on the farms where I came from in Ireland they thought you were off your nut!'

I can think of three other Irishmen who are great characters; Eamonn Coghlan, Ray Flynn and more recently John Downes. In the Southern in 2001, at Parliament Hill Fields, there was a very close finish at the end of the very muddy senior nine-mile race. Downes was third behind Shaftesbury's Nick Francis and Hounslow's Sam Haughian (who was later to come second and only a second behind Birchfield's Mike Oppenshaw in the 'National'). In the Southern, only three seconds separated the first three home. Downes, the 'rugged' London Irish runner, who had a spell with the strong Salford Athletic club, had been one of the top UK and Ireland cross country runners half a dozen years earlier, before he suffered injuries that plagued him. In fact he seriously thought he would retire from the sport, as he wandered around on crutches, but one of the things, more than anything, that encouraged him to return to racing was a chance remark. It was made by a friend of his having a conversation over in Dublin with someone. 'You know John Downes is badly injured. He is thinking of retiring altogether!' his friend said. The man turned round and with a broad Irish accent shot back with, 'God created three types of men. The soft, the hard men and John Downes!' Another surprising success story, after physical setbacks concerned Glynn Tromans of Coventry Godiva, the 'National' cross country champion in 2000. He had the second of two heart operations in 1997 to straighten out some problems that were plaguing him and, within a short time returned to international standard athletics.

Besides recognising Ron Hill's unusual longevity as a distance man, I can see Gerry North, the English 'National' champion of 1962, with a white handkerchief wrapped round one of his hands, running in his Blackpool, Belgrave and later Portsmouth colours. I can picture him now and see his light frame bounding over the countryside; that was an abiding memory. Elswick Harrier Harry Matthews would not only point to Bob Peart and Mick McLeod in his club as great characters, but even more so to Jim Alder in the north-east. Alder, the Commonwealth Marathon Champion of 1966, had a terribly tough start in life. As an orphan with no money, he fought his way up to the top in international sport. Alder is now the 'fiery' adviser to Morpeth Harriers, who had the talented Hudspith brothers (Mark and Ian) in their team when they won the National Six Stage road relay in millennium year.

Gently eccentric characters, who were fine clubmen in the 1970s, included a squad from Hercules & Wimbledon – Mike Beevor, Dave Smallbone, Steve Badgery, Mike Fuller, Bas Collins and Mike Kortenray; I am sure the Holt twins, both internationals for Hercules, would agree with that! Mike Beevor ran later for Luton and came sixth in the National of 1975. He represented England a few times. In the 1970s, we quite often went out for runs together from Tower Hill, along Jamaica Road and around Southwark Park. He helped me, in those days, to improve from 59 to 56 minutes for 10 miles on the road. Mike reminisced, 'It's funny, although I know there are more financial opportunities if you do well now, that cannot replace the fun we had. The banter with Freary "Big Mike", the Stewarts, Bedford, Holden etc. The laughs at Lauriston and the fun at the City of London Poly (School of Navigation, now London Guildhall University). Real sincere friendships that count for a lot.' Mike looked back to his early days, 'Casting my mind back to when as a boy, I enjoyed going to the White City and watching Hewson, Rawson, Peter Hildreth, Eric Shirley, John Disley, Bullivant, Ibbotson, Ken Mathews, Mike Fleet, Radford, Segal, Chataway, etc.'

I feel one might add that there were two world-dominant milers who lit up the White City in the 1960s and they were Jim Ryun (USA) and Kip Keino (Kenya) of course. I suppose, looking back even further for me, as a 9 or 10 year old in 1949/50, it was the excitement and pure anticipation of what was to come. Hearing the brass band playing inside the old White City Stadium. I remember that, as we approached the stadium in my father's car. Then, to see the National teams for those duel meets as the athletes came out onto the track, marching proudly behind their respective flags. There was John Roberts, a tall, rangy runner who, in his South London days, could run fast and talk a lot about a good race, as did Charlie Walker, Bill Kerr, John Thresher, and Charlie Dabbs, all from Belgrave. Alex Mineyko and Rory Allen of Poly were two flamboyant characters who are hard to forget, two great eccentrics. North London's Irishman Tom Ryan, was unusual to say the least. He used to pick up a pneumatic drill, work on the road in the City of London and then, without changing from his work clothes, join in with club runners and run along the Thames Embankment.

One cannot forget that immensely talented Tony Simmons, with his shoulder-length black hair, and his short but efficient stride pattern. He ran as an international for Wales and England over the years. Another in his era was Colin Moxsom, who ran for Woodford Green then Haringey. He was a blond bespectacled runner, who had a strong cockney accent. I thought of him as the 'the Michael Caine of athletics'. In Highgate there was Ray Appleby, a clock repairer and maker, who swore the run he would take you on was a 10 miler but it always ended up by being an 'Appleby 12, 14 or even 17!' He successfully coached Shaftesbury's Dominic Bannister. Highgate's running motivator of the late 1950s and early 1960s was influential clothes designer, and ex-naval man, Ted Fosbrook. He was an unusual character who introduced me to Highgate Harriers, of which I was made a life member in 1982. Then there was John Galloway, a jazz fanatic, who owned a greyhound that he kept in his flat, and had a mynah bird that would talk to you on the phone. His antics are legendary, as were other extraordinary Highgate personalities, Richard Cox, Tom Mainwaring, John Molloy, who became a good veteran in Australia, and Victor Sills, a Middlesex Champion who had difficulties getting his pole onto the trains. So much so that even the *Daily Mirror* picked up a story on that fact.

I always remember the relaxed Walthamstow Athletic Club, where they had their fair share of characters like Arthur Pointer, Ronnie Howe, Terry Wellard, Alan and Pauline Rich. There was Gerry Archer and Gerry Elmore from Hillingdon and Shaftesbury respectively, who tended to finish just ahead of me in the Championship cross country races or the Metropolitan leagues. When I overtook John Atkinson of Barnet, in those days, he often used to say, 'You going to interview me?!' A veteran known for his sense of humour was Mike Robinson of Havering AC, as countless people in Essex would substantiate. Stan Allen, a runner and coach, was another with a quick sense of humour and well known in the South London area. Alec Randall, a tall, bearded, ex-policeman, used to like to run nearly everywhere. As a vet in his mid 40s, he ran two 2:45 marathons in two days, and managed to fit in time playing in a brass band. Another ex-policeman, who used to be on the beat round my area at Crystal Palace, was John Jeffrey, who was an 800m runner for the Met Police and then ran some good marathons before

27

his back gave out. He is now a top official with Belgrave Harriers. Alec Randall, was a friend of South London's Mike Quinn, a veteran cross country rival of mine who had the irritating habit of choosing the worst steep downhill, narrow pathways of Farthing Down to rush past you. A tactic that more than often worked well for him.

Another unforgettable man I met was Scotsman John Ross, who ran under 60 seconds for 400 metres indoors when he was over 60 in 2001. The Edinburgh man was a fine track and field all rounder, a real bundle of energy and enthusiasm. Another person that struck me as a personality was Sheila Allen of Houghton AC, a successful road and cross country runner in the North East, and Bronwen Cardy-Wise from Wales, who won three gold medals in the over 45 in the World Veteran Games of 1999. She was another with a lovely personality. On the veteran scene two remarkable eccentrics are John Treadwell (an over 55 National Veteran Champion on the track and road in 2000) the brother of international Bob Treadwell. John came into athletics as a veteran, having travelled the world for many years. He entered the sport as a means of mental and physical therapy, after a ghastly accident in an explosives factory, when he was badly burned. When he attends the major veteran meetings he always sleeps outdoors, sometimes not even in a tent! Another who goes to those same veteran meetings is Clifford Taylor, who competes as an over 65 all round field events man. Clifford, a collector of antique books among other things. He also sleeps outdoors at many of the same meetings. Paul Taylor of Woodstock was someone else that stood out because, every time he finished his eighteen London to Brighton road races, always well up the field of finishers, he relaxed by the side of the road with the first of a few pints of Guinness and a cigarette. About that race he always declared, 'I enjoyed that – love the Brighton.'

On the international side, there's that fine marathon man of the 1960s and 1970s Colin Kirkham from Coventry Godiva, who belonged to the same club as that interesting personality of the late 1960s and early 1970s Dick Taylor. Kirkham could tell you a lot of stories about runners in his club. One in particular was Steffan White, the 1997 National Cross Country Senior Champion. White is a man who really makes training runs with his club fun.

Of course there was Mary Rand and Lillian Board, illustrated by the media as the 'Golden Girls' of the 1960s. They should never be left out, with their striking, looks and vivacious personalities. (Not to forget Mary Peters the 1972 pentathlon champion, a wonderful effervescent personality.) Lillian Board was the outstanding athlete of the 1969 European Games in Athens and will always be remembered for her bubbly disposition. It was a great loss to athletics when she was cut down by a fatal illness, while still in her prime. Bill Nankeville, and Brian Hewson were handsome stylish runners, winning middle distance races in the 1950s at the White City, often with consummate ease. On the sprinting side in those days there were great runners originating from the West Indies like popular Emanuel McDonald Bailey, Arthur Wint and Herb Mckenley. They all caught the imagination. They were liquid movers, like Don Quarrie in the 1970s, from the same Isles; a man with an immaculate bend running technique over 200 metres. In the States names that are bound to be remembered are Olympic Champions Wilma Rudolph (1960) – Jutta Heine (Germany) and Dorothy Hyman (GB) were Europe's best at that time – Florence Griffith Joyner 'Flo-Jo' (1988) and Marion Jones (2000).

From November 2000 to August 2001, I asked a random selection of athletes and ex-athletes, who did they feel were the 'great characters' in the sport over the years?

Martin Howard, who was a club runner with Highgate Harriers, has been President of the North of Thames and North London Athletic Associations as well as having done numerous jobs as an official on committees: 'Frank Salvat was the greatest character I ever met. He was just so outlandish. When he was forced to go up to the army health and recruitment board for conscription, he was just getting ready to run in the Olympics in Rome (1960). You could pass him by on the street and think nothing of it. He had one eye, beak nose; the original seven stone weakling. He was so skinny. The army doctor said,

"Mr Salvat what do you do for exercise?" "Well I read a bit." That was all he said, and the doctors immediately failed him. Within two months he was running in the Rome Olympics. He ran around four minutes for a mile, within weeks of going up for conscription. As a runner I was close to a group that trained with him.' Martin Howard continued, 'It was said that he got so drunk with beer one time, that when he arrived by coach for his leg in the London to Brighton road relay, in order that he could run his stage, they had to point him in the right direction. He then proceeded to break the stage, record!' (Frank Salvat won the AAA's 3 miles in 1960 with a time of 13:33.00.)

Jack Heywood was an international in the 1950s. He had a debilitating back disorder which meant he could only bend a quarter of the way down to touch his toes, and was rejected by the forces for National Service. He still had a successful time in the sport. He did point out that quite a lot of British runners did well at athletics in his day because they had the opportunity to train while doing their National Service. Sport was encouraged because of inter-services rivalry. Sometimes they would let you 'knock off' work at 4 o'clock, which gave more time to run. In the case of Emil Zatopek, one of Jack's heroes, he was in the army, in the days when he was racing well. That, one would have thought, would have given him a certain advantage, but not much of one if you realised he was obviously deprived of facilities and good food, especially at a time when he started to blossom out as a fine senior runner. His country had been under Nazi occupation for six years, which included time before the Second World War and, all through it. Other characters in Jack Heywood's view included Frank Salvat and Bruce Tulloh.

One race that marked Jack Heywood out as being a potential international was after he had won the Surrey Youth cross country Championships. He went on the following year to win the Surrey Junior, beating South London's Mick Firth and Peter Driver. The latter went on to be a Commonwealth Champion and was always remembered in his club as being 'The Perfect Gentleman'. Anyway, at the time, Firth and Driver were already in South London Harriers senior team. Heywood also remembered the time Pirie was so dehydrated that he collapsed in the last lap of the AAA's 6 miles at the White City. That was in 1955 when Ken Norris won, and Frank Sando overtook Heywood on the last lap to gain the silver.

'I went with two other sixteen-year-old Herne Hill Harriers to watch the 1948 Olympics. We saw this guy (Zatopek) run round in absolute agony and beat the opposition in the 10,000m. In the 5000m Zatopek got beaten by Gaston Reiff of Belgium, who sprinted by him. The supposition was that he would not do that a second time. Zatopek's ethic, as you know, was hard work, and all the clubs like our club Herne Hill were being advised to take it easy in training. Train three days a week, which is what I did, and yet there was this guy doing phenomenal distances, which we did not believe at the time! We then all wanted to be little Zatopeks!' (Zatopek's wife Dana won the 1952 Olympic javelin in Helsinki with 50.47 metres the year Emile won the 5, 10 and the marathon.)

Mick Firth, who ran third and fourth in the 'National' in the 1950s remembers a Southern in 1958. It was well into the race at the time, 'I was running along at the front with Frank Sando and suddenly Stan Eldon shot past us. "Oh! He'll come back," Frank said. Sometime after, near Kenwood we realised he was not going to come back and, I said to Frank, "And I'm not going to be third!"' (In 1958 Stan Eldon won the AAA's 3 and 6 mile.)

'Gordon Pirie was undoubtedly the greatest character. He was the forerunner of modern middle distance running in this country. He was inspired by Emile Zatopek and had pictures of him all over his bedroom as the man to beat, then Kuts came along and beat them both. Stan Eldon was quite a character and Mike Maynard was a great guy too.' (Another Herne Hill Harrier, just after the time that Mike Maynard was among the best UK cross country runners, was a man who was a great youth leader, Don Taylor. He set a UK National 10,000m record of 28:52.4 back on the 23rd of August, 1963.)

Mike Marlowe ran 4:11.1 for a mile in 1959 and coached his son from Bracknell, Gary Marlowe, who ran 1:46.1 for 800m: 'Zatopek, he was outstanding. The coach Geoff Dyson was a real character never to be forgotten. Harry Hicks, of Hampstead

Harriers was an excellent runner. I remember him sprinting into the stadium at Chiswick with Arthur Keily, in order to get a place on the Olympic marathon team in 1956. Harry has put an awful lot into athletics as a runner and official.'

Maureen Smith, who was the second runner after Diane Leather to break 5 minutes for the mile, the night Derek Ibbotson broke the men's mile world record in 1957, said: 'To me the characters were June Bridgland, who had a tragic accident falling off a train to her death, Madeline Ibbotson and Joy Jordan.' (Joy Jordan, a Commonwealth bronze medallist and UK 800m record holder, was five times WAAA's 800m Champion 1958–1962 and Madeline Ibbotson won the Women's National in 1963–1964.)

Pam Jones from Ilford AC has been a World and National Veteran Champion, and was sixth in the Women's National cross country in the 1960s behind winner Pam Davies. (Davies won that four times and Rita Ridley, who was married to Clive Ridley of Walthamstow, won it five times.) 'I followed Zatopek when I was young. He was quite an inspiration because he ran a lot over here. I went to the White City to watch him. In my era Diane Leather was the woman that impressed me. It seemed every race I ran against her she won. She was untouchable at the time.' (Diane Leather was noted particularly for being the first woman to break 5 minutes for the mile in 1954, the same, year as Roger Bannister was the first man to break 4 minutes for the mile. Leather ran a world record for 1500m with 4:30.0 and 4:29.7 in 1957.)

Mike Barratt, 'The Evergreen' runner from Ealing, Southall and Middlesex, was a character in his own right, as illustrated in *The Winning Edge*. He was President of the North of Thames Association in 2000. He won the senior North of Thames cross country Championships in 1953 and, was second to Ken Norris half a dozen times in the Middlesex senior Championships. He beat international Tim Briault to win it once. In his mid-40s, in 1978, he became a triple gold medallist in the European Veteran Championships in Italy. 'Not that many characters now in recent years are there! Very stereotyped now. All very serious about it. Obviously Gordon Pirie, there was a character and Dave

32

Bedford of course. They are the outstanding characters, if you are talking of the top line.'

Andy Ferguson, an 'effervescent' Scot, was Middlesex and Southern junior cross country champion in 1949, and was third in the AAA's 3 miles in a Scottish Native record of 14:11.2, in 1950, the same time incidentally that the great Finn Paavo Nurmi did when breaking the world record in Stockholm in 1923. In Andy Ferguson's AAA's race Lucien Theys of Belgium won in 14:09.0. That was the year before Roy Beckett, coached by *Athletics Weekly* Editor Jimmy Green, won in 14:02.6. Andy Ferguson also achieved a time of 2:39.48 in the London Marathon of 1982 at 53 years of age! 'I remember running against Zatopek at Wembley and congratulating him on winning. I can also remember running against Miles Atkinson and Walter Hesketh.' Andy continued, 'It was Gordon Pirie for me. He always wanted to put over his viewpoint. He was a great character. Since then, two runners have stood out as characters for what they achieved. Dave Bedford won the senior Southern 9 mile cross country Championships at Parliament Hill Fields, on the 20th of February, 1970, in the mud and in the drizzle, and before changing out of his shorts and vest, talked to some of the press. Someone said, "The Southern Junior is now on." "Oh well," he said, "I might as well do it." Off he ran and won that too! The other memory was to see his clubmate Julian Goater, a fairly heavy man. He simply floated over the mud and easily won the senior National of 1991.' (1. Julian Goater 44:39; 2. Dave Clarke, in his breakthrough race 46:34; 3. Mick Mcleod 46:58 and Dave Moorcroft 47:00 fourth after starting late. Marathon runner Steve Jones was fifth.)

Peter Hildreth was the most consistently good UK high hurdler in the 1950s, and then became athletics correspondent for the *Sunday Telegraph* among other things. He pointed out that when he was competing intensively as an international he had a full time job. He had to squeeze all his racing abroad into his three weeks' holiday allocation for the year! Not like today where athletes can go away for months for warm weather training. His feelings about sport these days was that so much money at the highest level helps corrupt sport. Peter Hildreth's ideas of the supreme Champion and the greatest characters were as follows: 'Herb Elliott (Australia) with the three years when he was undefeated over 1500/mile stands out for me. He was single-minded and had an eccentric coach in Percy Cerutty. As far as characters I met, Frank Salvat stood out and, in my event Paul Vine, whose father Lawrence Vine was a high court judge.' (In 1955–56 Paul Vine was AAA's 220 yds hurdles Champion.)

Geoff Harrold, 61, is still competing well as a veteran and is London Marathon Publicity officer. He was editor of *Athletics Monthly, Marathon & Distance Runner* and now *Veterans News*. He remembers winning the South London Harriers '30' mile road race in 1977 for two reasons. Firstly Tom Richards, who was second in the Olympic marathon of 1948, handed him the prize, and it was the same day in 1977 that Steve Ovett won the 1500m in the World Cup. Harrold ran 10 miles in 49:47 and the marathon in 2:22.46. 'My biggest hero was Herb Elliott and then there was Ron Clarke. Peter Browne [AAA's 800m Champion and many times world veteran champion] a great character and a good example of dedication and getting the performances out. Ron Franklin is someone who has had the sheer enthusiasm and enjoyment for the sport over so many years.'

Ken Norris of Thames Valley Harriers was fifth in the Olympic 5000m at Melbourne in 1956. Norris McWhirter's *Athletics World* showed the first five of the 20 finishers as 1. Vladimir Kuts (USSR) 28:45.6; 2. Jozsef Kovacs (Hungary) 28:52.4; 3. Allen Lawrence (Australia) 28:53.6; 4. Zdzislaw Kryzykowiak (Poland) 29:0.0; 5. Ken Norris (GB) 29:05. In the match where Great Britain was beaten by Hungary in Budapest in 1956 Ken Norris beat Jozsef Kovacs, the Olympic silver medallist in 29:56.4 to Kovacs' 29:56.8. In 1954 Ken Norris won the Southern cross country from Frank Sando and Peter Driver, which was on the same day as Fred Norris won the Northern. Ken Norris won the 'National' senior in 1956 and the AAA's 6 mile in 1955. Essex Beagles 'battler' George Knight won in 1957.

'The one that immediately comes to mind is Zatopek. He was a giant! Bedford made a massive impact and Pirie. Coe and Ovett and to a lesser extent Steve Cram. Frank Sando too, but he was very self-effacing. He would blend into the background. He would never push himself forward. A very great runner. He won the International "World" cross country twice, in front of me both times.

'Athletics was more fun in those days. There is no question about that. People are very money orientated now. There doesn't seem to be the same camaraderie. We trained in groups, although I used to do a lot of training on my own. At least three times a week I had someone else I would train with part of the time. If I went down the track to do 20×400 I had seven or eight people start out with me. After half a dozen some dropped out, others came back in and joined me for the last half-dozen.'

A lot of the characters in the middle and long distances, at that time, did the premier British road relay: The London to Brighton. 'The sort of drama you had with people collapsing. My own club we had a guy who collapsed and did not finish his leg. Somebody from Belgrave collapsed on the penultimate stage going up Pyecombe Hill. We had a wonderful race in 1955–56 when Jim Peters ran the eighth stage for Essex Beagles and, at the end of that he had $4\frac{1}{2}$ minutes lead on the second club, he retorted "That's not enough!" I was running on Pyecombe Hill on the eleventh stage. When I took off we were $3\frac{1}{2}$ minutes behind. I took off in sixth place. I took us up to third. I chopped a huge chunk off the stage record. We were $1\frac{1}{4}$ minutes behind. Alec Olney ran the last leg for us, a great runner in his day. He caught the guy in the finishing funnel and passed him. It looked impossible when I set off, that we could not possibly catch them, as we were $3\frac{1}{2}$ minutes behind, but we did! We had that sort of drama. The London to Brighton stopped in about 1968 and they re-routed it partly, so they avoided going along the main A23 at Mitcham and put it through all the back streets so it came out beyond Purley, but then the police said "Enough is enough" as more and more people were getting cars.

'In its height in the 1950s the number of cars were limited, while each club would have about $1\frac{1}{2}$ coaches per club and a couple of cars. It built up and up and one could understand the police saying it was too dangerous.'

Barrie Saunders was a TVH 10 mile Champion back in the

1950s, in a race where he beat Terry Stacey, who went on to come third in the North of Thames senior Championships. 'The character who I will always remember was not even an athlete and that was Alf Mignot' (something his clubmate Ray Crosbie would agree about). 'Alf's tremendous enthusiasm. The way he cheered everyone on, pushed them, needled the opposition.' (In the Thames Valley Harriers road relay at one time Jack Heywood went off in the lead on the anchor leg for Herne Hill. Ken Norris of Alf's club pursued him, having been 100 yards back at the take over. As the leg progressed with Ken Norris threatening, Alf Mignot, on his bicycle, came alongside Heywood and insisted 'Don't worry John, Ken's given up!' That was a clever bit of needling from Alf but Jack Heywood did not fall for it and, managed to get home first!)

Barrie Saunders continues, 'Alf was a tremendous person to have around. When you arrived you felt there was somebody there who was over the top with you.' (The late Pat Holland of Highgate, father of the three Holland brothers, had a powerful voice that could be heard for a great deal of distance and, of course, Ron Bentley of Tipton and Stan Long of Gateshead fitted into that category too; as cheerleaders for their clubs.)

Barrie Saunders added, 'In an athletic sense Ken Norris was a formidable athlete. You never gave him an inch or he would take the proverbial mile, so cunning and crafty. I remember when Norris retired he made a remark to me, "I never lost a race I should have won. I have won an awful lot of races I should not have done," which sums him up nicely. Norris took a tremendous interest in everybody. Afterwards he would come up and say, "Where did you finish? What did you do? Well done!" and encourage you.'

George Harrison, the well known Hertfordshire coach, in 1962 came third in the AAA's Marathon and, among other things, coaches the St Albans School team. Looking at that team in 2001, it certainly has runners with potential in it. To mention just two, Pete Murphy and Tom Bedford, who like father Dave, is an ardent football supporter as well. George Harrison looks back: 'Franky Salvat at the 5000m at the Rome Olympics, Mel Batty and Dave Bedford what characters they were! I got on

36

very well with Brian Kilby, Arthur and Joe Keily. All the marathon runners of the 1960s They were all great. I remember running the Walton "15" and being with Arthur and Joe and, at the half-way stage they turned round and said "Who are thee then?" I said "George Harrison" and they said "George Harrison, pleased to meet you." When I tell kids that today, that's what they used to do, they don't believe it. I think they were characters then. I don't know whether there are so many now, as it is so competitive, money at the end not a canteen of cutlery.

'I have had characters in my squad like Adrian Stewart, Michael O'Reilly, James Clarke and Paul Herbert, all great characters in their own era but, I think you have to go back to the 1960s when you find the real characters about. Harry Hicks, Frank Sando, and Gordon Pirie, and Frank Salvat, a character and a half. Eric Shirley looked after Frank, as he only had one eye. Frank going off course many a time in the cross-country races and Eric had to put him on course.'

An interesting point George brought up about it being so 'competitive' these days. It also takes up an inordinate amount of time training-wise, if you want to be at or near the top in the sport. **Alison Wyeth** from the successful Parkside club where the late Sylvia Parker coached, who was fifth in the World 3000m Championship in Stuttgart in 1993 just behind Sonia O'Sullivan, remarked, after finishing fourth (at 36), in the Women's National cross country Championship 2000: 'Athletics is a strain. I have a 2½-year-old son' (partner is John Nuttall the 1996 'National' champion) 'and a full time job as Preston College Development Manager. Athletics takes up the whole of your life and you can't do anything else.'

John Dorgan, Secretary for London Irish Athletic club for over forty years: 'Jim Hogan and his comments. Noel Carroll, Frank Murphy and Ronnie Delany who is a good after dinner speaker. Pete Fagan was a character too.'

Terry Driscoll, who as a club runner did 52.8/4:30 for 400/mile before going on to coach and team manage with the Highgate Harriers: 'The greatest athlete, to my mind, was Peter Snell. He won the 800 and 1500 at the Tokyo Olympics. There was no one else like him.' **John Davies**, from New Zealand, who was third behind Snell in the 1500 metres in Tokyo talked about Snell when he retired in 1965. Snell had won the 800/mile in the 1962 Commonwealth at Perth, as well as taking the gold in the Olympic 800 title in 1956 narrowly beating the Belgian Roger Moens.

'A week before Tokyo Peter found it hard to dip below 1:50.0 for a half; he was criticised. But Snell, with Arthur Lydiard his coach, soon put the bogey to rest. Way back at Perth he was criticised for running "slow" but Peter wanted to make sure of his win. Shouldn't tactics play any part now? He was beaten by Jim Ryun in the States though, clocking only 0.1 slower; he was criticised for bad tactics. But is anyone invincible? Herb Elliott was beaten by Snell in their only meeting. As a close friend I was overjoyed at his triumphs in Tokyo, even though I was one of his rivals. Although his times will sometime pass into oblivion, the era of Snell will remain with many until their dying day. Certainly I shall miss him. Quiet, likeable, always looking on the bright side, never despairing, Peter Snell is of a type so rare in the world today. A King.'

(After Snell's world mile record of 3:54.1 in 1964, the next to go on the books was by 'stylish' Michel Jazy of France, who had come second to Herb Elliott at the Olympics in Rome in 1956. Jazy ran a world mile record of 3:53.6 on the 9th of June, 1965.) Terry Driscoll continues, 'As far as a characters ... Frank Salvat. I think Steve Cram was a bit of a character too. As far as potential, Karl Palmer whom I coached.' (Palmer came third in the National youth cross-country of 1983. Paul Taylor, who at the time was coached by Cliff Stainton of Copeland, and was later a member of Border AC, won the race.) 'Palmer had amazing potential but he hardly ever trained and in fact, between the National and the World junior cross country, when he was first English junior home, he did no training at all!'

Jack Fitzgerald, now in his late 70s, ran a best of 1 hr 55 min for 20 miles on the road. He also won the Surrey '20'. Bridget Cushen, who was third in the National behind Pam Davies and Rita Ridley at Aldershot in 1969, when coached by Frank Horwill, was advised by Jack Fitzgerald when she won the European vets marathon in 1978. (Bridget Cushen is currently the UK's delegate on the council for the World Association of veteran athletes.)

'Ron Franklin was one of the greatest characters over many years.' (Welsh international Franklin was a successful distance runner from Thames Valley Harriers. A racing vegetarian, who has beaten a lot of the best in the UK on the road in his day. He was third behind Brian Kilby and Brian Cooke in the AAA's Marathon of 1961 and, at 41, came third behind winner Bernie Plain in the Welsh 10,000m. He beat outstanding veteran, Derek Turnbull, the New Zealand sheep farmer when he won the 1979 National M50 vets 5000m in 16:26.0.) Fitzgerald continued, 'Ron Hill you obviously have to say. I have a special regard for Hugh Jones as a person, a marvellous bloke. The important factor is what the athlete is like as a person!' (International marathon man Jones won the London Marathon in 1982. He was second once in the National cross-country and, when he ran for Liverpool University, achieved the fastest ever time on record in the Imperial Colleges Hyde Park Road Relay.)

Joyce Smith, and her husband Bryan, do tireless work as officials now. Joyce was undoubtedly one of the UK's greats of all time. She won the first London Marathon in 1981, was the International 'World' cross country champion in 1972 and third in the European 3000m of 1974. 'Dave Bedford brought the crowds back to athletics. There was Coe and Ovett.' Joyce felt that the media tend to make the personalities.

Mike Puddifoot ran for TVH then Shaftesbury as a veteran. He did 29:12 for 10k on the track: 'David Bedford, no end of stories about him. After he had done a second session on one of his days he phoned up Ian Stewart, found out he was going to do a session. Dave jumped on his motorbike, rushed up to Birmingham and did his third session of the day with Ian.

'Henry Rono. I watched him doing a session with Bob Parker's group. They were doing 2:40 to 2:45 for 1000s and Rono gave them 15 seconds start then cruised by them each time.' (Rono achieved a 3000, 5000, 10,000 and steeplechase world record all in 1978. He was inspired by Kip Keino in Kenya.)

Adrian Stewart, who ran for Highgate Harriers and then

39

Haringey, was once the fastest 3000m youth in the country and became an international junior cross-country runner, before becoming a good senior club runner. 'Dave Bedford was a character. He was years ahead of his time and Tony Simmons. I went for runs over 15 miles on Sundays with the Shaftesbury runners and because Dave was there, with all the fun and games, the long runs felt more like 3 mile runs.'

Eric Nash, one of the top officials in the UK, has been involved in athletics for a great many years. Two of his most recent postings were ECCU President in 2000 and Southern President in 2001. He has known and met athletes of all standards for countless years. 'Australian Ron Clarke. He was a metronome. Brilliant runner but it never seemed to work for him in the major competitions but he really was a tremendous runner. For characters, you have got to say Dave Bedford.'

Outstanding cross country men in the 1970s, and 1980s at least would include such men as Rossendale's Dave Lewis, Grenville and Graham Tuck, Tim Hutchings and Dave Clarke. Certainly the latter four have trained from Lauriston Cottage, Wimbledon, running across the Common and into Richmond Park. Clarke ran from there more than most in the last twenty-five odd years. His coach John Sullivan did, when he was in the strong Hercules team of the mid-70s. **Mike Puddifoot** points to some unexpected high-profile runners from abroad who have run out from 'The Cottage' at some time or other, 'Malinowski from Poland, Mark Winzenreid and Marty Liquori from the United States.'

Phil Hernon, who ran for Woodford Green and now a distance and cross country veteran for Orion Harriers: 'First of all I followed David Hemery and Kip Keino. A personality for me was Andy Carter who came third in the European 800 of 1971 and then, as far as I can remember, went on to win an Emsley Carr Mile. Seb Coe and Geoff Capes are two more. For me people like coach Gerry Shaw, who brings the kids through at Orion Harriers, should be admired.' Phil gave his opinion on athletics today. 'I feel a great part of the sport has been destroyed with a lack of tracks, facilities and competition. Too elitist now!'

40

Martin Cadwallder ran 48:53 for 10 miles on the road. He ran in the Wolverhampton and Bilston team that came 8th in the National six stage of 1980 and 7th in the 12 stage of 1981. 'As far as characters Bedford has got to be by far. If he could have run the marathon at his peak he would have run 2:7 because he would have blasted it from the start. Someone else is Mick Mcleod. He was a good racer and confident of his ability. He was a hard man with a good sprint finish. 1500m upwards.' (Silver in Moscow Olympics over 10,000.) 'He could also run a 1:50 half. It was those two as far as I am concerned but someone I would like to mention that was good was Roger Clarke from the RAF. He was third behind Dixon and Bedford in that National at Parliament Hill in 1973 and came 5th in the international "World" cross that year. As he was considered solely as a cross-country man no one remembers what he achieved. Nearly everybody knows Dave Bedford but Roger Clarke was one of the top runners but he was not a famous person. One of our biggest talents was Micky Morton who won the World Junior cross country and ran 3:42.0 and 8 minutes for 3000m as a junior. He was at the top for a short time and he then disappeared off the scene.' (Micky Morton was coached by Gerry Barnes of Blackburn Harriers. Morton won the National Youth cross country in 1977 before going on to win the World Junior cross in 1978.)

Nigel Gates runs for the successful Brighton & Hove veterans team, and was still winning major international veteran events at 47. At 39 he was ninth in the 'National' cross country! 'For the greatest character, it's David Bedford isn't it?' Nigel then points out about one of the greatest racers in his opinion, 'Brendan Foster had mental strength and ability. He faced up to pressure races. When he did the trials to make the team, who was he racing? Ian Stewart, Ian McCafferty and people like that. It was always possible he would not make the team. He still went out and did it and then performed well in the Championships.' He quipped, 'I beat Brendan in the National cross-country once!' (Nigel Gates is a teacher at a school for special needs, which is the same type of position Jonathan Kilsby, the talented Shaftesbury veteran runner holds.)

Dave Moorcroft, the Chief Executive of UK Athletics, ex-5000m world record holder and previously Commonwealth 1500 and 5000m Champion, about the characters he found inspiring: 'Chris Chataway when I was very young, Kip Keino, Jim Ryun, Brendan Foster and nowadays probably Paula Radcliffe. Chris visited me at primary school and he fascinated me as a person. I thought "That person is a world record holder" and, even then, I liked running. Kip Keino was the smoothest thing I had seen and was the first of the best Africans. Jim Ryun because I thought he was so much on top of his running and so in control. Brendan Foster because I think I needed that influence at that time of my career. Someone with that iron determination. He was a role model, a person I could aspire to beating. I raced him when he was towards the end of his career. He would often come down to my distance (1500). It was great for my confidence. And Paula because she has got an attitude that is fantastic. The best we can do is to get the very best out of ourselves and she just epitomises that. People like Chataway and Keino were removed from my career really but it helps enormously with your own career when you have got somebody who is a role model you can relate to as well. Brendan Foster was inspirational in many ways but beatable. There was that feeling "If he can do it, I can do it". In the 1970s to 1980s we had loads of these. Cram could look at Ovett and Coe and have that same relationship with them. I think nowadays women are looking at Paula and saying to themselves, "I may not be as good as Paula but I am going to have the same attitude". Maybe the men have not quite got the same role models we were so lucky to have.'

George Richardson, who has been racing for Loughton AC since 1952, said: 'The most remarkable thing I saw was when Tony Simmons was doing a long training run, for one of the "big" marathons. He ran through 10 miles, in about 90th place in the "Finchley 20" in about 58–59 minutes, then ran 48 minutes for the last 10 giving him a time around 1:46 to 1:47.'

Tony Edwards, who has been Captain of the Dulwich Runners: 'Keith Penny had a stroke so he cannot race any longer and is a forgotten man. Keith Penny of Cambridge

Harriers was a great and very modest person. He dominated road running for ten years. He was a fantastic road runner like his wife Glynnis. The only one who could regularly have the edge on Keith was Aldershot's Bernie Ford.' (Nine interesting guys from Kent were good around that time. For Invicta East Kent AC, Mick Gratton, Nick Brawn, Peter Brenchley, Merv Brameld, Eddy Broad, Ian Macmillan, John Wilkins, Jon Wigley, who used to be Assistant Editor of *Athletics Weekly*, and for Medway AC, Vic Smith and Richard Newbold.)

Tim Morphy, a Folkestone AC runner, has run around the 3 hour mark in the London. 27 years ago he started up The Boxing Day, 3 mile 'Fell'-like road race and fun run at Saltwood. The race now attracts well over 400 people for the 3 o'clock start. Two who have won the race are Mike Gratton, after winning the London Marathon in 1983 and former European 800m indoor Champion Steve Heard. Tim remarks: 'Mike Gratton is an outstanding personality and a nice person.'

Regarding Cliff Temple (the late Cliff Temple, was *Sunday Times* Athletics Correspondent and well known coach), Morphy remarked, 'Cliff, to me, was someone I can never forget. His enthusiasm as a coach and as a club runner. He was a great loss to the sport.' (That is something I know Dave Moorcroft would totally agree with. Strangely enough, I can remember in 1974 finishing the Finchley 20 in 2 hrs 3 min 7 sec, just two seconds behind Cliff and a couple of seconds ahead of race walker Paul Nihill. Also, in the Tonbridge 10 I did 58 min 6 sec one year and I was a second behind Cliff at the finish.)

Triple Olympic Champion Seb Coe epitomised the single mind of a winner, and appeared to be only interested in that aspect of competition, but not a lot of people realised Seb Coe had a passion for helping out his club mates, both at Haringey, and before that at Hallamshire Harriers and Loughborough University. That gave him tremendous pleasure. **Gerrard Long** was the Captain of Loughborough University when his friend Tim Hutchings and Seb Coe were there, Long having been a 1:50/3:48 800/1500 man. Long's three 'athletic offspring' are with Highgate Harriers, Becky, Ben and Alex Long, all with potential. About Loughborough and Coe's efforts that Long appreciated so much: 'I remember when Seb Coe had to beat international Gary Cooke on the last leg of the final event, the 4×400. Loughborough were trailing the AAA's team and Seb had to overhaul international Gary Cooke (who married top sprinter Kathy Smallwood), to win the match outright. Seb threw everything into it and won in a thrilling finish.'

Jason Henderson, 31, who ran 1:54 for 800m and is the Editor of *Athletics Weekly*: 'At the age of 11, I was so excited by watching Sebastian Coe gliding across the television screen and winning the 1980 Olympics that I went out and bought four athletic magazines and they included one from America. Looking back now I know Steve Ovett was an admirable runner too.

'Of the people I have interviewed Gerrard Hartmann the physio impressed me most because he really makes people believe that he really has cured them.'

Steve Roe, who once ran a 2:32 marathon in his Herne Hill days, and is now a Kent athletics writer, gave his opinion of Ovett's attitude to the sport: 'Steve Ovett is the greatest character as far as I am concerned. He had a laid back attitude. He always downsized his performances. What did it matter if you had a gold medal when there are children in hospital, people unable to walk. What is achieved is purely history.'

Richard Priestly, who was President of Highgate Harriers in 1993 and manager of the track and field team in 2001. 'At the start it was Steve Ovett who inspired me to run. Without a shadow of doubt he was the greatest character for me. Another one was Kriss Akabusi. He should be invited to come back as an ambassador for the sport as he would have a lot to contribute.'

Andy Catton, whose father Jim Catton of Ilford AC was a good distance runner in the days of Jim Peters. Andy was an international track, cross-country and road runner and went on to win international veteran road events. 'My greatest performance was coming nineteenth in the Senior "National" when "everybody but everybody" ran the National; The Who's Who of British Athletics. It did not matter whether you were a track runner or road or country runner, everybody ran the National in

44

the middle 70s. Ian Thompson dipped me on the line that year.' (Andy was one place higher when Nick Rose won from Ken Newton, Steve Kenyon and Barry Smith in 1980.) Andy continued, 'The Cambridge 10 when I ran 47:30 solo was a memory as it was one of those days when everything went superbly well.

'Two guys stand out, Steve Ovett was one. To my mind he is still the greatest 1500/miler that there has ever been. I think his talent was untapped. I don't think he ever showed his best. To me Steve was the better athlete than Seb or Cramie. I think it is a great shame but I don't think he ever fulfilled his potential. The other one was John Walker, the New Zealand Olympic Champion, who gave everything in every race he ever did.' (Walker has the record for running the most sub-four minutes miles – well over 100.) 'Those two stand out. As far as characters are concerned there was Nicky Lees and Neil Coupland, real eccentrics but fantastic talents. John Batchelor was another character from my Ilford club. During the 70s there were so many immensely talented athletes and every club had a dozen characters.'

Robin Dickson (58) has enjoyed running for 50 years. He is a member of Croydon Harriers and runs as a veteran for Thames Hare & Hounds as well. His best 5k on the track is 14:51. 'Steve Ovett stands out for me as far as characters go that I have seen, and two others that I admire are Seb Coe and Sonia O'Sullivan. As far as the current set of British distance runners are concerned I think the best is Keith Cullen because he is good on the road, track and country and a very unpretentious and friendly character.'

Tony Harran has been club running for 22 years and, like his father Mick, competes for Herne Hill Harriers. It was just after Tony came third for his second-claim club South London and, as the first veteran over 40 in the Gordon Pirie 10 mile cross-country race, he said, 'Steve Ovett is the one that stands out. He was unconventional and, as far as characters go Barry Attwell is a character, a great eccentric. People have said that if he had only trained he could have run under 28 minutes for 10,000 metres.'

Something Tony and Mick remembered hearing was part of a conversation Mick Mcleod was having on the phone, after the National of 1979 at Luton. It went something like this: 'Now for the bad news Gateshead won the team event! Now for the good news I won!' (Luton 1979. 1. Mick Mcleod 47:10; 2. Bernie Ford 47:12*; 3. Nick Rose 47:13; 4. Steve Kenyon 47:16; 5. Julian Goater 47:34; 6. Steve Ovett 47:41; 7. Barry Smith 47:45; 8. Tony Simmons 47:56. 1555 finished. Team: 1. Gateshead 198, 2. Airdale & Spen Valley 276, and 3. Tipton 291.)

In the case of **Bernie Ford*** he remembers his favourite 'National' when he won at Leeds on the 4th of March, 1978. 1. Bernie Ford 41:34; 2. Ian Stewart 41:37; 3. Tony Simmons 41:52; 4. Steve Ovett 42:24 with Steve Kenyon and David Black the next home. 'That race started – in fact, there was a story behind it, which started back in January on a training week in Portugal. I seem to recall that there was myself, Ian, Brendan and Mick Mcleod. We were out on a long run and Brendan casually remarked "I think Ovett is going to win the National this year, no one is going to touch him!" I remember Ian looking at me and not saying anything but I could see from his look that he was not impressed. When we had finished he took me aside and said, "Steve is not going to win it. We have to stop him from winning." From that moment on I think we both trained like men possessed. Tony as well, I think, knew that Steve was after the race, obviously because both he and Steve were coached by Harry Wilson. So the three of us went into the race with one objective and that was to make sure that if we did not win it one of the other two would, but it certainly was not going to be Steve. Tony set off at a tremendous lick and Steve got a bit of a bad start and so he never got on terms, but I was very pleased with that race.'

Tony Simmons won the 'National' in 1975 and so what did that mean to him? 'That was the race I dearly wanted to win to emulate such great runners as Mel Batty, Dick Taylor, Mike Tagg and Dave Bedford. As it turned out Bernie Ford gave me a very hard race for 7 miles and then on the last lap I found it very easy and I just waited again for the last 800 metres to go before I put in the final effort. Winning that race has been one of my life-long ambitions.' One of the names Tony mentions is Mike Tagg, who won the International 'World' cross country at Vichy, where England won all the team prizes. Looking back to that race in March 1970, the year after Tagg achieved a silver in the European 10,000, one realised that he certainly beat an impressive collection of runners. Out of the 103 finishers in the International 'World' cross, the first few were 1. Mike Tagg (England) 36:39.8; 2. Gaston Roelants (Belgium) 36:41.8; 3. Trevor Wright (England) 36:44.6; 4. Dick Taylor (England) 36:50.8; 5. Noel Tijou (France) 37:03.2; 6. Ricky Wilde (England) 37:07.0; 7. Mike Turner (England) 37:09.8; just behind that were Zaddem, Javier Alvarez Salgado, Jordan, Rault, Lachie Stewart, Puttemans and Mike Baxter.

In the early to middle 1960s Mike Turner and Tim Johnston were two of the main runners of possibly the strongest Cambridge University distance group ever and Turner was captain of a successful England cross-country team. Liverpool Harrier Turner was still running well and around the '20' mark in the 'Nationals' in the 1970s. About that race in 1978 that Ford won, **Mike Turner** points out, 'I think at the start of the "National" now, you definitely must run faster. Take the 1978 race as a good illustration. I stood about 600 metres from the start and watched them appear up the hill and they were really belting along. And people who were at the front were people who could keep up in a fast 1500 metres race, there is no question about that. That is the first thing, you have got to run faster it seems to me. One obvious reason, of course, is the fields have been increasing in numbers. If you increase the size of the base of the pyramid in the front of the field it is going to be that much sharper and it is going to be pushed into going faster and faster.' (The marked difference would be that in 1978 there were 1379 finishers; 1977 1368; 1976 1214; 1975 1053; 1974 968; 1972 887; 1971 851 according to *Athletics Weekly*.)

Tony Milovsorov, the National Senior Cross Country Manager from 1996–2001, gained 51 'National' team medals for Tipton Harriers. He ran a 2:09:54 personal best in the London of 1989 (when Douglas Wakiihuri of Kenya won in 2:09:06 from popular Australian Steve Moneghetti 2:09.06). About that personal best performance: 'I remember that six months before Kim McDonald said that I might get down to 2:12 but, back in 1983, I had that self-belief that one day, with the help of Bud Baldaro's training, I could get down to sub-2:10!

'As a kid I painted a picture of the Munich Olympics for my O-level Art, and so two people that stood out for me then were Lasse Viren and Ian Stewart. Viren had the mental ability to win when it mattered most. Ian I admired because of his determination and his great "Do or Die" runs. He had the guts and gave everything. He became tactically aware with the ability to take on the best in the world. Ron Bentley with his 24-hour run was someone I admired and recently Haile Gebrselassie. Regarding characters in my club, the people who love the club so much they have put the club before personal ambition. Two who I could name were Steve Portman and Steve Davies, who lived outside the area; they tried hard and gave everything to Tipton. As far as the greatest character I could mention it would be Stevie Binns of Bingley Harriers. He could make you laugh till your sides ached. To be in his company for an hour was such fun, as he came out with all his stories.' (Stevie Binns was a Commonwealth silver medallist and also a good international on the road and country in the 1980s and early 1990s.)

Ricky Goad, a 2:29 marathon runner from Basildon and now a veteran cross-country runner with Orion Harriers: 'David Bedford and his Southern double, Brendan Foster. Bernie Ford and Tony Simmons racing it out in the National of 1977. Barry Watson and the way he won the 1976 Olympic trial. He went away from such good runners in relentless fashion.' (Watson won from Jeff Norman at Rotherham.) 'All those people in those events were great runners.

'For characters, reading about Steffan White of Coventry in your last book. It sounds that he is a character. The strongest character mentally that I have ever met was Eamonn Martin who, after being an English Schoolboy Champion, fell away with injuries finishing well down in the 100 to 300s in major senior championships but he never gave up, eventually coming through to the top of the pile.'

In 2000, Eamon Martin looks back: 'My favourite races include the first time I won the "National" (1984 from Roger Hackney and Julian Goater). The British 10,000m record (27:23.06) in Oslo, 1990. For those particular races I thought I was in exceptional shape. The London Marathon win in 1993 in 2:10.50 was a good run but does not compare to the other two results. I ran well on the day in the marathon but it was the fame and the things that went with it – plus the fact that it was my first marathon – that was pleasing. But it was a fantastic thrill to win the National because I thought it would always be a struggle for me to win it. Then at Newark (1992) I won it again! I was probably in the best cross country shape I have ever been in (40:29 from Luton's Billy Dee, 40:56 with Sam Carey third) and I went on to finish 17th in the World CC Championships.'

Alex Rowe from Wesham Road Runners, a 52:12 '10' miler, had just come in second to Nigel Gates in the BVAF 10 mile Road Champs at Brockwell Park in 2000: 'Richard Nerurkar in recent years has been one that has caught my imagination. Gary Staines was magic when he was running well. When you watched him, you saw he had excellent style as a smooth runner, particularly when he ran 46 minutes odd in the Ballycotton 10. Pinto of Portugal and Anton of Spain were others who impressed me.'

Competitively one of Bingley Harrier Nerurkar's best performances was when he won the 1993 World Cup Marathon in San Sebastian in 2:10.03 from Sverino Bernardini (Italy) 2:10.12 and Kebede Gemechu (Ethiopia) 2:10.16. Gary Staines was the European 5000 silver medallist in 1990 in 13:22.45 just behind Salvatore Antibo of Italy (13:22.0).

Rachid Banouas the coach to Algerian middle distance runner Ali Saidi-Sief, talked in glowing terms to me about the runner he advises. That was just after Ali had won the Dream Mile in the Golden League Grand Prix meeting in the Bislett Stadium, Oslo on July 13, 2001. It was a personal best time for Ali Saidi-Sief of 3:48.23 with Kenyan Bernard Lagat (3:48.57) and Olympic Champion Noah Negeny (3:50.29) second and third. He thought his man capable of breaking the world mile record at the Bislett Games in 2002, helped by the wonderful atmosphere in the Stadium in Oslo.

'Ali is a very good sportsman with very good qualities. His methodology is the same as 1996 Olympic Champion Noureddine Morceli with his whole approach to athletics. However, as a coach, I feel having the Olympic and World Championships one year after another is too much. Ali's best event is the 5000 and he will do that in 2002.' [Olympic result in Sydney. 1. Million Wolde (Ethiopia) 13:35.49; 2. Ali Saidi-Sief (13:36.20); 3. Brahim Lahlafi (Morocco) 13:36.47.] According to Press comment, unfortunately Ali Saidi-Sief was declared to have tested positive for a banned substance and did not compete on the world scene for the rest of 2001. That may have robbed him of being possibly the only one to really test middle distance runner Hicham El Guerrouj over 5000 or 1500m for some time.

Scott Tompsett, a 23-year-old Hillingdon AC runner, who came 7th in the National Junior of 1997 the same position he got in the Senior Southern of 2001: 'Gebrselassie is impressive with his sheer consistency and guts. Coe to me was another one with that ability. Dave Bedford was a great running character with the clubs.'

Andy Morcombe, 35, a claims manager for Miller Insurance brokers in the City of London, is team captain for Sutton Harriers. He loves running in Richmond Park and on the North Downs. He has run 64.00/3:10 for 10 miles/Marathon: 'To me Gebrselassie is an amazing athlete, as he always seems to be able to find another gear. Of the UK runners I admire Jon Brown, I still think he has a great future and, as he said, it was a level playing field when he came fourth in the Olympic Final.' (Sydney 2000: 1. Gezahgne Abera (Ethiopia) 2:10.11; 2. Eric Wainaina (Kenya) 2:10.31; 3. Tesfaye Tolla (Ethiopia) 2:10.31; 4. Jon Brown (UK) 2:11.17; 5. Giacomo Leone (Italy) 2:12.14; 6. Martin Fiz (Spain) 2:13.06; 7. Abdelkader El Mouaziz (Maroc) 2:13:29. Abera went on to win the World Marathon the following year in Edmonton (2:12.42).

Hayley Yelling, the international from Borough of Hounslow said, after winning the Southern in 2001: 'In sport the greatest character is Steve Redgrave the rower. Another one could be

50

considered a character is Jo Pavey who succeeded despite of all the injuries she had to contend with.' (Jo Pavey ran a personal best time of 14:58.27 to come 12th in the Olympic 5000m final in Sydney 2000.)

Andy Hayward, of the Road Runners Club, ran 7 hrs 27 min for the London to Brighton road race, as a newcomer, in 1998. 'Paula Radcliffe (Bedford & County AC) after her fourth in the Sydney Olympics. It was difficult for her to motivate herself again but she did in the Great North Run. After going clear she showed such spirit by going for the record, even though she was left to do it on her own.' Her time for the half-marathon on October 22nd was 67:07, a European Best, with Tegla Laroupe of Kenya 2nd in 70:07. On the 12th of November in Vera Cruz, Mexico, Paula Radcliffe won the World Half Marathon Championships in 69:07 from Susan Chekemei (Kenya) 69:40. (Chekemei went on to do a world's best of 65:44 in Lisbon in 2001.) Lidia Slavuteanu-Simon was third in 70:24. Then on the 24th of March, 2001 Paula Radcliffe ran one of the best races of her life in the mud at Ostend, to fight off the challenge of 1999 World 10,000 Champion Gete Wami of Ethiopia in the home straight and win the senior World cross country Championships. Her husband, middle distance runner Gary Lough, who trains with her, was first to congratulate her. The next day over the short course Paula was outsprinted by Gete Wami for the gold, but Paula had already achieved her aim. Mohammed Mourhit the Moroccan running for Belgium easily won the men's long race and Kenya were the successful team yet again.

Sharon Murphy, at the age of 15, was the youngest for the UK ever to run in the World Junior cross-country. She also had achieved a win in the English Schools 1500m. 'A lot of talent,' said her coach Ossie Arif, who ran 2:16.35 for a marathon in 1987. Sharon Murphy never fulfilled her potential in her early 20s because of a throat problem but, at 24, she won the London cross-country championship in November 2000. It was straight after that race, in torrential rain, that she was quick to answer which runner she felt was a great character: 'Paula Radcliffe. We were on the team together as juniors. Before that when I was young it was Liz McColgan.' Liz McColgan's outstanding run was in Rome in the World 10,000m Championships in 1991, in 78% humidity, 27°C. She ran away from the field to win in 31:14.31. Another person Sharon Murphy admired was Welsh steeplechaser Christian Stephenson.

Lucy Elliott, who was 18th of 144 in the world cross country in Turin in 1997: 'Paula Radcliffe is the first person that comes to mind. She is so tough. As far as characters, not quite so many around these days. One that I think of was in my club, Dave Bedford!'

Nick Bideau, the successful coach in Melbourne, Australia, thought his partner Sonia O'Sullivan (they were expecting their second child in 2001) was and could be a great athlete again. We talked together in the Raddison Plaza Hotel in Oslo in 2001: 'I saw her do 6×400 in 60 seconds with a minute recovery between each. I said that, if I did, that in training I would expect to do 3:50 for 1500. Her reply, "How do you know I won't?"' Bideau has run 3:54/14.36/2:35 for 1500/5000/marathon. He pointed out: 'Sonia was World Champion in 95; ran a great 3000 at Crystal Palace the year before; was double World cross country Champion in 1998, beat Szabo (the Olympic Champion in Sydney) that year in Budapest over 5000m. In her first ever 10,000 she beat Ribeiro. To do all that you have to be super-talented. Sonia is a tall, strong and powerful runner.'

Danielle Sanderson was the first woman in the London to Brighton in 2000 and also won the BVAF 10 miles in Brockwell Park from Alison Fletcher of Dulwich Runners. Sanderson, who was born on 26.10.62 spent her formative years at Brighton where her father Justine Myers was a well known doctor in the Jewish community. As an international, she ran the marathon in 2:36.29 (she was 11th in the European of 1992). Veteran race walker Harvey Jaquest from Watford advised her, as he did with John Merriman, who obtained places in the 1958 and 1962 Commonwealth Games 3 and 6 miles. 'My heroines nowadays would be people like Paula Radcliffe, such determination, such grit. You believe genuinely she is not taking any performance-enhancing drugs, and getting those results by determination and hard work. She sets her mind to things and achieves them.

Another one is Richard Nerurkar because I could trust his results as the product of hard work.'

John Sullivan, who coached at North London AC and now Woodford Green AC. Some of those he coached were Steve Crabb, Gerry Odlin, Wendy Hoyte and now sprinters Tyrone Edgar and Monu Miah, the AAA's, 2000 under 17 Champion over the 100/200: 'I have always admired Daley Thompson. When the chips were down he always rose to the occasion. He showed what a true Champion he was. Emile Zatopek is another one I think had that special ingredient.' John looked back on an ironical situation, regarding a race with a future world record holder. 'I was at Brook Farm, North London, for an inter-club trophy cross-country race. In the race, after a while, I was running along in eighth or ninth place with this sixteen-year-old. He was sticking with me and I thought "No way will I let this youngster beat me!" I then decided to move through and won the race. The *Evening Standard* put in that night, "35-year-old John Sullivan wins Trophy". I was annoyed they mentioned my age! The sixteen-year-old I had been running with turned out to be Dave Bedford, who finished fifth in the race!'

John Goodbody is a very good writer on sport in *The Times* and in the issue of 29/9/2000, Goodbody, in order to illustrate how the decathlon as an event has moved on, pointed out that Canvey Island's Dean Macey, who was fourth in the Sydney Olympics behind winner Erki Nool (from Estonia who scored 8641 and was coached by Daley Thompson) scored 8567 points, compared to 8522 scored by Daley Thompson when winning in Moscow in 1980! On 26–7/5/2001 at Gotzis, Roman Sebrle set a world record of 9026, wiping fellow Czech Thomas Dvorak's 1999 mark of 8994 off the books. Sebrle did 4.21 for his last of the ten events, the 1500m. Decathlete **Snowy Brooks** said: 'Incredible for 15 stone men to do such things or to even break 4:30 at the end of such a gruelling set of disciplines.'

Ollie Flynn, the race walker, won the Commonwealth gold for 30k in the 1978 Edmonton Games in 2:22.04 from Willii Sawall (2:22.59) and Tim Erickson (2:26.34) both from Australia. Flynn, who is an ardent follower of all athletic events was also 14th in the 1976 Olympic 20k in Montreal. 'Paul

Nihill's longevity. He was the antithesis of an Olympic athlete. He was a hard competitor being an ex-boxer. His type of fight reminded you of Henry Cooper. Peter Tancred the discus thrower was a great personality in his own right. Dave Bedford was another. Adrian Metcalfe, the 400m runner who went into television. Geoff Capes was a budgerigar breeder. Physical variance to his private pastimes. Don Thompson "The Mighty Mouse" (1.68m/57kg) who won the walking gold medal in an Olympic record in Rome (4:22.30). After not finishing the 50k because of the heat in the 1956 Olympics at Melbourne he decided to build up his resistance by boiling kettles in his bathroom, to simulate the heat and humidity he would have to encounter at the next Olympics in Rome.' The heat was something that so many found impossible to deal with. It worked for Thompson as he was the only UK gold medallist for track and field in 1960. 'Zatopek "Immortal" a free spirit. Not only a very great athlete but more important as a person with integrity in a repressive system that abused him. The tragedy of his life was the IAAF honoured him in death rather than in life.'

Ollie Flynn mentions Adrian Metcalfe, who comes up strongly in a conversation with **James Mayo** who has run 1:48.6/3:44 for 800/1500 in recent times. Mayo, whose brother is middle distance runner Tom Mayo, was inspired by his uncle Adrian Metcalfe. 'He had yellow jaundice after the Olympics of 1964, after achieving a silver medal in the 4×400 relay. He inspired me first of all then I went on from there. I found a distance I was relatively good at and then admired Peter Elliott, Seb Coe and Ovett.' (Adrian Metcalfe never had a chance to reach his peak before retiring and in 1961 he held the British 400m record of 45.7 jointly with 1962 European Champion Robbie Brightwell.)

Dave Cropper is married to ex-international Pat Lowe. Cropper won his heat in the 1968 Mexico Olympics in 1:47.9 and ran 1:47.6 in the semi final. He was AAA's Champion in 1969. 'The people who impressed me were Brightwell and Cooper as a duo. Robbie was quite meticulous in his preparation and dealing with athletes when he was coaching. John was very happy-go-lucky. Together they made a good duo. When I knew them I was at a very impressionable age and those are the two who come to mind. I have a lot of admiration for Robbie. We did not run together as Robbie finished in 64 and my first international was in 65. It was not someone I knew as a peer. He retired when I really broke through. I often felt that, if I could have brought his discipline to my talent, we could have been all right!' (Brightwell anchored GB to silver medals in 1964 Olympics in Tokyo and gained silver in the Commonwealth, besides gaining a gold in the European. John Cooper was runner up to American Rex Cawley in the Olympic 400m hurdles in Tokyo.)

The hurdler **Gary Oakes**, who ran for Haringey AC, was third in the 400m hurdles in the 1980 Olympics in Moscow. 1. Volker Beck (GDR) 48:70; 2. Vasiliy Arkhpyenko (URS) 48:86; 3. Gary Oakes (GB) 49.11. Oakes is married to Heather Hunte who was a UK Champion and Olympic relay medallist. 'Tom Johnson my coach, when I started with him said, "Go away and read David Hemery's book *Another Hurdle*." Hemery was inspiring. He set out over two years to achieve an Olympic gold medal. Michael Johnson was another one who planned his running strategy so well.' (Johnson from the United States a 200 and 400m Olympic Champion, at the time of writing, holds the world record for both distances.) Gary added, 'The biggest characters in the sport are the ones who are less talented but work just as hard. You see them down the gym and on the tracks all the time. They have to be admired as characters.'

Mike Belligham, a field eventer from Cambridge Harriers, who was the 1960 AAA's Junior discus Champion looks at all the events: 'Al Oerter. He was certainly one of the greatest. He stands out. He made a comeback, after gaining four Olympic gold medals at his event, to compete in his, 40s and 50s as a World veteran Champion.'

Al Oerter's philosophy: 'I remember so many competitions BUT the only trophy I have ever kept in my return to athletics was in 1976. It was a little competition in Massachusetts where I was travelling with a friend. We saw a sign posted up pointing to a high school field saying that there would be a track and field meet there that evening and those wishing to compete should show up at 6 o'clock. The cost would be 50 cents. Somebody loaned me a discus and I just happen to have some jogging shoes; I used them and threw something like 181 feet (about 55m), winning the competition. I won my little trophy for my 50 cents and it was one of the first feelings I had of what track and field was really about for me! The whole thing just happened. I just happened to drive by the high school that had the advertisement up. I just happened to find somebody who would loan me a discus. It was not the Olympics that were the important thing in this sport any longer. I really enjoyed that evening of competing with a gathering of people who wanted to throw as far as they could possibly throw, enjoy the competition and try to encourage one another to throw further. It was a country fair kind of environment that I totally enjoyed.'

I had a conversation on the phone with **Melvyn Watman** on 25th of July, 2001. Watman is considered one of the world's top athletics statisticians and writers on the sport for over forty years. I asked him as to who he thought was the greatest pole vaulter over the years. 'Sergey Bubka dominated world vaulting more than anyone in history,' was Mel's immediate answer to that. Regarding women's pole vaulting he said that international pole vaulting has only come into being in the middle 90s. It has become a popular, developing event, with a very good image. There has been good publicity and people like Stacey Dragila from the United States have enhanced its reputation as a spectacle. Because it is relatively new records are going more easily. Janine Whitlock has broken the British record about 33 times, if you add her indoor to her outdoor performances. Before the fibreglass pole was used, Cornelius Warmerdam, 'The vaulting vicar' Rev Bob Richards and Don 'Tarzan' Bragg were outstanding and then came charismatic characters with the fibreglass pole like Bob Seagren, also from the United States. As far as the United Kingdom was concerned Mike Bull, a thoughtful personality, who competed for Northern Ireland, was the UK athlete on the fringes of world class and Mike Hooper also did a lot for UK vaulting. It is noted that Allan Williams, according to another athletics authority **Dave Cocksedge**, was an international till he was 27 with a best of 5.25 for the vault and then came back into competition as a veteran and competed in the over 45s in 2000. (Sergey Bubka from the Ukraine, born 4.12.63, had done the 23 best vaults of all time listed in the *International Athletics Annual* 2001. Cornelius Warmerdam was the first 15-footer in 1940. Bob Richards won the Olympic Gold for the USA in 1952 and 1956; Don Bragg was first over 16ft; John Pennel first over 17ft.)

John Pennel looked back: 'I thought it was a pretty dramatic event to start with, and I think it still is. I looked at newsreels of Richards, Bragg, Gutowski, Graham and Martyn and I used to think when I was at high school nobody can jump that height! We put up the bar at 15ft and then looked at it, and we thought surely nobody can go that high! So those athletes doing it were impressive as hell to me.' (Bob Seagren was the Olympic Champion in 1968. Mike Bull was the 1966 and 1967 AAA's Champion and 1970 Commonwealth Champion. He broke the British record 11 times, ending up with a best of 5.25. Brian Hooper broke the UK record 15 times and had a best of 5.59 and 5.01 as a veteran over 40.) Stacey Dragila was born 25.3.71 in Auburn, California and won the 2000 Olympic title for the USA with 4.60m.

My Satisfying Result

Athletics being so personal to the individual, often the best result in life that an athlete feels he had may not be shared by the public and can be a surprise when you talk to the athlete concerned.

Take Trinidad & Tobago sprinter Ato Boldon (born 30/12/73 in Port of Spain). He was third in both the 100 and 200m in the Olympic Games in 2000. He obtained a silver and bronze medal in the World Championships the year before. In Stuttgart in 1997 he ran 9.90/19.97 for the 100/200 at the same meeting, but Ato told me at the Press Centre in the Bislett Stadium in 2001: 'The best personal satisfaction for me was the Commonwealth Games 1998 when I did 9.98 without a doubt. It was into the

57

wind on a track that was really slow and it was not considered the performance of the Games because of all the controversy surrounding the race.'

17th of September 1998 Kuala Lumpur, Malaysia: 1. Ato Boldon (T&T) 9.88; 2. Frank Fredricks (Namibia) 9.96; 3. Obadale Thompson (Barbados) 10.00; 4. Matt Shirvington (Australia) 10.03; 5. Darren Campbell (England) 10.08; 6. Eric Nkansah (Ghana) 10.18; 7. Chris Donaldson (New Zealand) 10.19 and 8. Marlon Devonish (England) 10:22.

Getting the Best out of Yourself

Nick Bideau was an adviser to Sydney Olympic 400m Champion Cathy Freeman from 1990 till April 2000. (Peter Fortune coached her through to her Olympic glory.) About her qualities he said, 'Unbelievable capacity to get to the start line and deliver the maximum. Just a fantastic competitor. To be relaxed and get the best out of herself. Really lift and go to that new level on the big occasions. She always ran her best races in the Championships every year.

'Five weeks before the World Championships in Athens in 1997 Sandie Richards had been a bit down after her run in Stuttgart. I invited her to come and train with us till the World Championships in Athens. Things fell into place and the training worked. Cathy was first and Sandie second.' 1. Cathy Freeman (Australia) 49:77; 2. Sandie Richards (Jamaica) 49:79 and 3. Jearl Miles-Clark (USA) 49:90.

The All Rounder

Ex-international decathlete **Nick Phipps**, was in the Great Britain Bobsleigh team from 1979 to 1992. Since then he has competed for Woking AC and was second with 7230 points in the World Veterans Championships decathlon at Durban in 1997. Now at 49 years old, he commented in July 2001 at Battersea Park, where he was doing some coaching: 'I love to keep competing for as long as I can despite having injuries in the last two years. Veteran competition is good competition.'

Regarding the great all rounders of all-time he was quite emphatic about that: 'For the men Daley Thompson. No comparison with anybody. For the women Jackie Joyner Kersee (USA) with her 7291 points.' (Born East St Louis, Illinois, USA 3rd of March, 1962. Her 7291 points were achieved on 24/9/88 in Seoul in the Olympic Games, 12.69/1.86/15.80/22.56/ 7.27/45.66/2:08.51.)

Those Who Stand Out?

Stan Greenberg, Athletics Historian, statistician, Assistant to the BBC Athletics Team, Sports Editor of the *Guinness Book of Records* in 1982 has seen 230 World Records achieved since 1948. 'Viktor Saneyev (USSR) with his three Olympic gold medals and a silver in four Olympics of doing the triple jump. An event that you can easily get injured in yet he achieved those results. Al Oerter and Janis Lusis are two more that spring to mind. Emil Zatopek, a lovely man to talk to, and there was that great legend Jesse Owens, someone I admire in athletics history.'

4

'The Hard Men'

Roy Fowler

Roy Fowler, with his sterling qualities as a tough racer, epitomised the type of runner who could succeed over the more naturally gifted, time and again. In many ways he fitted into the same mould as his personal heroes Emil Zatopek and Gordon Pirie. I remember going to Perry Bar, Birmingham on the 27th of March, 1977, on a gloomy damp day and, after a hell of a trip facing the vagaries of the Sunday train service from London. The day turned out to be quite an inspiring one. I went to see Roy Fowler win the National Veterans cross country Championships for the third consecutive year. In the underrated event, he had surprisingly good opposition. A resurgent Nat Fisher from Harlow, Gerry North, Ron Gomez (Vale of Aylesbury), Dick Cooper (Worcester), Harry Clayton (Bristol), Eric Austin (Tipton) and Bob Slowe (Highgate). Those were the ones up front for much of the race. He threw off the challenge of Fisher and North in the closing stages. About that fact he explained, 'I remember what Zatopek said, 'When you think you have nothing left, the others have nothing left, and if you can play your last ace you may have a chance of pulling it off." With that in mind he went for it.' Roy, who liked to have a glass of sherry with a raw egg before he started his early morning training runs, had been doing 90–110 miles a week and had recently been racing against a younger international Mike Tagg. Fowler went on to win his final National Vets cross country in 1979, again beating Fisher and Harry Clayton (who still races

60

as a vet). Wirral, once more, were dominant team victors. Since those days the most consistent veteran cross-country runners in the 40–49 group have been Aldershot's 'Taff' Davies in the 1980s and then Nigel Gates in the 1990s. In 1975, before those races, Fowler won three gold medals in the first Veteran World Championship in Toronto. Eric Austin and Arthur Walsham of Northern Vets were two notable category winners in the marathon. Two years later in Gothenburg, Roy won the 10,000m from Ron Gomez and was second to Gaston Roelants in the 5000m.

In 1976 I went up to the Potteries to have a nice long talk with Roy. We went for a five mile run to begin with. Howard Williams, the top Essex official, who attended every Metropolitan League in the history of the event, will recall how I had made the first 60, so as far as I was concerned, I was running well at the time. Being able to train with Roy, I had decided to wear my fastest 'flat' shoes. Roy wore heavy army boots. He still had to wait for me three times on the run, before we washed ourselves down in cold water in Roy's sink!

Red-haired Roy ran for City of Stoke in his prime. He was born at Leek in March 1934. In his job, he was constantly up a ladder painting and decorating, not really conducive to being a top athlete on a heavy mileage, but that never put Roy off. His racing weight was 57kg and he was 1.65m tall (5'5"). He ran without his teeth in, which gave you the impression he was either grimacing with pain or purely smiling at the opposition. One national newspaper reporter was a trifle inaccurate when he wrote once. 'Fowler was gritting his teeth with determination!' He is married and all his children, Anthony, Paul and Jane, have been good runners.

Roy Fowler looks back in March 1976. 'First of all the doctor advised me on medical grounds to go running. I was a very weak child and up to about 4 or 5 years of age I had not started school at all because of ill-health. Then I had double pneumonia again and eventually finished up having it three times so I only did three years at school in all my life – the rest of the time was spent in an out of hospital for one thing or another. On medical advice I was told to get out in the fresh air as much as possible and run about and try and strengthen my lungs and my heart and that was how I eventually got very keen and enjoyed running. At the age of 14 I won my first cross-country race at school and just after that I joined Leek Athletic Club. We are now trying to form a club in the area. I found a lad a few months ago who had never raced in his life; I trained him and he won a County title and finished 11th in the Inter-Counties for his age. His name is Andrew Wilton, and there you have a case of a lad who was very healthy because he lives in the hills and loves to run. He reminds me of Maurice Herriott (silver in 1964 Olympic steeple) in his very young days. It proves to me there is a lot of talent here and that is why we are trying to form this new athletics club.' (Staffs Moorlands became the club. In the case of Andy Wilton, he went on as a senior to be a vital cog in the winning Tipton teams in the 'National' cross country and road relay teams of the 1980s. He was 7th in the National of 1986.)

'I work with ten athletes locally. One of them is Glen Harvey, a junior international. This lad was dropping out of races and it just was not there, but within 12 months of training we eventually got this young lad running 25 to 26 miles and when I say run I mean run. This lad was in the coal mine at the time, at 17, down the pit and he was training at 4 in the morning and then again at night. Now he is in college and studying for a degree in coal mining and I think Glen Harvey will one day be something a little bit different. He is now very fast and very fit.'

In 1980 at Sutton Coldfield Glen Harvey was 39th the National senior and Mike Tagg 26th to take Staffs Moorlands AC into fourth place over all, three points behind Invicta. Tipton won from Gateshead and Nick Rose was first past the post.

Ferdie Gilson who was running for Surrey and in the 30s in the Intercounties in 1961 before he hit a stone, hidden under the snow said, 'That 1961 Inter-counties at Blackpool was Roy Fowler's big breakthrough. Bruce Tulloh came second.'

In 1963 Basil Heatley, who went on to gain the silver medal in the Olympic marathon the following year won the 'National' for the third time and led Coventry Godiva to team victory from

62

Portsmouth and Derby & County. Roy Fowler finished second ten seconds behind Heatley. Behind that came Eddy Strong, Tim Briault, Tim Johnston, Brian Craig, Mike Bullivant, Mike Turner, Alan Simpson, Don Taylor, Juan Taylor and Gerry North. John Farrington won the junior race from Billy Adcocks, who became one of the UK's finest ever marathon runners. Roy Fowler went on to beat Gaston Roelants, in the International 'World' cross country, which Roelants won on four occasions.

Now for the 'hard man's story'. Reflecting on the race with Roelants: 'I had some terrible pains in my legs; they told me there was nothing wrong but that it was just the amount of hard training that I was doing and what with doing 9 hours a day on my legs as a painter decorator it was just strain and nothing to worry about. I was doing around 85 to 90 miles a week. I had finished second in the National, but Basil Heatley came up to me two days before the race and said, "Roy, you can win this International." I said, "What do you mean, Basil, you are the British Champion." "Yes," he says, "but to run 9 miles cross-country in the National is one thing, to win over 10,000m against a man like Roelants is another. I think you are the one with the type of temperament to go with him." I bunked out with Basil in San Sebastian and we planned together; we trained twice a day before the International. There were over 60,000 people at that race and the weather was terrifically hot. I remember warming up and everything was spinning round, it was so hot.

'Any road, away we went and I remember there was Michel Jazy there, Roelants and a lot of very good competition. After a mile there were only three of us in the race – I know I had never run so fast in my life, but I had never trained so hard as I had for that race. I had to stay with Roelants whatever happened, and the race was on! I was like a cart horse, so they told me afterwards, and Roelants was flying over the ground; as a steeplechaser he also had an advantage when we took the obstacles. Coming back around for the last lap we were joined by Mariano Haro (Spain), and I attacked with everything I had got. I went up through the apple orchard, down over the stream and over a ramp with about six or seven foot drop at the other side, and I took it perfectly. I was away, but to my amazement Roelants came up, looked at me and flew down the home straight with at least 20 yards on me. I attacked again and got up to Roelants' shoulder, and this carried on five times down the home straight! Eventually I remembered Emil Zatopek's saying, "When you think you have got nothing left the others have got nothing left at all and if you can play your last ace you may have a chance of pulling it off." It happened with him, he said, in the 1952 Olympic 5000m. So, with this in mind, I threw everything I had into the last 500–600 yards and I don't remember anything, it was as though I was in a coma; and I went through the tape and fell on the floor. When they brought me round they said that Roelants had stopped and walked in and that was the end of that race.

'Previously in the "National" we had 200 yards of cement path to run up at Cambridge and it was there I believe I fractured both tibias. I felt pain in the International – I could not sleep at night without sleeping tablets because my legs were burning all the time – but the fractures in the tibia did not show till about two months after! It was after the International that I went in plaster for another six months on and off on my right leg then the left leg played up a lot more, so they x-rayed my left leg. I did no training then for 12 months at all! I returned to the England cross-country team in 1966 (El Ghazi of France won, England won the team) and then after that I was 3rd in the 1968 International in Tunis. (Mohamed Gammoudi of Tunisia won and as more often than not in those days England won the team event.) In the Tunis race I had felt a sharp pain in my big toe but did not think anything about it when I hit the front with 2 miles to go. I felt well and confident and thought I could win the race. Then the pain in my big toe got worse and worse and I remember just glancing down as I was running round and I saw a dirty mark on my shoe and I knew then that my foot was bleeding and I could not take it any more. Gammoudi put an effort in and I still had second place with 110 yards to go when Ron Hill took me again. After that I had a slight operation to take a bit of steel out of my toe. That went by, and then I got a pain in my achilles tendon and I eventually went lame; I could not walk at all. I saw a specialist in London who operated and I was off athletics for six to eight months and then it was a slow fight back.

'As my wife had just commented that the World Veteran Championships were coming up in two to three years time it got me mobile again and so I had to push on, plus the team wanting me in the six-man National Road Relay. In fact in athletics it is being needed that has been the greatest thing of all. George Dunn and many more have always come up and said we have got to win the race, we need you, and that is it. Though I say it myself I was third in the European Championships but I don't think one official from the British Board came up and said well done Roy Fowler, but that's another story! I feel I am a person who has to be needed.

'The British athlete gets up in the morning at 6.30, does his 8 to 10 miles, comes back, washes and shaves and goes to work. He has about half an hour for dinner, then at night he is on the highway again. Don't forget most athletes will do this for six or seven years before they ever win so much as an area title. For instance, I trained twice a day from when I was 21 and I did not obtain a title of any description till I was 27, yet I still trained twice a day every day – Saturday and Sunday too. I even came out of night school at 9, walked home and went training for an hour at 10.30, and was still up at 5.30 to get my session in. The British athlete does not want a soap box to stand on to shout "I have done this" or "I have done that", he just wants someone to say thank you, and I think it means a lot. I remember when I won the Inter-County Cross Country Championships at Blackpool for the second time, and the man who presented me with that medal was Jack Crump, shortly before he died. There had been a lot of sneers and talk about Jack Crump but I always remember his words: "Roy we want men like you in the England team. You are the men who are going to win medals." That gave me a terrific lift.'

In the 1962 Commonwealth Games in Perth, Australia, Ron Clarke, the Australian multi-distance record holder broke through as a senior. Clarke came second to Murray Halberg in the 3 miles. Halberg was an amazing runner, who had a withered arm from an accident earlier in his life. He was the Rome 5000m Olympic Champion. At Perth, Bruce Kidd of Canada was third and Bruce Tulloh fourth. Tulloh won the European 5000m title in Belgrade, barefoot in 14:0.6. The first 8 in the 10,000m in Belgrade were 1. Pytor Bolotnikov (SU) 28:54.0; 2. Friedrich Janke (EG) 29:01.6; 3. Roy Fowler (GB) 29:02.0; 4. Martin Hyman (GB) 29.02.0; 5. Robert Bogey (Fr) 29:02.6; 6. Leonid Ivanov (SU) 29:04.8; 7. Franc Cervan (Yug) 29:07.6; 8. Mike Bullivant 29:13.4.

'Just before I left England I had a 2 mile race; in that I had a groin injury. The British Board decided they would take me over and see what Johnny Johnston, who was the physiotherapist with the team, could do about it, so away we went to Belgrade and I settled down with some easy jogging but the right leg was very painful. I was lame, so I just did the easy jogging and had massage. I had a talk with Mike Bullivant and Martin Hyman and they said all I can do is set off at a reasonable speed and hope the groin stood up to it; with that in mind I thought right, I am going to go nice and steady and not get put off by anybody. At 5000m I remember looking across the track and thinking I hadn't a chance; I was next to last, 200 yards behind. Then, for some unknown reason, I started to "tick" and the laps became like running 50 yards instead of quarters. Eventually, with 2 miles to go, I got with Bullivant, Hyman, Bogey and the Russian. With seven laps to go there started being a "punch up" – Bogey got very rough and he hit Martin Hyman in the solar plexus and nearly put him out altogether, Bullivant got knocked over onto the grass two or three times, and then I rolled into Bullivant. We went into the final three laps and Hyman did not come at all which left me stuck out there on my own and then I realised Hyman was after a medal as well as me. Bogey then took me with 200 yards to go and so did Hyman. I got very close to them at the top bend and now the leg was dead and I could not feel a thing – I flew round Hyman and Bogey and I sprinted down the home straight and I missed being second in the European Championships as much as Tony Simmons missed being first in that dramatic finish in Rome (1974)! After the race I had an internal haemorrhage which had to be nicked and drained off. My groin was bleeding internally, the leg was severely swollen and my briefs had to be cut away from my leg. Any road, it was a great race and it was what I had trained for, and I was very happy and content.

'I had now to get myself ready for the Empire Games in Australia. I was now second fastest man in the world over 6 miles and I was very confident. The only trouble was the weather. We could not even get up to train for 8 in the morning as the weather was so hot and we had just got no life in us at all. In addition I had got sunburnt on my feet and they were all swollen. I will never forget the race as long as I live. The temperature was 92°F in the shade and the track was bone hard, a combination of ashes and iron-ore. We cut our spikes down to an eighth of an inch and sharpened them up but my spikes never went into that track at all. I kept coming through till I eventually got up to fifth place and all at once I noticed that in the race, out of 33 starters, there were only 12 athletes left in the field, and then there were only 9 – all the rest were lying about on the ground, or on the track. I finished the race eighth and was admitted to hospital for 10 days in which I never came out. After all that I keep saying it shows how good and respected the British athlete is: Mel Batty, Martin Hyman, Mike Bullivant, John Merriman and I all finished! It really was a terrible race.'

1. Bruce Kidd (Canada) 28:26.6 (Games Record); 2. Dave Power (Australia) 28:34.0; 3. John Merriman (Wales) 28:40.8; the next three were Maghee (New Zealand), Hyman and Batty.

John Bourne, whose famous sports shop Bourne Sports (Stoke on Trent) is now 32 years old, did a marathon inside 3 hours a couple of times: 'Roy Fowler was my hero. He was so tough and strong. I used to watch him as a kid winning all the local events, and that inspired me to take up running in the first place.'

Andy Holden

I can remember days in the 1980s visiting Tipton Legends Tony Milovsorov, Allan Rushmer and Andy Holden for lengthy stories I did for Geoff Harrold, who was the editor of *Marathon and Distance Runner*, sadly a magazine no longer in existence. Harrold is currently publicity officer of the London Marathon and is a good veteran runner. In Andy Holden's case, it was in the summer late in the morning when I arrived in Birmingham and we had two or three pints before lunch. I ended up in the evening in a pub drinking Wilsons beer with Andy, Tony Coyne and Brian Clifton. Brian became a devoted manager of the Tipton team in the 1990s. The club had much success on the road and country under his management. He took me in his car as a special favour to get the last train back to London. That was from some obscure station. After many pints I don't remember which. I was woken up at Paddington by half a dozen Pakistani gentlemen in the early hours of the morning. They had obviously got on somewhere along the way. I first met Andy in 1970 but it was in May 1998 that we last talked at Sutton Coldfield. Those reflections from the 1980s and again in 1998 I will recall for you.

Andy Holden, who has his own dental practice, is one of the greatest UK club athletes of all time. That's what people in the Midlands would acknowledge. He has and is putting so much into sport. As a junior (at 19 he ran 8:42 for the 3000m steeplechase) and as an early senior he took Birmingham University to the most prestigious University road and cross country titles, and was recently president of their athletic club. He won the National Junior from Dave Bedford in 1969 at Parliament Hill. Among other things he became 3000m steeplechase British record holder and had some good international marathon wins, but explains: 'If the atmosphere of today prevailed I might have taken up the marathon in 1973–74. But in those days it was not the done thing. There were one or two athletes who did it. Don Faircloth ran marathons in his early 20s and Graham Taylor (1966 AAA's Champion) was another. I suppose Ronnie Hill was the only one who ran consistently over the marathon for a number of years. I did not change to the marathon very readily, in fact, in those days it was more or less the end of your progression when you changed to the marathon. I probably delayed running marathons but the marathon was not regarded in the same light as it is today.'

I noticed Andy had a couple of good results quite close together in 1980 over long distances. He was second in 1:41.36 in the North Staffs Road runners 20 miles on the 23rd of March behind winner John Graham of Birchfield, with Ian Stewart third. In the AAA's marathon at Milton Keynes in early May he was third in 2:15.18 behind Ian Thompson, the Luton, European and Commonwealth marathon champion of 1974 (2:14.00) with Dave Black of Tamworth second (2:14.28.). Thompson told Mel Watman for *Athletics Weekly*, 'It wasn't a course for fast times and the wind was very trying.' The next runners in after Holden were Yakata Taketomi of Japan, Chris Garforth, John McLaughlin, Dave Cannon, Ian Ray, Malcolm East, Trevor Wright, Mike Longthorn, Mike Gratton, Stan Curren and Hugh Jones.

As a Tipton Harrier, Holden never lost his enthusiasm for competition and went on, after his very full international and high quality club running days, to become National Veterans Cross Country Champion (Over 40) at Silksworth, Newcastle in 1989. In that undulating race, after a mile completed Colin Youngson, the Scottish marathon runner from Aberdeen had a good 100 metres on Andy, who was running in third place at the time, but Holden eventually worked his way up to the front and won well.

In recent years we had not seen Andy about in veteran competitions, till suddenly there he was at Sutton Park on the 22nd May, 1998 in the National Veterans Road Relay, running the anchor leg for Tipton in the over 50s race, his red hair, green and white hooped vest, the slightly crouched style with the familiar low leg action creating that famous ground-eating stride that was once so familiar around the world. That was all unmistakable. He took his club from thirteenth to finish tenth out of the 42 clubs that started.

'That was the first time I have run in two years. I have been injured for twenty months and I could not get more than seven days of consecutive running in. Basically, I have damaged my achilles and since the lay-off I have a lot of pulled hamstrings, knees and calf problems. They dragged me out for this one, even though I do enjoy running.'

The real pleasure recently for him has been with his coaching which he also has a talent for, as others testify when they see him at Tipton Sports Centre track. 'I have got a squad I train. Under 17s right down to Under 9s. I am concentrating on the Under 17s and a couple of lads are just over 17. When we had the McDonalds relays one lad I coach, Phillip Nicol, ran the fastest lap in the Under 15s. He was also second in the Inter-Counties this year (1998). There is another 17-year-old called Mark Andrew who has not been running quite two years yet, and he is now County potential.

'It's great to be involved with them really and with my sons who like running. Joe has just turned 12 and ran personal bests this year, 2:30 and 5:11 for 800 and 1500m. He is showing good potential and has got a really good temperament. My elder son Tom is more an 800/1500m runner whereas Joe is more a cross-country type.'

Andy looks back over the years and points to his happiest memories as a runner. 'I made the Olympics and the Commonwealth Games when I was fairly young. But even further back I remember the first time I ran the National Cross Country and finished third in the Youths race just behind Tony Simmons (Graves Park, Sheffield, 1996) completely out of the blue. That will always remain as an incredible experience. That was the year Mike Turner and Ron Hill fought out a very close finish in the senior race.' That gave him the appetite for the sport which he never really lost.

'I had been training hard to do that. I thought then, I had got the potential and it gave me the appetite to train hard and get up with the best boys around, I suppose I was lucky with the peer group of juniors I grew up with because there were such classy lads around. The Stewarts, Brendan Foster and Tony Simmons and people like that. I had to race amongst them as a youth and junior. It got me to a pretty good level and in fact as a junior I was knocking on the door of the senior scene. I ran the senior international when I was still a junior. I went to university at Birmingham. I had five good years there, training to become a dentist. Mal Thomas (1972 National winner) was at the university and between us we knocked out some good sessions and knocked down some beers as well! Big "Gino" Griffiths was there and he was a leader on the beer stakes and we knocked him into shape as a runner eventually!'

In the International 'World' cross country in 1971 at San Sebastian, England won the senior team and were first junior team. Nick Rose won from Ray Smedley (a sub four-minute miler) with Scotland's John Brown third. Doris Brown of the USA won the women's race and, Joyce Smith led England to victory in third place.) England Men: 1. Dave Bedford (38:42.8); 2. Trevor Wright (39:05.2); 5. Pete Standing (39:19.5); 15. Tony Simmons (39:55. 2); 16. Frank Briscoe (39:56.3); 17. Andy Holden (39:57.2) and non-scorers 18. Mike Beevor (39:58.3); John Caine 28, and Alan Blinston 29.

'That was magic really, Dave Bedford ran away with the race and Trevor Wright was second, Peter Standing ran out of his skull for fifth and there were four of us running for the last three places, Mike Beevor, Frank Briscoe and Tony Simmons and myself. We were coming down the home straight and into a very strong head wind, it was about six inches deep in mud and there were four Englishman in the middle teens fighting and punching each other. I got in front, Tony blocked me and I had Mike Beevor on one side and Frank Briscoe on the other – holding them back.'

England being victorious in the 'World' cross country? Older people would say 'Not like that now!' but, the younger people around today would say 'There were no Kenyans and not so many countries competing then!' (1) That is only half the story. Belgian, Omer Van Noten, the triple 'Over 50' World veteran Champion at Gateshead in 1999, said that in those days he could not make the Belgian team because what he termed as the 'White Kenyans' were beating him. His countrymen were that good and, were spearheaded by such men as Karel Lismont, Emiel Puttemans and Roelants etc, so he got to about 11th in the National Championships but could not get any further! (2) In San Sebastian who were the English up against in the IAAF 'World' cross country that could be considered among the best in the world at the time, outside of the UK runners? Noel Tijou, Lucien Rault and Michel Bernard (France), Mariano Haro and

Javier Alvarez Selgado (Spain), Rod Dixon and Eddie Gray (NZ), Pekka Paivarinta (Finland), and Gaston Roelants, Willy Polleunis, Karel Lismont (Belgium). (3) The team result indicates a fair spread of countries: 1. England 56; 2. Belgium 174; 3. France 185; 4. New Zealand 192; 5. Spain 196; 6. Morocco 213. Other countries behind that included Finland, Eire, Poland, Switzerland, Italy, and Algeria.

Ron Bentley has been one of the great motivators for Tipton over the last 40 years and he ran 135 marathons (only two over three hours). He also held the World 24 hour Track record when he covered 165 miles 545 yards at Walton 1973. He was noted as being a good relay racer for the club too, so his appreciation of Andy Holden's effect on joining Tipton was very relevant.

'In the early days he used to train with our lads and they would drink together. We had Allan Rushmer (Commonwealth bronze 1966) but we wanted one more top liner to win the National Road Relay, as we had never won it. We had already won the National cross country. We needed one more runner and Andy was the bloke. When he joined that was the turning point. From then on we won everything because Andy was the main one in the team. Rushmer and Holden were the top two runners and people like Tony Milovsorov were coming through.

'Andy Holden had got greater qualities than people thought because he was the sort of man who could run things like the Isle of Man and have three wins and the second fastest time in the relay in four races in two days and things like that.

'He went through a bad patch, probably drinking too much. He knew I ran the Two Bridges and said, "I would like to run the Two Bridges" and he ran like a maniac. At 20 miles he dropped out. He said, "I am coming back next year to win this!" He came back the year after and broke the record that still stands today and from then onwards he went all the way through again. He got his interest ebbing back. He got married, got the kids.

'It was when we had Holden, Rushmer and Mike Kearns who were mates, we were never out of the first three in the National road relay for ten years!

'Till then we had got a good "engine room" but we had not got the stars like that to carry us through.

'Then later there was Ian Stewart who trained along the canals on a Sunday morning as did Brian Cole, Rushmer and Paul Venmore. Stewart was a very hard man and he destroyed a few runners in his time by them trying to run with him.'

Without a doubt one of the most exciting races ever held at Crystal Palace Stadium was the Coca Cola Invitation meeting on the 10th of September, 1971 when novice steeplechaser David Bedford raced against the British No. 1 Andy Holden, with a good supporting cast of specialist steeplechasers such as Gareth Bryan Jones, Ron McAndrew and John Bicourt. The end result was that Bedford and Holden had a titanic battle and both men became the first ever UK athletes to run inside 8:30. Bedford winning in 8:28.6. Andy takes up the story:

'David had never really run one seriously before and he was up for it. I had come back after having a bit of a downer in the European. It ended up a tremendous race, out of the blue really. Dave went off after the start like a maniac and I eventually caught him. He gave this great huge leap at the last barrier and managed to get a couple of yards on me. I could not quite claw it back. It was great as there were 18,000 people shouting. You can't buy memories like that!'

David Bedford recalls, 'I felt more like an entertainer than an athlete. Everyone was so involved and athletics is all about involvement. That was fantastic to see. I don't think it will be quite the same again. I have had some really great memories running at Crystal Palace and the crowd going berserk. To know you can raise that kind of feeling in people. It's very satisfying.'

Andy Holden had a distinctive style in the steeplechase, appearing to have a check mark before the jumps. He would suddenly lean forward a little way out, before hurdling over the barrier.

'It was a mental check mark. I used to do a little skip and that gave me a perspective on the hurdles so I could judge the right leg length. It was one of those things that developed by accident. I used to train with John Jackson and we did our steeplechase sessions at either Preston or Kirkby, both were particularly windy tracks. Down the back straight with the wind behind me I picked the hurdles up all right but when I got into the wind it was more difficult and that little stutter and skip, enabled me to find the perspective on the hurdle.'

'Bad boy' gives Britain a break

BEDFORD BEATS THE WORLD

by Sydney Hulls

Those were the words that were emblazoned in banner headlines right across the front page of the *Daily Express*, on Saturday 14th of July, 1973. Dave Bedford had shown his detractors once again he could prove them wrong. He ran the AAA's 10,000m at Crystal Palace in a new world record of 27 min 30.8 sec. The previous world record of 27:38.4 was set by Lasse Viren of Finland in the 1972 Olympic Final. In Bedford's world record race Tony Simmons was second and Bernie Pain, the Welsh marathon runner third.

Bedford, looking back in 1976, said, 'When I ran 27:30.8 (half way 13:39.4), it was not a shot in the dark. I had been training well and was not surprised at the time I did but, when I ran in Christchurch (1974), until two weeks before the Games I felt far fitter than I had been when I set the world record and was thinking of a time around 27:10. I firmly believed I could run that time; it was not just a pipe dream and I had evidence in my training to say that I was going to do that. Unfortunately, the leg injury came on again two weeks before the Games, probably due to the hard and fast work I was doing, and I was unable to prove that.'

Back to Andy Holden. In his days as a senior there were many quality runners in the UK, particularly in the 1970s. Did Andy think there were more good runners about than there are now?

'I think there were. The reasons for it were manyfold. There were a lot in the country who ran around the country as kids. I can't think of my children doing what I did when I was eight or nine years old, running round the streets when it was pitch black and nobody batting an eyelid. I don't think that exists any more. A lot of the kids are ferried everywhere in cars. I used to run to and from school when I was eight or nine. I probably did six or seven miles a day, without thinking about it as training but it gave you that basic running background. I think there were a lot of people like that around in those days which meant there were a lot of good runners all coming through together. You don't get that intensity now. There are good runners but I think the runners with the best potential tend to end up playing football these days. A lot of school teachers don't give them the time out like they used to do. Obviously it affects the runners coming through into the sport. You are not getting the depth, therefore you are not getting the level of competition. When I was one of the best juniors I had the likes of Tony Simmons and Ian Stewart to run against. You had to be pretty damn good to do well!'

Andy Holden concluded about the top runners today: 'In my day we ran for the sake of running, whereas nowadays they run for a livelihood which puts a different slant on things. They pick and choose where they are willing to race.'

5

Six Outstanding Medal Races

Most athletics enthusiasts can look back with relish on their best and most vivid memories of Championship races. Whether they were there in person, or watching TV or listening to the radio. For me it was the European Games, 1500m final, on a warm evening in Athens in September 1969, when John Whetton ran a brilliantly tactical race to beat Frank Murphy and Henryk Szordykowski. Regarding television spectacles, to see Haile Gebrselassie out-kick another great runner, Paul Tergat, for the second time in an Olympic 10,000m final, at Sydney 2000 was another abiding memory. It was Sydney where Kathy Freeman, with the total expectation of her home fans and the tremendous pressure she was under, still managed to win the 400m final. That was a truly outstanding achievement.

Obviously, revolutionary races that changed the course of an event for the future, should be considered as important to the history of athletics. In 1971 in Helsinki, Juha Vaatainen outsprinted Jurgen Haase, over 10,000. Haase had won the event in the two previous Europeans. It was off the previous laps of 69.2 and 65.2 when Dave Bedford was leading, Vaatainen ran a 54.00 last lap. He sprinted to victory in a total time of 27:52.8. From then on in major Championships one realised, to win over 10,000m, a runner needed the vestiges of great speed in order to be able to challenge for gold in the final lap. Cuban Alberto Juantorena 'White Lightning' won both the 400m and the 800m in Montreal in 1976. That showed what raw power was needed to win a future Olympic 800m.

Jack Lovelock, the 1936 Olympic 1500m Champion from

New Zealand was deeply admired as a runner by Frank Horwill, the coach, who was one of the founder members of the British Milers Club. Another who thought Lovelock impressive was Clive Cope, once a club sub-two minute half miler. Cope said, 'Referring to Jack Lovelock, I read about that famous Harold Abrahams commentary ... To me it was possibly the greatest 1500m ever run, at those 1936 Olympics.' Jack Lovelock, a Rhodes scholar at Exeter College, took off with 300 metres remaining and was not caught, even by the 1934 World Mile record holder, American, Glen Cunningham. The result in Berlin was 1. Jack Lovelock 3:47.8; 2. Glen Cunningham (USA) 3:48.4; 3. Luigi Beccalli (Italy – 1932 Olympic Champion) 3:49.2. Archi San Romani (USA) was fourth, fifth Phil Edwards (Canada) and sixth Jerry Cornes (GB – 1932 silver medallist).

One of Lovelock's main rivals was a modest, bespectacled solicitor called Sydney Wooderson, who was coached by Albert Hill the 1920 800/1500 Olympic Champion. Sydney beat Jack Lovelock in the AAA's mile in 1935 and 1936. Wooderson's best ever times were 1:48.4 (WR 1938) for 800m and 4.04.2 for a mile. The latter was achieved coming second to Arne Anderson (4.03.8) in 1945. Anderson like Gunder Haegg was a world mile record holder from Sweden. Before he ended his career Wooderson won the 'National' in 1948.

The amazing thing was his two gold medals were achieved each side of World War II. In 1938 in Paris, Sydney Wooderson won the European Games 1500m in 3:53.6, from Joseph Mostert (Belgium) 3:54.5; and 3. Luigi Beccali (Italy) 3:55.2 (Beccali won in 1934 in 3:54.6). Just before turning 33 in 1946, Sydney won the European 5000m in Oslo, a race that might be considered Wooderson's best performance. He beat two rising stars who were future Olympic Champions, Zatopek and Reiff, as well as the 'Flying Dutchman' Willy Slijkhuis (multi-gold medal sprinter/hurdler Fanny Blankers-Koen was nicknamed the 'Flying Dutch woman'). Slijkhuis won the European 1500m in 1950 and was a bronze medallist in the Olympic 1500/5000 in 1948.

In order to give a true illustration of each of the six chosen races, the winners gave their own account to me of what happened in each case.

Race 1. European 5000m Final, 23rd of August 1946

'During the war I had not had any contact with my coach and I really took over myself, training on his lines but I was self-coached from 1940. I think there were two reasons why I changed over to the long distance. I was just a little bit bored doing miles and miles every year; secondly I was over 30, so I felt I should go to a longer distance. Perhaps I had not got the speed of a younger man like Lennart Strand who was the top miler and or 1500m man in those days.

'I obviously went to Oslo for those Championships with the sole idea of winning and I knew my chief opponent again was going to be Slijkhuis and he was. In some ways it was a very similar race to the AAA 3 mile I had at the White City, but he started his sprint in the European much earlier – with 400m to go whereas before it was with 200 left. In the European I shot him in the beginning of the back straight and found it much easier to win than I had done at the White City. In the AAA's, I had led most of the way until the last bend but on the last lap I eased slightly and he shot past me; then coming into the straight I sprinted past him and won by a few yards. At Oslo, with the great number of first class competitors, it was really that they were leading most of the way and I gradually eased up from the back of the field to tenth, third, and then second behind Slijkhuis – and as I say, on the last lap I shot past him on the back straight.'

1. Sydney Wooderson (GB) 14:08.6; 2. Willem Slijkhuis (Hol) 14:14.0; 3. Evert Nyberg (Swe) 14:23.2; 4. Viljo Heino (Fin) 14:24.4; 5. Emil Zatopek (CSR) 14:25.8; 6. Gaston Reiff (Bel) 14:45.8 (six of ten finalists).

A long serving member of Sydney's club, Blackheath Harriers, was Ken Daniel, a good middle distance and cross-country runner for the club.

'The majority of people think of Sydney Wooderson as something special. The times he ran on cinder tracks in those days. Especially when you realise his training. Sunday morning session was to go for a 10 mile walk. What would he have done if he did the training sessions of today's runners!' (It was amazing to think Sydney Wooderson did not receive great public recognition for what he achieved in sport till he was well into his 80s and then was awarded an MBE.)

In 1964, I was 24 and went round the world on three P&O liners (the whole time away from my home in North West London, took 3½ months). It was with the express intention of taking in the Tokyo Olympic Games. Everything went fine, except for the fact that I challenged a rugby player to a couple of races on board ship (the SS *Iberia*), just before Hawaii. Although I might have had a victory by the odd inch in the second race, my right arm went through a glass hydrant protector situated at the end of the deck. Consequently, I had 60 stitches in my right arm. Fortunately the man I challenged was the assistant surgeon on the boat! However, I had an unforgettable time in Tokyo and my spirits were only slightly dampened by the accident. The most exciting race was undoubtedly the 10,000m, which was a straight final between 35 runners.

Race 2. Olympic 10,000m Tokyo, 14th of October 1964, cloudy, 18.4°C/68°F

Australian world record holder Ron Clarke and his clubmate Tony Coyle were in the line up and another favourite Gerry Lindgren, who had won the American Trials from Billy Mills and Ron Larrieu, was strongly favoured too. There were two previous Olympic Champions Murray Halberg and Pytor Bolotnikov. Halberg, although topping the world lists over 5000m the previous year, was suffering from a virus. Those were the favoured athletes before the race.

In the closing few laps Ron Clarke, Billy Mills, Tunisian Mohamed Gammoudi, and Mamo Wolde (the latter two became future Olympic Champions) were the only ones in a group well clear of the rest. Wolde then fell away and a rather rough last lap developed, caused by the leaders almost running into the back of a lapped runner. The race for first place was not decided till the last 100 metres, when Mills sprinted clear.

Billy Mills said, 'I had high hopes of making the team in the first place and when training was going well in February last year, I thought then that I could possibly win the 10,000 metres – but if I made the team. Still a lot happened in the intervening months. Nevertheless I got to Tokyo. After the 10,000m had actually started I felt that any one of some ten athletes in the field could win – and of course I was one of them. Then, after dropping the pack and realising that Halberg and several other great runners were not with us with only five laps to go, I was fairly sure of getting a medal, and perhaps the gold.

'Before the race started I had made up my mind to go with the leaders. I knew almost certainly that Clarke would be one of those and counted on Halberg being up there too. Once Clarke moved I was prepared to go with him. Even so, I was not prepared for such a fast first 5000 (14:04.6) but once everybody else dropped and I was still there, it was merely a matter of hanging on. I hung on for a couple of laps by the skin of my teeth then it started to come easy and I actually felt I was as much in control of the race as Clarke, even though he led most of the way.'

The incident in the last lap

'I think Clarke, finding himself boxed in, as we were lapping a runner. He was at my shoulder, panicked momentarily leaving himself one of three choices. 1. He could have stopped and come round; 2. He could have speeded up and pushed through (I would not let him get ahead because I had him on the inside, but I was not doing anything illegal); or 3. He could have pushed me out. As I say, I think he panicked momentarily and did push me out because, let's face it, he must have been scared as I would be in his position, that he might lose the race then and there.

'I was bumped, but I am quite sure in my own mind that it was unintentional. Gammoudi must have been in a similar

80

position as Clarke but seized the opportunity more readily as, seeing the gap as Clarke bumped me wide, and just as I was about to move in on Clarke again, Gammoudi, with his momentum unimpeded, did the only thing he could do other than stopping dead, and flashed ahead between us.'

Ron Clarke said, 'I think the move that won the race was when Billy Mills got knocked back behind. Straight away he "hit the trail" on us. To my mind, anyone who comes off the bend with two blokes in front of him has a tremendous advantage. Billy was knocked when he was already going pretty hard for home, I think, and it put him behind in what proved to be the most advantageous position.'

Mohamed Gammoudi was the Mediterranean Games Champion but it was the first of three Olympics where he gained a medal. 'I thought I would finish about fifth or sixth. I was very nervous and had not slept for three days before the event, whereas in Mexico [where he gained a bronze and a gold in the 5000] I felt stronger and more confident. At the bell in the final of the 5000m I knew I was going to win, though it was a tough race until the last stride.'

Tokyo: 1. Billy Mills (US) 28:24.4; 2. Mohamed Gammoudi (Tunisia) 28:24.8; 3. Ron Clarke (Australia) 28:25.8; 4. Mamo Wolde (Ethiopia) 28:31.8; 5. Leonid Ivanov (USSR) 28:53.2; 6. Kokichi Tsuburaya (Japan) 28:59.4.

Billy Mills had an interesting background. He was half Sioux Indian and born on a reservation. It was at Pine Ridge School, South Dakota that he did some boxing. That was something his father had done. His parents died early in his life. He was orphaned at 12. He graduated from Haskell Indian High School and went to Kansas University where Wes Santee and Ron Delany had been his heroes.

Billy told me about his fluctuating form as a runner at Kansas. There was a good film on Billy Mills called *Running Brave*. In that he was depicted as having suffered with quite a lot of prejudice against him in his college days, being of Indian extraction. However, he won through and became the Olympic Champion. At that time he was 26 years old and in the Marine Corps, as a Marine Motor Pool Officer.

'In a way I was very lucky to make the Olympic team after all the planning. I opened the 64 season well and came through tremendously about May, then I injured myself, missed the National Championships, but I gradually got back to my old form. Then I had some trouble with "dropping arches" which caused considerable pain in both my feet and shins and I was forced to wear shin splints. During the sixteen weeks from mid-May to Mid-September I had to lay off training for more than six weeks with these injuries and for the rest, the only training I used to do was long, easy running which, as it turned out, proved to be the best thing for me. Because of these injuries I was not able to sprint and though I did some sessions 330s on grass, my longer runs were mainly on the road, with no track work at all. This training in fact built up my stamina and strength to a far greater degree than would have been the case (I think) through track training and racing.'

Specifically in Billy's case, I thought I would outline what type of training he would have done for the Olympic Games, when injuries were not pressing.

'It is difficult to outline a "schedule" from the training I have done as this is the first year I have trained (or tried to) right through non-stop since I began running. In the past I have trained for only nine months of the year, 5 sessions a week totalling about 40 miles. Also, I do not know what my session is going to be before I start; I go according to how I feel and do not worry beforehand. However, a typical week's training before the Olympics was something like this: Monday 15 miles steady; Tuesday (morning) 10 miles, (afternoon) 6×330 with 20 sec interval on grass; Wednesday 10 miles; Thursday (morning) more 330s on grass, (afternoon) 2×330, 1×880, 2×330 – three times; Friday an easy one-hour run; Saturday an easy 45-minutes run; Sunday a long run, around 15 to 20 miles. I seldom finish a session tired. I love to swim and enjoy taking a good swim a couple of days before a race (I did this in Tokyo before the 10,000) because I find it relaxes me, eases my tired muscles.'

Race 3. 800m European Championships, Athens, 18th of September 1969

So often in life one reads in the papers about great successes and terrible disasters that make the news. In 1969 the most obvious example of a Greek Tragedy athletics-wise happened, to a vivacious and attractive girl from Ealing, London (born 13.12.48). It is quite often said that in life you pay for your happiness but in the case of **Lillian Board** it was with her life. Hailed as the outstanding runner in the European Games in Athens, she was given a special award for her performances. (She modestly felt it should have gone to the French lady Nicole Duclos from France, who won the 400m in 51.7.) The downside was that Lillian was very ill by the end of the year and died of cancer. Among her successes were winning the 400m in the European Cup, (53.7) in Kiev on the 15th of September 1967. In the Olympics in Mexico City in 1968, she came second in the 400m final. Running in lane 1 she was pipped by France's Collette Besson who had been running out in lane 5. Besson was timed at 52.00 (an Olympic record) just one tenth ahead of Lillian Board. In Athens in 1969 Lillian overhauled Besson on the anchor leg in the 4×400m. It was a world record of 3:30.8 for Great Britain and their team was Rosemary Stirling (Commonwealth 800 Champion of 1970), Pat Lowe (married to 800m runner Dave Cropper), Janet Simpson (fourth in Mexico individual). Lillian had won the 800m beating European Champion Vera Nikolic of Yugoslavia who won the European of 1966 and 1971!

My interview with Lillian, expressing herself in such a characteristic way, was published in *Athletics Arena* 1970. The editor was the Coach, Charlie Elliott.

'The person who worried me most was Vera Nikolic. I knew that if she went out fantastically fast – if she covered the first 200 metres in 26–27 she would probably not win, but would certainly play havoc with the pace. One would be running, and wondering "supposing we do let her get away" (one has those races where you say "Oh, let her go", and you find that she, whoever she might be, has been allowed to get too far away) "and she could win?". I made up my mind not to think about that, and just let the race unfold – that was my big problem. I still thought "Please God, don't let Vera go off like a rocket, because if she goes too fast I won't know what to do about the pace", then "shall I sit tight with the others or shall I wait until Silai [2nd in Mexico] goes; will she go after Nikolic, or shall I go after Vera myself?", so you see you can have three different races going through your mind.

'Well, the gun went for the start of the final – and Vera did not go off fast, she stayed in the bunch and I was sitting on Vera's shoulder and (it doesn't matter who it is) I just like sitting in on the shoulder of the leader, helping her, and sharing the lead – if she doesn't mind, of course. That's how the race went then, until the end of the first lap. Silai came up, and I faltered momentarily over someone (I can't remember who it was), I don't know why, and let her get a couple of metres ahead of me – we all have such long strides, and it is easy to get a spiking without knowing it, and I did get a slight spiking, I felt something – and so on round to the 600 metres mark. I thought, suddenly, "I am feeling a bit fatigued, or the pace is quickening?" so I started to move a bit faster, too. All the time now, with just that 200 metres left of the race my mind was ticking away ... "Keep with the leaders, and if you are with them with 100 metres to go, you'll win" ... "Yes, that sounds easy..."

'On that last 200 metres Nikolic and Silai began to pull away slightly, and I put in that extra effort, quickening my pace to stay with them. "I must stay with them, I must". Then we were there – 100 metres to go; "It's all over". I made a move out into the third lane, dropping back slightly as I made the move – and then I went for that finishing line. "Please don't let them catch me before I get to the tape" ... and they didn't.'

1. Lillian Board (GB) 2:01.4; 2. Annelise Damm-Olesen (Den) 2:02.6; 3. Vera Nikolic (Yug) 2:02.6; 4. Barbara Wieck (EG) 2:02.7; 5. Ileana Silai (Rum) 2:03.0; 6. Pat Lowe (GB, 2nd in 1971) 2:03.4; 7. Anne-Marie Nenzell (Swe) 2:05.2; 8. Ilja Keizer-Laman (Hol) 2:05.2.

Lillian Board's personal heroes were Anne Packer (1964 Olympic 800m Champion), swimmer Anita Lonsbrough and

Mary Rand, who became a great friend of hers. Lillian's parents were very supportive all her life and George Board, her Father, took a particular interest in her sport.

'There are so many parents who used to go down to the track week-in and week-out, and yet they didn't ask "Why?" "How?" and "What?", about what their children were doing. For instance, 8×220 yards for such-and-such an event, and I feel that such parents are simply handing-out schedules. But Daddy went into all the ins and outs of it all, and this has rubbed off on me. As I have said on a couple of occasions, if a coach does well enough he eventually works himself out of a job to a certain extent. Daddy was working in Birmingham for at least three weeks before Athens, and my last three weeks in England before the Championships was done without a coach, virtually on my own and I could write and tell him all I had done and at weekends he could see me.'

Race 4. Olympic 5000m at Munich at 15:10, 10th of September 1972

In the first few days of my stay in Munich I realised it was a good place to be at Olympic time with all that smooth beer and sizzling German sausages. All of those feelings were seriously jolted when there was a horrific attack on the Israeli athletes in the Olympic Village and consequently, 12 athletes or coaches lost their lives.

After a day's mourning with no Olympic sport, the 5000m final had been put forward the extra day. One of the world's most charismatic distance athletes Steve Prefontaine, arrived at the final, determined to win the race, and start his run for home about a mile before the finish. Steve Prefontaine, from Coos Bay, Oregon, was the subject of a film called *Without Limits* directed by Robert Towne. Prefontaine had a very strong following Stateside. Another one with a great following from the UK was Dave Bedford who was also in the line-up too but, like Sviridov and Alvarez, only led briefly. Dave's day would come when breaking the 10,000m world record the following year.

Perhaps Prefontaine added most to the drama of the race. Prefontaine was coached by Bill Bowerman, and his great friend Frank Shorter won the marathon at the same games. The race was very tactical in the early stages. Prefontaine threw in a 62 lap after the previous one being a 67, and then wound things up even more with a 61.2 lap, but there were still two laps to go. Lasse Viren was in control with Gammoudi and Prefontaine close at hand, looking to be the only ones with medal chances. Ian Stewart was also trying to get in the picture.

Viren won with wily racer Gammoudi second. The latter obtained medals at three Olympics. Ian Stewart finished fast to take the bronze. Stewart went on to have a field day in 1974 when he achieved a European indoor title as well as winning the world cross country. As for Prefontaine, he went on to run some brilliant races back in America, till sadly he had a fatal car accident, when only just 24 years of age, and before he could be the big medal hope for the USA in the 1976 Olympics.

Munich. All the finishers: 1. Lasse Viren (Fin) 13:26.4 (OR); 2. Mohamed Gammoudi (Tun) 13:27.4; 3. Ian Stewart (GB) 13:27.6; 4. Steve Prefontaine (USA) 13:28.4; 5. Emile Puttemans (Bel) 13:30.8; 6. Harald Norpoth (WG) 13:32.6; 7. Per Halle (Nor) 13:34.4; 8. Nikolay Sviridov (Sov) 13:39.4, 9. Frank Eisenberg (EG) 13:40.8; 10. Javier Alvarez (Spa) 13:41.8; 11. Ian McCafferty (GB) 13:43.2; 12. Dave Bedford (GB) 13:43.2; 14. Juha Vaatainen (Fin) 13:53.8.

Lasse Viren, who won the double again in Montreal, was coached by Rolf Haikkola. Viren considered his first breakthrough came when winning the Finnish 5000m in 1969 in 14:10. He was born at Myrskyla on 22.7.49 and followed a great Finnish distance tradition after such names as Hannes Kolehmainen, Paavo Nurmi, Ville Ritola, Ilmari Salminen, Veikko Karvonen and Juha Vaatainen.

Lasse Viren said, 'At Munich in the 5000m I thought Puttemans, Stewart, McCafferty were the dangers. I had planned after 300m I would lead, then I would start to run fast, but all the other runners were around me so I did not have the chance to lead and I had to wait. So it was three laps left that I started to pass the other runners and make for the lead position. I knew all the time they were all there. I knew Prefontaine was going to run very fast but it did not work because I thought it was just Prefontaine talking.'

Winter training before the Olympics: 'I ran 200 kilometres in a week. I think my best time to train was about six in the evening and I trained about six in the morning as well. As a policeman I work in the day. I travel about driving a police car and I have to be in the office too.' In the summer: 'On the track I used to run 10×200m speed training in one day's session. When I first started training it was not so hard and it was not so much. I did not then need to train as I do now [talking in 1973 through his interpreter Pirkko Hannula]. I was training 120 to 130 kilometres a week then.'

Ian Stewart said, 'A lot of people thought the 5000m heats were a formality. When it is two through and the two fastest losers, though, you can't hanky panky about in it. I reckon that was the toughest qualifying round in the whole Games I think that was a real cut-throat, nasty thing to do. Any other qualifying round, you could afford to make a slight slip somewhere.

'In the Olympic Final you can't say there is only one man. Especially that final. It was the most open final of the lot. For instance, in the 400m hurdles you could say it was David Hemery, John Akki Bua or Ralph Mann. Those were the ones for the medals. In the 5000, there were any of a half dozen who could have won it. One would look down the list and say Viren looks good, Prefontaine has some good qualifications, and so on. And each one would have equally good qualifications to be there, and the right to win the medal. I thought Mohamed Gammoudi would win the 10,000 if he had stayed on his feet. [Gammoudi fell mid way through the race.] But I thought I would have beaten him in the final of the 5000 because I was only one point off him. I did not run well. It is not often I slip in a big Games, but I did there, and I could have kicked myself for doing so. With 800 metres to go, I was on Prefontaine. Viren came past with Gammoudi on the back of him, and I could not get out. I stepped out to get behind Gammoudi, with 600 metres to go, and just to get around Prefontaine. And as I tried to get around him, Prefontaine came out sideways and knocked me almost into the third lane. I lost a hell of a lot of ground there – 10 to 15 yards. Things went even more wrong for Prefontaine early on.

'He came up to me and said, "It's not fast enough." And I said, "What are you going to do about it?" This was after two laps. I was faster than he was, so I was all right.

'There was only one other runner like me, and that was Viren, because both of us are very long kickers and we will kick from a long way out. On our day, we are very close in that relationship.

'If somebody said to me, "How would you run that race again?" I would say I'd run exactly the same. The only thing I would not do again is let that bloody gap develop, because if I had come out of the bend with Viren and Gammoudi I would have beaten them. I don't think there was anyone in that field who could cover that last 100 yards faster than I.

'It was when I was hit and lost two seconds that things did not go right. But I would not run the race any differently. I could give Bedford 10 yards with 600 to go, but not Viren, Gammoudi or Prefontaine in that race. I thought with 200 to go I was not going to get anything, and when I came off the bend I did not think I was going to get a medal. But I went past Prefontaine 10 yards from the line, and I was eight-tenths up on him when I crossed the line. I would like to have had a watch on my last 100!'

Race 5. Olympic 1500m Final, Montreal, Saturday 31st of July 1976

John Walker at his best was a magnificent athlete. The first man to break 3:50 for a mile. The New Zealander was wonderful to watch. His long hair flowing behind him, his raking stride and his great strength enabled him to grind the opposition into the tartan, particularly in the 1975 to 1977 seasons. **Eamonn Coghlan**, who was twice fourth in the Olympic 1500 final and held the indoor mile world record, was the first man over 40 to run under 4 minutes for a mile (3:58.8 indoors in 1994). Like the American Steve Scott, Coghlan was a great rival of Walker's on the indoor circuits. He remarks, 'John ran 3:55 at 38 and when he retired as an elite runner he retired with an achilles injury and although he had had some time off, he under-estimated what it would take to get back to 4 minute mile shape at 40. He went straight into quality work with an achilles ten-don injury which was a big mistake. I have no doubt in my mind that John Walker would have been the first over 40 to run a sub-four minute mile had he maintained his fitness between his elite years and the vet year but he didn't. I was the one who persevered because I badly wanted to achieve that goal.'

John Walker was noted for being a great ambassador for New Zealand sport who did not suffer fools gladly. It was sad that a man with such talent and so much to give, should end up in his 40s with Parkinson's disease. He was born on the 12th of January 1952 in Papukura, New Zealand, and his racing weight was 74kg. His height was 1.83m.

John Walker's breakthrough came when he was only 20. He ran 3:38 for 1500m in an international race back in New Zealand in 1973 and the following year, still rather inexperi-enced, he ran 3:33.52 for 1500m, inside the old world record but second to Filbert Bayi of Tanzania who ran 3:32.16. It was in those Commonwealth Games in Christchurch he ran 1:44.9 for third place in the 800m final. The following year in 1975 he ran his mile world record of 3:49.4. Whenever Bayi met Walker again, he never got near beating him but Bayi was robbed of having the chance of racing against him in the 1976 Olympics, when the Tanzanians were part of 22 countries that pulled out of the Montreal Games. The reason for that was the New Zealand rugby team's planned tour of apartheid South Africa. Walker was then clear favourite for the 1500m but had his own problems, as he felt the immense pressure on him and the fact that some people were not wanting the New Zealand team to be at the Olympics.

In the Olympic final Dave Moorcroft, who went on to break the 5000 world record, led in 62.5 for the first lap from Rick Wohlhuter, who achieved a bronze in the 800m. Walker was back in seventh and Ivo Van Damme, who was second in the

800m brought up the rear. It was Eamonn Coghlan who led at the 1200m mark. Walker's stretch-kick came with 250 remaining in a 52.6 lap, when Ivo Van Damme was in second place. Paul-Heinz Wellman just got home ahead of Coghlan to take the bronze. Coghlan was later to have his share of the glory taking the World Championship 5000m in 1983.

John Walker comes in about the final, 'Well, I think personally the only reason why everybody was saying Bayi was the big thing was because he is a front runner – but basically he was no different to anybody else. I had to accept that he was just another competitor; I think that is how you had to regard the whole field. That is what I did to start with but because he ran from the front, was so good and the world record holder, I had trained specifically (for the previous year). I was learning to run from the front just in case Bayi did not turn up, so I had two plans. Once I had heard he had withdrawn, it did not upset me but it just knocked me back a little bit for the simple reason that I thought look, there goes the one guy who could ensure the pace was fast. I could not see anybody else leading!

'Thomas Wessinghage was one that surprised me by not making it. Coghlan I had never run against before the Olympics; I had heard a lot about him but the best time he had for 800 was 1:48 and I thought if it was going to be a fast race then he would not win and I thought he might get third or fourth.

'Rick Wohlhuter was very fast and had very good leg speed but I thought if he went through and ran three heats of the 800m and three heats of the 1500 then he would be very tired.

'I think when you have been sitting in the Olympic Village for 2½ weeks, facing four walls, and criticism from reporters, and finally you go out there, you run, then you win, naturally it is going to be a hell of a relief. It's all over ... four years of really hard work. It is everything a person has dreamed about, winning the Olympic gold medal, and that's it, it's all finished.'

1. John Walker (New Zealand) 3:39.2; 2. Ivo Van Damme (Belgium) 3:39.3; 3. Paul-Heinz Wellmann (West Germany) 3:39.3; 4. Eamonn Coghlan (Republic of Ireland) 3:39.5; 5. Frank Clement (UK) 3:39.7; 6. Rick Wohlhuter (USA) 3:40.6; 7. David Moorcroft (UK) 3:40.9; 8. Graham Crouch (Australia)

3:41.8; 9. Janus Zemen (Hungary) 3:43.0. Ivo Van Damme, just a few months later, was killed in a car crash.

John Walker, who was coached by Arch Jelley, went into a bit of self-analysis when I commented that some people thought he had not got speed.

'I have not really got terrific speed as my best 400 metres is only 48.9, but 200s and 400s are things I don't really run that much of. When it comes to running say a 600 metres I would not be as fast as Juantorena or Wohlhuter or any of those guys, but where I do make up is on strength. Now I know that I can finish over the last 200 metres in a 1500 metres just as fast if not faster than anyone else and I don't care if they have 1:42 speed because I feel I can match them with a combination of strength and speed. If you are going to run 800 metres then you train specifically for the 800 and you run 200s, 400s, 600s, 500s and that sort of stuff. I trained to be a 1500 metre runner.'

Now to jump from my interview with him in 1976 to the next one in 1985 that was published in *Marathon & Distance Runner*, editor Geoff Harrold.

'If I look back at 12 years of running I can't complain at all. For a start I never set out to be the Olympic Champion or world record holder. My main forte was cross country running [John was fourth in the world cross at Rabat in 1975 when Ian Stewart won]. I think like a lot of English fellows, we are brought up on the cross country club background, and this helps a lot.

'I thought Cram was very beatable in the 1982 Commonwealth Games. I ran 50.8 for my last quarter, so you are talking about sprinting. [1st Steve Cram 3:42.37; 2nd John Walker 3:43.11; 3rd Mike Boit (Kenya) 3:43.33.] I got behind Mike Boit but I thought the rest of the field was with us and I got stuck in behind him when Cram took off and I realised half way down the straight that Boit was going nowhere.

'Normally Boit moves out and lets people through on the inside. I think I could have sprinted with Cram that day because Cram was not in that great shape. I had run 1:46 in the final of the 800, I was in very good shape and I think if I could have beaten him any day it was that day, but it was not to be. But I did not take the Commonwealth Games too seriously as I had been road racing in the United States a month before and was doing everything possible wrong. I got to the Commonwealth Games in not that great a shape and just raced myself back into shape.

'The 1981 World Cup was particularly satisfying for me as I had really come to the end of my season a long time before that. A few weeks before I was finishing only sixth or seventh in races and I was really getting tired. My coach finally arrived and changed my training around. We went back on the track for four days and really did some solid speed work. I improved immensely off that and ended up running 3:35 which was a big surprise to me. I finished like a train down the home straight. It was very surprising.' (1. Steve Ovett 3:34.95; 2. John Walker 3:35.09; 3. Olaf Beyer (EG) 3:35.58.)

'A race that no one remembers is when I broke the world indoor 1500m record at the 1977 TAC Championships (3:37.3). My first clash against Bayi after the so called Bayi-Walker thing had been building up for three years, also happened indoors and I beat the guy by about 70 metres. It was just like the Ovett-Coe thing.

'In 1982 I ran 3:49.08 just after running 3:49.7 which means I should have been running 3:47 back in 1975. Probably my only regret now is that I never chased the world record again. It will [would have been] very hard for Cram too because, once you have broken a world record you become very complacent and you think well it's mine, and I don't want to have to go through it again. I know very well in '75 when I went for it I was not peaking particularly, I had already run 13 races. I think if I had gone for it in '76 instead of running the 2000 metres I could have run 3:47 – I am sure of it. If I had run the mile that night instead of the 2000 I would have smashed the world record again quite considerably.

'I love racing. I hate training. I hate getting injured. I can race every day of the week and I thrive on it. The harder the races and the more I have, the better I become. That is what really has stood me in good stead over the years. I improve off racing, I don't improve off training. I can have a race one day, come out the next day and come out the third day and run better on

92

that day than I did on the first day. I have got no problem with that, and that is why, in the 1976 Olympics for instance, I was sharper and better in the final than I was when I ran in the heats. But even if I had run 3:47 for the mile it would have been broken by now [talking in 1985]. It would have just given me a little bit more satisfaction knowing that I was a bit better than I really was. I raced far too many times, and I ran all over the damn place. I was too accessible to meet promoters. If someone rang me up I could not say "No". The athlete today is managed a lot differently. They pick their races, they become more elusive and, of course, they make a hell of a lot more money by doing so.

'Too many of the other magazines [unlike *Marathon & Distance Runner*] that I read today are utter rubbish. I saw a new one a couple of weeks ago and it is never going to make it for me. There are never enough in depth human interest articles – the same repetitive articles time after time. You get too much statistical stuff – people are not interested in statistics. Kids get inspiration from reading about the greats, not some dilapidated 65-year-old who happens to run 3:50 for a damn marathon!

'I think Sebastian Coe is the most majestic runner I have ever seen, anywhere in the world. If you can compare an athlete to a thoroughbred he has certainly been it.'

Jimmy Carter, President of the United States, withdrew his team from Olympic competition in 1980 because of the invasion by the USSR in Afghanistan, and several other countries went along with it. Consequently, subject to selection, such contenders as Thomas Wessinghage and Willy Wulbeck from Germany were not present, Mike Boit and James Maina of Kenya (unbeaten over 800 in 1979) were two more plus Don Paige and Steve Scott of the United States. However, Sebastian Coe had headed the rankings in both events in the *Track & Field News 1980* for 1979. Ovett was rated No 2 in the 1500m.

Race 6. Olympic 1500m Final, Moscow 1st of August 1980

1. Seb Coe (UK) 3:38.4; 2. Jurgen Straub (GDR) 3:38.8; 3. Steve Ovett (UK) 3:39.0; 4. Andreas Busse (GDR) 3:40.2; 5. Vittorio Fontenella (Italy) 3:40.4; 6. Josef Plachy (Cze) 3:40.7; 7. Jose Marajo (Fr) 3:41.5; 8. Steve Cram (UK) 3:42.0; 9. Dragan Zdravkovic (Yug) 3:43.1.

Jurgen Straub revved up the pace after 700 metres with Seb Coe just behind him, handily placed, Steve Ovett was next. It was coming into the home straight that Coe and Straub were together. Coe accelerated with 80 metres remaining, with Straub holding off Ovett for the silver. Steve Ovett had already won the 800m in 1:45.4 with Coe second in 1:45.9 and Nikolai Kirov of the USSR third.

Coe had considered that he was a better 800m runner than 1500 man, but lost several major championships over the 800m distance. Having said that, before he retired he still won a World Cup and a European Championships over 800m. Ovett appeared to have a very relaxed style but bags of strength. He was overjoyed to win the 800 with such a fine runner as Coe behind him. However, that put paid to his 1500 metre chances because Coe was expressly motivated, after losing the 800m, and Straub was up for the best medal he could possibly get in the 1500m. Steve Ovett explained how difficult it was to go for a second gold medal after the 800 win.

'After winning the 800m, it was coming to terms with the deflation after achieving an Olympic gold medal, and then re-motivating myself again.'

After losing the 800m and then going all out again for the 1500m, Coe really had to work at it mentally. 'It was a tough three days, a lot of soul searching. My father Peter and I had to sit down and could have panicked. He was quite right to criticise. I expect criticism from him where I won't accept it from other people. I know when I have run badly. The one thing that I am very proud about is that that the battle plan for the 800 – which should have worked except that for various reasons I was not just running very well that day – was the plan we stuck to for the 1500m.

'Whereas everybody was screaming, writing letters, telling me, "Go from 400m! 600m! 800m! Go from the gun!" I have been told what some of the pundits in the press box said when they saw the dawdle for the first two laps, "The guy has not got any brains" was just one of them.

'You go into a race knowing you have certain strengths and if an opportunity arises you grasp it with both hands. But you must also go in with the intellectual adaptability to know that there was no point in carrying a plan through just to be a sacrificial offering over the last 100 metres.'

In the mid to late 1970s and in the 1980s the United Kingdom had a load of world class, two-lap racers and milers. Obviously Steve Ovett's purple patch did not last quite as long as Seb Coe's, partly because of an injury when he ran into some railings, among other things, but both were astonishing when they broke world record after world record. For instance, in 1981 Ovett ran a world mile record of 3:48:00 just two days before Coe ran 3:47:33, which took Ovett's world record off the books. Then there came Steve Cram who improved the time to 3:46:32. There were Frank Clement, Dave Moorcroft, Peter Elliott, as championship performers, as well as Graham Williamson, an overshadowed and forgotten man. Here is just one of Williamson's results. It was in the wet and windy conditions at Meadowbank, Scotland, in August 1982 at the Iveco International Games: 1 Williamson (E) in 3:52:66; 2. Ray Flynn (Irl) 3:53:87; 3. Richie Harris (USA) 3:53:99; 4. Tim Hutchings (E) 3:54:53; 5. Colin Reitz (E) 3:55:41; 6. Jack Buckner (E) 3:55:91. Almost classed as a side show to the great runs of Coe, Ovett and Cram!

Peter Elliott, the Olympic 800m silver medallist of 1988 and a Commonwealth gold medallist in the 1500 in 1990 told me in April 2001, 'I remember watching Coe and Ovett in the Olympic Games in Moscow. They were the role models and heroes with Steve Cram following on, then you find yourself lining up against them, fighting for positions on the team. People said I came along at the wrong time but I would rather be part of that era than the one that's here now. The depth at 800/1500 – if you took away Cram, Seb and Steve there was

Tom McKean, John Gladwin, Steve Crabb, Rob Harrison, Gary Cooke, Ikem Billy, Tony Morrell and you could name more who could run 1:45 for 800m and that was because runners wanted to run those distances because of Coe, Ovett and Cram!'

In the spring of 1984, in a pub in Putney, Seb told me, 'We may yet have to adapt back to 1971 standard because there is no guarantee that some of the performances we are throwing out will continue.' That was great foresight on Lord Coe's behalf.

Sebastian Coe went on to win the Olympic gold in the 1500 at Los Angeles and was second, in 1:43:64, behind Joaquim Cruz of Cuba (1:43:00) which proved he did not always have the championship success despite, perhaps, having the most potential at the event in the world. We never saw Coe run against Said Aouita of Morocco, who was ranked top over 1500m and 5000m for the 1984 Olympic year. Aouita took the gold in the 5000m at Los Angeles. Could Aouita have beaten Coe that year if he had contested the 1500m with him? We will never know the answer. I feel Coe, sufficiently motivated, as was proved in Moscow, would probably have had the edge.

In Steve Ovett's case he had quite a range, winning even half marathons. He won a strongly contested Inter-Counties cross country Championships at Derby in 1978 in 37:49 from Steve Jones (38:00) and they were followed in by Alwyn Dewhurst, Trevor Wright, Bob Treadwell, Grenville Tuck, Graham Tuck and John Wheway. He also won the Commonwealth 5000m in Edinburgh in 1986 in 13:24.11, from Jack Buckner and Tim Hutchings.

One must not forget there was another player who became world class in 1981, called Sydney Maree. He had been a runner in the townships of South Africa and eventually was granted American citizenship. In 1983 he briefly held the 1500m world record of 3:31.24. Maree went on to come second in 13:01.5 behind Said Aouita who set a world record of 12:58.39 in the Bislett Games, Oslo in 1985. The previous best was by Dave Moorcroft who did 13:00.40 in 1982.

In Coe's book he mentioned a friend at Tapton School, Sheffield, who was suffering from a rare form of juvenile arthritis, he could hardly walk let alone run. That must have brought home to him just how lucky we athletes all are. He talked about that in 1984:

'It is a very important thing to come to terms with. There have been two people I have been quite close to, Danny and a little girl who I speak to a couple of times a week on the telephone. She was involved in a horrific accident and she lost parts of a limb and parts of her face. She started ringing me up after the 1980 Games – she is fourteen now.

'You worry bitterly about an achilles tendon that is sore or a touch of shin splints, ligament or knee problems that keep you side-lined for six weeks – then you get on the phone to a kid like that, who is in the process of having a plastic limb fitted and her face remodelled and all sorts of inherent problems. That brings you down to earth. It's not a question, "There for the grace of God..." It is not that, it is just simply that you can lose perspective about your own situation. It is a very sobering thought.

'When Steve Ovett came out with exactly that comment a few years ago, about the work he does with handicapped kids in Brighton, I knew what he meant. It puts the whole thing into perspective. Other people who are around you are close to you, can find it very difficult to put it into that kind of perspective.'

6

Enjoyment – Perspective – Belief

Enjoyment

Before illustrating some of the pleasurable things about running, there are just as captivating situations for the field event exponents. Hugh Richardson, the ex-international hammer thrower, became a National Veteran Champion, advised by outstanding UK National coach Wilf Paish. Richardson, now a retired Leeds solicitor, was a cross-country runner at university before turning to his consuming hobbies of training, competing or putting together vast amounts of field event data. He particularly cited an incident in *The Winning Edge* of pure enjoyment when out training. He recollects throwing the hammer in a field with the sun warming his back and just a kestrel hovering above. It was that pure pleasure of unleashing the hammer in such ideal surroundings that he loved.

I can remember times through the last 35-odd years when the running life was good. The other side of 50 when the body was still receptive to faster action. It was feeling the legs moving smoothly over the tarmac, as one almost effortlessly travelled along the country roads at six minute mile pace. There was the 'Longcross' run at Virginia Water in the late spring, when all the leaves of the trees from above would enclose you. I remember the gently undulating surface through Trumps Green, and Lyne followed by a good last half mile up the long drive at Lyne Place Manor, where my stepfather John Leaf used to live. Another time was when I ran with Al Sowden (once the Highgate club half-mile Champion, who was in those days a

4:16 miler). It was after starting out from Parliament Hill Fields that we ran up and on to Hampstead Heath. Al liked to stop on the run, just to appreciate the views from the highest points on the Heath.

There were the back roads, behind the holiday seaside resorts in Italy, Greece, Spain and Portugal. It was those winding lanes, through valleys of citrus and olive groves and the smell of the wild flowers and birds singing on brilliant summer days. It was all virgin territory and I was unlikely to go that way again. That made the situation all the more poignant.

For hard distance trainer Dave Bedford there were moments, even though he did say to me, when he was training for the big championships, it was 99% drudgery and 1% inspiration. It is the 1% we will concentrate on here.

'I remember when I first went to St Moritz before the Olympic Games. About 3 miles out of St Moritz we were climbing a great pass for a long time and I decided I needed a bit of a stretch and a jog, as we had been driving all the way and so I put my gear on and ran the last 3 or 4 miles in. As we suddenly came over this col, capped with snow on either side, there in front was St Moritz in the valley. It looked like dreamland from there and that was certainly exhilarating. I was going into a new life for another six or seven weeks and that was exhilarating seeing the place I was going to live and train and work in. That was great. There obviously have been times, especially Sunday morning runs with your clubmates after the race the day before, and they don't need to tell you how well you ran because you read about it in the paper yourself that morning – that kind of feeling is good and it is days like that when you think you can never lose again.'

Stephen Moore, that fine ultra-distance runner from Hertford & Ware, retired in his early 50s as an executive with a London City bank. He then went to live in the Peak District because he loved it so.

Sebastian Coe had something to say about running there: 'The Peak District to me is ultimate delight and my family home is in Sheffield, is just on the edge of the peaks. In the summer it is lovely and in the winter it's pure Wagner –

very bleak, a bit bare at times. It is a lovely area to hide away in.'

John Whetton, who was the 'King of The Boards' because of his international success indoors, was European 1500m Champion and made two Olympic finals.

'Were I to think about athletics all the time I would want to pack it up, and I have felt that sometimes [talking in 1969–70]. The answer is to take your mind off it, and that is why if I have something beautiful and stimulating to think about I want to continue. That is why I enjoy Sherwood Forest so much. Without the forest I think I would have finished running a long time ago. I like to feel I am part of the environment: if I am enclosed by trees and bushes, I somehow feel part of it. Of course there is always the point that, when training in the woods or forest land, the running can hardly be boring since the environment is changing continually. Maybe short trees, tall trees or no trees, soft grass or pine needles. Now and again you will scare a rabbit out of its hole or suddenly find a pheasant swooping down close to you. All this adds interest to one's training session, and takes one's mind off the hard work and, honestly, I feel that if I cannot think about aesthetic things in training I do become bored.'

Perspective: Some good advice from a champion

Derek Ibbotson was a great personality in the 1950s. He broke the world record for the mile on the 19th of July, 1957. It was when I was in my last term at Langley school near Norwich that I found a wireless in another dormitory broadcasting the race. There were several boys huddled over the set listening intently to that world record race. Roy Moor the journalist wrote in the *News Chronicle*:

'The voice boomed over the loudspeakers at London's White City last night: "Ibbotson's time is 3 min 57.2 seconds – a new world record for the mile" and beaming Derek, undistressed by his fantastic record said, "Not bad for a young lad". It was the first time four runners beat 4 minutes for a mile in the same

100

race.' [1. Derek Ibbotson 3:57.2; 2. Ron Delany (Eire) 3:58:8; 3. Stanslav Jungwirth (CZE) 3:59.1 and fourth Yorkshire's Ken Wood 3:59.3. Mike Blagrove led at the 880 in 1:55.8. 5th and 6th were Stefan Lewandowski of Poland (Polish record of 4:00.6 and Alan Gordon of GB 4:03.4.]

In 1962 Derek Ibbotson said, 'When people write me off and say I am finished I have tremendous determination. "I'll show the beggars" – that is why I succeed to get back where people think I'm more or less finished.

'I had great inspiration from the thoughts of breaking world records. I always wanted to become a world record holder, a lot of drive inside me. I have never had a coach. I have admired lots of runners but have never been inspired by them. I have always wanted to become the best in the world.

'The main thing, when you are young, is not to be worried by reputations and size because world champions come in all shapes and sizes. When you are young you think a big lad is bound to beat you. This may be true when you are 16, 17 or 18 years old but when you get older there are lots of things that come into it. It's what you have in the heart and in the mind that counts because mind can plan a race well, to make up for the little lack of physique.' ('Ibbo' was 5'9½" and 147 lbs.)

Dave Moorcroft was a Commonwealth 1500/5000m Champion and ran a world 5000m record of 13:00.42 in Oslo in 1982. He became Executive Chairman of UK Athletics. It was after he had run in the 1976 Montreal 1500m Olympic final as a promising 'star of the future' that he said: 'There are a number of factors involved in athletics. It satisfies the competitive urge. It satisfies your social motivation in terms of meeting people and expressing yourself. But I think the over-riding thing about it is that I just use the self-expression the way in which you use something you have got in a particular way to express your personality, yourself, your qualities... As a form of expression it is rather like art, in that you utilise what you have got in a particular way through your training, through your approach, through your general life, and you put it all together in a package called a race and during that race you utilise everything you have gained, all your talent, and express yourself in a creative

101

way during that particular period. Running is a very exhilarating sport; and it also can be very frustrating and annoying but at its best it's very exhilarating whether it is an Olympic final, whether it is training on a lousy wet day, whether it is training on a beautiful day, running through the forest, or whatever it is. Each individual effort you do, training or racing, has got its own sort of qualities and there is a definite magic about the whole thing really, difficult to put into words.'

Belief

Innocent Egbunike, from Nigeria, who studied at Azusa Pacific College in the USA, was twice an Olympic 400 metres finalist and came second in the world championships of 1987. That year he ran a personal best of 44.17 for 400m. In 1987 he showed his steadfast belief in being a Christian.

'Now, I think I can run a lot better with God's grace. No matter how much I hurt, being a Christian I can go through the pain. This year, more especially I say "to beat me is to destroy me" because I know I have worked hard – I have put in many hours training.' How right he was, as he ran 12 times under 45 seconds and his time of 44.17 in Zurich was an All African and Commonwealth record (which still stands in 2002) and he traded wins with world record holder Butch Reynolds.

'I shake the hands of my competitors and give them my best wishes. God has already picked the winner so I go there and do the best I can.'

One of the main individuals to bring tremendous interest for the sports fans in the various international arenas was Willie Banks from the United States. He started to get the crowd clapping as he stood at the start of the triple jump and as he ran down the runway. He achieved a world record triple jump of 17.97 metres at Indianapolis on the 16th of June, 1985. 'God had told me I was actually going to jump it. The whole thing was already preordained. There was not one single doubt in my mind.'

Nourredine Morceli, who was three times world 1500m

Championships outdoors and Olympic Champion in 1996 achieved quite a few world records from 1992–1995 inclusive. He is a devout Muslim.

'Within me is something special, and why I have the ability is coming from God. I thank God for it, because without God I would never be who I am and never make it to the top. I get my power from God and I am a very religious man. It is forbidden to drink alcohol and a lot of things that could effect athletic performance. Praying is very important. If you don't do that you don't keep in touch with God.'

David Hemery, who is currently the President of UK Athletics, won the 1968 Olympic 400m hurdles final in a world record of 48.12 in Mexico City with Gerhard Hennige of West Germany second and John Sherwood, the 1970 Commonwealth Champion third. Hemery was twice the Commonwealth high hurdles Champion. After his second high hurdles win in Edinburgh in 1970 he talked about his beliefs.

'The fact that I am a Christian has nothing to do specifically with my athletics. The fact that I am a Christian means to me that it should permeate through whatever I do – just concern for others. I do not approve of the way some people say "he's a Christian", labelling one rather like Doctor, Lawyer, and so on. To me it just means that I believe in God, and I personally think that the philosophy of Christ could not be bettered. He did a service to other people, he was concerned with them and did everything he possibly could for them – which to me is a most positive attitude to life. My beliefs do not mean standing up on a soap box saying "I am a Christian". It means nothing. I think that if you are living a constructive life and trying to get along with other people you are doing as much as anyone else. I would rather be known as someone who would do something for somebody else without wanting anything in return other than claiming a belief. I don't think that talking about it alone means anything: you have got to *act* on your beliefs.'

Edwin Moses, who was born Dayton, Ohio, in the USA, was an amazing 400m hurdler. He won 122 races on the trot at one stage of his career and it included the 1976 Olympic title in

47:64. His belief in God helped him through to being the greatest hurdler of his time.

'I think it had a definite influence. Being in the position I was not knowing exactly how well I could do, or just going in and hoping to become a champion. I think faith helped pull me through, gave me the energy and spirit at times when I did not think I could finish a workout.'

Jonathan Edwards, the 2000 Sydney Olympic triple jump Champion, who won the triple jump in the World Championships in Edmonton in 2001 with 17.92, told me in London after he broke the world record with a mark of 18.29 on the 7th of August, 1995, 'About what has happened to me is almost humbling. God has chosen to bless me in a very special way. I look at myself and I am not particularly striking to look at physically. These other guys can probably do better things than me in many respects in training. Its just a kind of funny feeling!

'The fundamental thing about a Christian belief is that you believe in Christ died and rose again and paid the price for our sins, because man is alienated from God, so what I have as a Christian is fundamentally a relationship with God, and God will look after me. You might say that might make me a less good athlete because it is not my primary drive to be the best or to have to earn money because otherwise I am going to be destitute, all these kind of things.

'I do love reading and I love studying the Bible. That's my passion really. My fundamental aim in life is to glorify God in what I do.'

Graham Bradbury competed as a boy for Surrey County and joined Hercules and Wimbledon AC as a 16-year-old. Bradbury is now semi-retired and in his mid-50s but competes at cross country for Hercules Wimbledon, South London Harriers and Vets AC. I talked to Graham after he was easily the first 'over 55' runner in the Gordon Pirie 10 miles cross country race at Coulsdon. Bradbury got married at 55 in Millennium year. He is a 'Lead' walker on routes for Age Concern. Jeremy Hemming talked to him for *Veterans Athletic Club Newsletter* in December 2000 and finished his particular article with Graham Bradbury quoting a Bible passage, Isaiah, Chapter 40, Verse 31:

Those who trust in the Lord's help
Will find their strength renewed.
They will rise on wings like eagles
They will run and not get weary
And walk and not grow weak

7

Veterans Athletics

Veteran athletic championships started at world level in 1975. The first to take place, the 'World, Masters Championships' was held in Toronto from the 12th to the 16th of August, 1975. However, the oldest veteran athletic club in the world is the Veterans AC, founded in 1931. In recent years they have held their various championships at Kingsmeadow, Lea Valley, Battersea and Wimbledon Common.

Jack Fitzgerald of Mitcham (Sutton & District AC) and John Hayward of Woodford Green AC, were two of the main instigators in organising the first International Veterans Track & Field meeting which was held at Crystal Palace in 1972. That year, when the veterans marathon was on in Cologne, Jack and John plus others, decided to have the World Veteran Championships in 1975. It has been run as a bi-annual event since then. Hazel Rider, a veteran competitor for Cambridge Harriers, when she saw that 'International' vets meeting at Crystal Palace was inspired enough to go ahead and help start a UK women's veteran athletic movement in the United Kingdom.

Fitzgerald remarked in 2001, 'The way the World Championships have grown is amazing. So many would have stopped competing long ago and retired from the sport if it had not been for the veteran movement being so active. From little acorns great oak trees grow.'

At the World Veterans Championship at Gateshead in 1999, I talked to many who competed. One person who has been a credit to veteran athletics with her whole attitude towards it was

106

Rosemary Chrimes, like her late husband Howard Payne, won a field event gold medal in the Commonwealth Games of 1970. Many times 'age' world record holder Chrimes did point out that it was a mammoth task organising the meeting at Gateshead. It was bursting at the seams and, like field events competitor **Bill Gentleman**, who was coach to Yvonne Murray, felt there may eventually have to be standards brought in to contain the situation.

Three people who may have benefited from world veteran events, had those World and National Championships been around in their time, were that brilliant high hurdler Donald Finlay, who at 40 in 1949 was still competing as an international. Finlay was an ace wartime pilot, whose time of 14.4 that he did for 110m hurdles on the 1st August, 1949, was the oldest world veteran record on the books till 2000. He won his eighth AAA's high hurdles title in 1949. There was Jack Holden, who at 42, was Commonwealth Marathon Champion in 1950 and Fred Norris, who won the 'National' of 1959, was still top class in his early 40s.

More recently, one of those choosing not to do the veteran Championships but being easily old enough to fill that category was Merlene Ottey. The Jamaican Queen of sprinting, Ottey made the 100 metres Olympic Final in Sydney at 40 and gained her eighth Olympic medal in the 4×100.

Sylvester Stein, Rob Bush and Guy Ogden have been outstanding veterans with Highgate Harriers. In Sylvester's case he has been gaining major veteran track medals since 1972. He was second in the over 75 100m in the National Championships at Bedford in 2000. In 2001 at Eaton he broke the British record for Over 80 200m with a time of 33.82.

In 1979, I talked to Sylvester, when he was 57, about the five-year groupings for veterans. 'The five-year gap is very necessary and reasonable. Anyone over 30, I would say, loses one per cent of one's speed per year – if you like, ten per cent per decade. If you look at the world records we are talking of about 10 seconds for a 100m at senior level, 11 seconds for 40-year-olds, 12 seconds for 50-year-olds, and about 13 seconds for 60-year-olds. So a man of 49 cannot compete with a man of 40 all

107

other things being equal. In the World Masters I will be the wrong end of my age group, nearly 59. I have a chance of medals in the 55–59 group but I would have no chance in the 50–54. The five year grouping is essential.'

Howard Williams, now 68, as a young person ran 52 minutes for 10 miles and ran 2:50:02 for the Isle of Wight Marathon in the 1960s, when 'Ghost' runner John Tarrant won in 2:47. Williams has organised every Metropolitan cross country League race since the start in 1968, with fields in excess of 200. About that well-contested event among the London clubs he remarked: 'Over 50% of the Metropolitan League fields are made up of veterans these days which is a dramatic increase in the amount of veterans that were in it fifteen years ago. That shows there are less youngsters coming in, which is a poor reflection on the sport.'

In road races there is a tremendous swing to veterans taking part. In 1999 out of 83 finishers in the London to Brighton road race (inside the new standard of 10 hours) 56 were veterans. They were led in by a M50 veteran Stephen Moore in 6:02:45 and bringing up the rear was John Fulcher (M55) in 9:55:09. Apparently in the gruelling 20th Tour of Tameside (2001) race 72% were veterans!

Pete Mulholland, a correspondent for *Athletics Weekly* told Dennis Williams, the inveterate and prolific veteran over 50 road racer that there were 14,000 'over 40' veterans entered in the London Marathon of 2001! That was a fact that Dennis found very hard to believe. Potentially, the fastest of those 14,000 was ex-international Paul Evans (40 on the 13th of April, 2001) – who should threaten many of the UK M40 records but, would find it hard to match the time done in the Paris Marathon by Moroccan born Mohamed Ezzher, of France, who ran an all time world veteran M40 best of 2:10:32!

Opinions on Veteran Athletics

Gowry Retchakan, who has had an impressive career as a hurdler, felt her most satisfying performances were doing a personal best of 54:63 in the semi-final of the Olympics in 1992, coming second in the World Cup in Cuba and winning five National Championships titles.

Gowry is married to well-known statistician Ian Hodge. After her international career ended she decided to compete for Highgate Harriers. In 2000 they were top of Southern League Division 3. She was 40 on the 21st of June that year and ran a 400m hurdles in 58.3 in a Southern league race, a time superior to any 'official' listed veteran record for her age. Why then did she not do veteran athletics? 'I feel I'll get all the competition I need with Highgate who are progressing through the leagues.'

Jenny Mathews, from Ashford AC, won the gold medal in the 'W35' 400 and 400 hurdles, in the World Veteran Championships in Gateshead in 1999. (As a matter of interest Virginia Mitchell was second in both those events, is wife of Woking AC's sprinter/hurdler/800m man Tony Mitchell, and the daughter of outstanding veteran Carina Graham.) Mathews came fourth in 58:4 in the AAA's Championship of 1999 and was a finalist in 2000. Jenny gained gold in the 400 hurdles in the World Vets in Brisbane 2001.

Veteran athletics still has got a bad image, in some ways, because the media show the much older athlete competing, which appears to them as much more dramatic news. That does not necessarily give a good impression of veteran athletics being a valid and vital part of the sport. In comes Jenny Mathews with her opinion straight after her hurdles win in Gateshead.

'I think the more younger people do it the less you will get that happening. There is an image that when you are a vet, you only take up veteran competition because you were no good as a senior. One just has to look around at World Veteran Championships at Gateshead to see Tom Petranoff throwing 70 metres in the javelin plus other performers like Sharon Gibson in the javelin, and Yvette Finikin in the triple. They would probably still make the International teams.' (If footage had been shown on National television of two multi-veteran World Champions, both in their late 40s, Nigel Gates or Dave Wilcock in action on the track with their flowing styles and youthful looks, it would soon have been realised that there was little to delineate between seeing open and veteran competition. That sort of thing would have given the right impression to those who read the papers or watch television.)

Judy Oakes of Croydon Harriers was 42 and seven months, when she competed in the shot in the Olympics at Sydney. She won 17 AAA's titles, competed in 12 European Cups. She won six concurrent Commonwealth medals. Ian Chadband in the *Evening Standard* pointed out that she had 87 appearances for Britain, three world power lifting titles and two European golds at weightlifting. Judy is coached by Mike Winch, who achieved a silver in the 1974 Commonwealth discus and was AAA's Champion the year before that.

'I think it is a personal thing as to whether you want to be involved in veterans athletics. I have spent so many years in the sport as a competitor, I think I am actually burnt out and would not be able to continue but a lot of people who take the sport up late – it's got its place and there is good camaraderie. It is great for making friends and meeting people, and travelling the world which is what I do, all right at a higher level but, never-theless, it is a great thing to keep people in the sport and bring new people into the sport and also, it has got to help all round because then, some of those people go out and help others by coaching or judging or just helping to raise funds or promote their local club. I think it has got its place because it gets mature people into the sport, who have a level head and have the time often, because they are retired, to help the sport in more ways than someone like myself who works and competes at a high level.

'As I say veterans athletics has got its place and it's great for people to win these things. I don't think it's right for me to start winning those veteran titles. I could not go out there and per-form at a level that I did not feel was not 101%.'

Zara Hyde-Peters, UK Athletics Technical Director of Endurance, had an unusual distinction in 2000, while studying for an MBA as a 37-year-old. She won the Indoor AAA's 3000m in January, British Students cross-country in February and then the British Veterans 5k on the road on the 28th of August. She felt that really being on the sharp end of 'Open'

110

competition, she would be unlikely to go into veteran track championships till she was 40 and expressly did the veteran road 5k at Havant because she wanted to help her club out. Her husband Mike was a guide to Paralympic Champion Bob Mathews in Sydney.

Tom Petranoff, from the United States, competed in the javelin for South Africa in 1992–93 but the rest of his international career he represented the United States. He has been a world record holder and silver medallist in the World Championship. Perhaps the most significant thing for veteran athletics is the fact that in 1999, after coming second in the American Championships, the same season, he competed in the World Veteran Championships at Gateshead. He won the M40 category with a, modest for him, impressive mark on a veteran scale of 73.32 metres.

'I suppose if you had asked me ten years ago, if I would be involved in veteran athletics I may have said, "I'll worry about that when I get there" or not have taken it as seriously as I have done.

'I have gotten a lot out of the sport. I have enjoyed twenty years really, where the sport has done a lot for me. I just feel I owe the sport something back. The very people that were my fan base, are the very people that are sitting here (in Gateshead) right now and some of them I have driven them into the sport, so to speak. Secondly it is about having fun, it's about friendship, It's about camaraderie, it is about making fun of each other, harassing each other. Having a beer together, but it is the social side I like as well. These people take their athletics very seriously. I just enjoy the buzz of it.'

Bill Collins holds the M40 200 world best of 21.86 (1992) whereas the man who missed the 1972 Olympic 100m final, Eddy Hart, ran a 10.6 hand-timed as a world best for over 40s in 1989. Collins was on the USA team that broke the 4×100m world record in the first World Cup in Dusseldorf in 1977 (Bill Collins, Steve Riddick, Cliff Wiley and Steve Williams 38.03). He won the 1999 M45 World Vets 100 in 11.2, beating prolific World Champion veteran sprinter Doctor Steve Peters and Wally Franklyn of the UK. Peters went on to win the 200 (22.12) and

400m (50.60). In the latter ex-Scottish international sprinter Alasdair Ross was second. Bill Collins went on to win four M50 gold medals in Brisbane.

'I love the camaraderie of veteran competition. You can talk right before a race and afterwards, which is really a beautiful thing,' said Bill Collins.

'The winning is nice but that is not the most important part. You meet great people and they feel the same about you. I look up to those older people in particular who can barely make it round the track.'

Al Oerter, four times the Olympic Discus gold medallist for the United States as an M40 threw a World Best of 69.46 in 1980. In the second World Vets Championships in Gothenburg in 1977, he won the Over 40 title with 60.36 beating Ludvik Danek (Cze 57.78) who was Olympic Champion in 1972 and was still throwing in international competitions. Al Oerter talked about coming back to throwing.

'When I decided to go back into competition I was determined to become as good as I possibly could, and compete both in open competition and veterans (or Masters as it is known in the States). When I went into my first Veteran Championships in the United States the question was "Who wasn't there?" I competed against perhaps one other Olympian in the entire competition and he was a decathlete. It was an environment many athletes found hostile. They could not conceive of the thought of competing at a lower level than they were used to. Evidently athletes have this sense of retiring at the peak of their form. And to accept anything less is very, very difficult.

'But why weren't they out there, enjoying something they had enjoyed for so long? Because that enjoyment was never really there. They found that the training regimen was very difficult. It was a forced environment because of coaches and physicians keeping them in some kind of form, when they really preferred to rest when they were injured. It became a difficult thing for them to get back into Masters competition in a way that was comfortable for them. However, I had always enjoyed it and nobody had ever forced me to do anything in my life. I could certainly accept a level of competition that was well below what

112

I had experienced in all of the Olympics that I had been at, so it became a natural thing for me to just start.'

Malcolm Fenton, coach to international Mark Proctor, won his first National Veterans title at 43 in the World Vets Championships in 1999. 'I never envisaged keeping on this long but I enjoy it and I am always competitive. I am still in the top 20 in the country as a normal person. I will just keep going. I have had a few nasty injuries but I am not going to be one of those people who says "I had to give up because of injury". That will never happen. I will give up when I have had enough.'

Guido Mueller, world over 60 300m hurdles record holder, was born in Stuttgart on the 22nd of September in 1938. As a young man he made the German National Final on three occasions. 'When you get older you start slowing down and I cannot do the same training at 60 that I did at 50.' He added, 'There is a tendency for people, particularly when they are retired with a pension, to be lazy and sit back in a chair but for veteran athletes it is different. They enjoy working out each day, taking up the challenge that old age brings to live life to the full.'

John Gilmour (born 3rd of May 1919) from Leeming, Western Australia, has had an outstanding, career as a veteran, which is amazing when you consider he had a very tough time as a prisoner of war in Japanese camps in the last war. It was when he was 61 that we first met in Hanover during the World Veterans Games. At those very well organised Championships 1979, he won the Over 60 – 800/1500/5000/10,000/Marathon. The first four events in World Age records. He gave his opinion then on veteran competition.

'I think it is a great thing because a lot of people today waste their life away by sitting around watching television. Television is the biggest bugbear in the home today, in my opinion. When people get home from work they switch it on and they even eat their meals in front of it. That goes on every day of the week, plus the fact that they are eating and drinking all the time with no exercise, whereas the beauty of veteran athletics is that you meet a lot of people and you get a feeling of competition against the other guys, it is the fact that you know that you are doing something for yourself, making you feel better within yourself and improving your own health, which I think is the greatest thing about it. Lots of guys I know who were 16 to 17 stone and today are 13 stone and they are wanting to run 26 miles. Before, they would even get their car to go a mile to buy a paper. Now, with veteran running and this fun running that has come into vogue, I reckon it is making everyone that much healthier.'

Charlie Dickinson won the European Veterans M50 5000m Championships in Finland in 2000. His first veteran win was at 40 in the Surrey Vets cross country at Richmond Park. 'After winning the European Vets race Omer Van Noten's friend came over and asked if Van Noten could have a photo taken of us both together. [The Belgian won three gold medals and a silver at Gateshead, four world titles in Japan in 1993.] Omer was so pleased for me that I had won. It was quite a humbling experience, as he is such a good runner. We have been good friends ever since.

'In veterans athletics people have respect for each other. It is just the fact you have seized the opportunity to win on a particular day. It really does not make you a better person.'

With that in mind it was a surprise for Charlie Dickinson that, when gathering people for the tribute to that modest and well-liked veteran runner, Laurie O'Hara (just before the National Vets cross country a couple of years back) the two people that phoned Charlie back, both enquired as to why he was racing at all at his age (48). His friend Arthur Bruce said cryptically 'Why not?' Charlie Dickinson noted that Mike Hager, that exceptional 51-year-old Tipton Harrier, was 59th of the 1227 finishers in the 'National' cross country of 2001. He thought that was an extremely noteworthy performance. He felt though that, besides some other unusually good placing of some younger men, for an over 50 runner to finish that high in the 'National' open, showed the standard of British cross-country running had gone down.

Les Presland, a naturally gifted athlete from Aldershot athletic club, despite being a very good club runner, competing from the age of 8, did not win a 'National' title till 1991, when he was over 50 cross country champion at Barnsley. He still runs well and was in contention for medals in National veteran road races in 2000. He achieved a World Best of 31:59:6 over 10,000m in the Berkshire Championships as an M50.

'I have never reached the very top, when you compare with say Dave Bedford. He achieved a world record and was the best in the world, but did he really enjoy his running? Whereas I am of slightly less capability but I have been racing since I was eight.

'I must enjoy my running more than Dave Bedford ever did, even more so that he had to run 150 miles a week plus, to do his performances. Okay, they were great achievements, but when I look back I am happy to have got only one English vest as a senior but still enjoy running after 40 years.' He was third M60 behind Harry Clayton and Brian Griffith in the BVAF 5k at Havant in 2000. The over 40 that day was won by Westbury's Peter Docherty, from Chris Buckley, both were advised by well known Irish veteran George Blackburn. Peter Hyde, after winning a couple of BVAF cross-countries won the over 50 category.

I thought I would give a mention to another outstanding runner who has been blazing through records and World Championship wins. **Ron Robertson**, a fruit farmer from New Zealand. M55 world records 1500 (4:12.5); 3000m (8:57:28); 5000 (15:41.72); 3000m steeplechase (9:59.8) and an M50 10,000m record of 31:01.9. He took up running after playing soccer at 39.

'Many people ask what would I have done if I had taken up running earlier but that's academic.'

Tony Simmons, born at Maesteg in Wales, now coaching, had a strong international career following a European under 18 mile record of 4:03.1 and eventually went on to win National Vets titles and a couple of Home Veteran Internationals.

Tony looks back: 'You drift along. Actually, between 30 and 32 I found it very, very difficult to compete. At the back of my mind I wanted to give up running anyway; I had reached my peak. It took me five years to adjust to the fact that I was going to be a normal club athlete. Club athletes I had never thought

115

of before were beating me, but I was taking it. Really it became quite challenging in the end.

'After a long period of time I knew I was either going to have to get out of the sport completely or start preparing to race correctly. I had done a lot of competition with a lot of stress, and I thought let's really enjoy the sport. It is not all about winning, gaining medals, world records or whatever. At the end of the day I found I did not want to give up athletics because I enjoyed the people, the company and the atmosphere. I decided I still wanted to be an athlete.

'It is a different attitude now to running to when I started [talking in 1990]. If you trained then on the road you were considered quite weird. You had to be quite a good runner, then, even to run through the streets. Now the joggers are coming out and keeping fit has become an accepted way of life. I have never run to keep fit, or be slim, or anything like that. I have always run to be a runner.'

Ken Crooke, 72, beat nine people in the 'National' in Durham. He has been competing since 1945 and attended all the World Veteran Championships which includes Brisbane in 2001. From 1989–1997 he was ECCU secretary. Ken Crooke was awarded the Torch Trophy for his long service to athletics and shares secretarial duties at Croydon AC with Mike Fleet, an ex-international half miler. 'Veteran athletics is more like old time athletics 50 years ago. Less stressful than open athletics.'

Dave Jones, from Ilford AC who ran 4:24 for a mile in the 1960s and is married to world class 'Over 60' vet Pam Jones, said, 'Veteran athletics is all about meeting up with people you used to run with years ago, in a late stage of life.'

The Breaks

There are athletes who have had huge breaks in their athletic life. Architect, **Don Adie** from Dulwich Runners, at the time of writing is 74, had 45 years out before coming back to athletics. In 2000 he was second to Welsh veteran international Bill Davies in the National over 70 5000m.

116

Derek Thomas, 70 years old, Cambridge Harrier, played for the very strong amateur football team Walthamstow Avenue before stopping sport for 21 years. He has achieved UK 800m records in the age groups right through from 50–55, 60–65, 65–70. 'The competition keeps me healthy and I love training,' he said.

Phil Lancaster, who was one of Coventry Godiva's first team runners in the 1960s, had 18 years out of athletics, playing hockey and cricket and then competed again at 50, became a home international veteran cross country champion for Elswick Harriers and, at 60, a double European Indoor Champion in 2001.

Alan Meddings, now running as an M70, was another person who had a long lay off from 1958–92. Brian Cook and Colin Simpson encouraged him to go into veterans athletics. Before that as a senior athlete, pressure of work, having such big distances to travel on public transport for training venues made him decide to retire, at a time he was bringing up a young family in his 20s too. He came back to sprinting again in his 60s. He achieved several World Veteran Championship wins which included Gateshead in 1999, M70, 100/200 13.48/27.3. When he was competing as a young man he was on Birchfield Harriers' relay teams with John Salisbury and Mike Rawson and remembers coming second to Emanuel 'Mac'Donald Bailey at the White City.

Charlie Williams was just four months short of his 70th birthday when he won the National over 65 400 title at Bedford in 2000, in a time of 66.56. It was interesting to note that the Trinidad born sprinter, who also ran for GB, was in a photo finish with Dave Sime of the United States, the Rome Olympic silver medallist, in Bordeaux back in 1956 and was timed at 10.3 for the 100m. He also ran a 9.4 for the 100 yards back in 1953.

Two great characters in veteran sprinting over the years were **Ron Taylor**, the seemingly invincible veteran sprinter, with his various striking costumes and effortless style of running, and **Bill Guy**, who won a couple of world golds in 1985. Byron Gray, the smooth Jamaican sprinter from Herne Hill Harriers, who coaches 400m man Graham Pope, would be sure to agree on my points about those two.

For the M55 100 gold in Rome in 1985 the story I heard was that it had been difficult for Guy's friends to get him out of bed for the final. He was still inebriated with strong liquor from a nightly session. They virtually had to help him to the start and pour him into the blocks. Somehow, Bill mustered everything he could together in that dash for the tape. At the finish, as he collapsed over the line, he raised one arm to the heavens. On asked why he pointed to the sky above. Bill said, 'God was my co-pilot.'

Evaun Williams in 1997 was a district nurse with Haringey Health Care and has a daughter Sharon Williams, who is an international sprinter. Some of Evaun's recent successes include five field event titles in the National Vets in Edinburgh in 1999 and a win in the weights pentathlon at Gateshead. 'I enjoy the camaraderie of veteran athletics. I like meeting people and we have good fun actually. I like the challenge and see how much the body can do.'

Bill Stoddart, who won the 1500 and 10,000 for M65 in the National Championships at Blackpool in 1977, was a Scottish International when he was young and ran in the world cross country. 'Veteran athletics for me is good because of the tremendous friendships. You work hard you play hard. The social side is good as well. Most of the trips abroad with the veterans I have gone with my wife and we have had nice nights out with Arthur Walsham and people like that.'

John Henson, who just got under the 50 seconds for a 400m, when winning the M40 400m in the European Veterans Championships at Brighton in 1984, won the World M55 200m final in 1999. Edwin Roberts who was third in the 1964 Olympic 200m, was the third fastest in those Games. Kermitt Bentham (TVH) was the next vet in the UK to break 50.00 in a veteran championship in 2000. He set a new British record of 49.55 at Eaton in 2001. Henson, like Mike Cordon and John Charlton competes in the Sheffield leagues. About old age and running he looks at it sensibly in a measured way. 'Realistically, I am now at an age where I have to listen to my body. If it is

Steve Backley, Oslo 13-7-01

Photo by Mark Shearman

Tipton's hardman Andy Holden
depicted in chapter 4

Photo by Jeremy Hemming

Lillian Board   Photo by Mark Shearman

Ato Boldon (Trinidad) Oslo 13-7-01
Photo by Mark Shearman

Seb Coe leads Steve Cram and Steve Ovett, Moscow 1500m   Photo by Mark Shearman

David Hemery, Mexico 1968 400m Hurdles   Photo by Mark Shearman

Jon Edwards, Edmonton

Carolyn Hunter-Rowe, Tourhout 8-8-93

Photo by Mark Shearman

Two Olympic champions battle it out in 2001. Allen Johnson (USA,1174) wins
the 110m Hurdles from Anier Garcia (Cuba)

Photo by Mark Shearman

Marion Jones
Photo by Mark Shearman

Richard Nerurkar wins, San
Sebastian 31-10-93
Photo by Mark Shearman

David Moorcroft   Photo by Mark Shearman

Paula Radcliffe, 'The women's role model'
Photo by Mark Shearman

Dave Bedford, 'The runner's runne
Photo by Mark Shearmar

Judy Oakes
Photo by Mark Shearman

Sonia O'Sullivan
Photo by Mark Shearman

Danielle Sanderson, Athens 1997
Photo by Mark Shearman

Khalid Skah (Morocco) World half
marathon, Oslo 24-9-94
Photo by Mark Shearman

Maria Mutola
(Mozambique, 562)
wins the 800m from
Stephanie Graf (Austria,
35) and Letitia Vriesde
(Surinam, 756)
Edmonton 2001
Photo by Mark Shearman

Earl Fee, a true athletics enig-
ma who ran 2 min 21.9 sec for
800m at 70 years of age
Photo by Jeremy Hemming

London to Brighton road race
25-9-83. Don Ritchie
(Scotland, 4) and Bruce
Fordyce (South Africa, 1)

Photo by Mark Shearman

Mark Steinle,
London marathon 22-4-01

Photo by Mark Shearman

Tommie Smith, Mexico 1968

Photo by Mark Shearman

Lasse Viren (Finland) after a training run in Finland, January 1980.

Photo by Mark Shearman

Joyce Smith (right) and Glynis Penny (left)

Photo by Mark Shearman

Bob Weir, Bremen 24-6-01

Photo by Mark Shearman

Left to right: Eric Smart, John Browne and David Elderfield in the National Vets
'M45' 100m in 2001

Photo by Jeremy Hemming

Gordon Pirie

Author on left in the London marathon 1984

Photo by Con Ellison

telling you to rest or take it easy, then you have got to obey it. When you are younger you can do more work. Now I stick to a lot of preparation and a lot of conditioning work and not so much actual running. Coaching the youngsters helps in that regard – it's really fun.'

Walter Wilkinson ran in the National Veterans Championships M55 800m in 2000 at Bedford. He had to beat two very good vets, John Treadwell and Reg Phipps, a specialist tactician who has a fantastic win record in the 50–59 age groups. Wilkinson did win the race in very windy conditions in 2:09.49. In his young days he won the Inter-Counties mile at Leicester in 1971 from Brendan Foster, Peter Stewart, Jim Douglas, and John Kirkbride and he won the AAA's 1500m at the White City in 1970 in 3:45.3. Why does Wilkinson like competing still? 'I just love racing, any kind of racing, since I was fourteen.' He even admitted, 'If I had been working all night in my job as a train driver, it made me a bit bad tempered and I could then put the aggression into the races.'

Sheila Carey won the world title at Gateshead for over 50 800/1500m, both from that great battler Pat Gallagher from Westbury. Carey was fourth in the Olympic 800m in Mexico (1968) and was fifth in the Olympic 1500 in Munich (1972) which was a British record of 4.04.81. What helps her to keep sufficiently motivated to compete at all at 50? 'As a teacher at a special school in Coventry I have to run with the children in order for them to be able to run. I am their teacher, coach and guide runner.'

Rod Parker, 81, from Salinas, California, the World Vets 100/200 sprint Champion at Gateshead, attributes vitamin E to the fact that he is still able to compete. 'I started taking it in 1946 on the advice of an American dietician. A lot of my colleagues have pacemakers or heart surgery but the fact that I have taken vitamin E over all these years has kept me from having those things.

'Another reason I compete at veteran athletics is that, when I was still a dentist at 45, I could see myself becoming a fat man with heart trouble so I started running. My first track meet was in 1980 and I have been running ever since.'

Tom McNab has performed as a veteran thrower, was the National Coach for the UK for seven years. He coached decathlete Peter Gabbett and advised Judy Vernon the Commonwealth hurdles champion of 1974 who is married to John Vernon. They both coach. John still enjoys competing as a long and triple jumper in veteran events. Tom's wife Pat McNab was a pioneer of hammer throwing on the veteran scene, as well as being previously an international pentathlete and hurdler. Tom McNab said, 'We tend to connect everything – including sex – with young people and almost remove the possibility of anybody but the young enjoying certain things. It is quite clear that older people like competing.

'The competition is as valid as anyone wants to make it. If people want to compete at 60, 70, or 80 then they should. There is nothing funny or farcical about it any more than there is about little kids of eight sprinting down a track. It is not funny, it is just different!'

Maeve Kyle, who ran in the Olympics of 1956, also ran in the European and Commonwealth Games. Her husband Sean Kyle has been a respected coach. Maeve Kyle won five over 50 world veteran championships gold medals in Hanover in 1979. Like race walker and statistician Colin Young, I thought Maeve's performances at those games were brilliant. She made the following observation at the time: 'There are three groups of people. There are people who have been at the top at Olympic level, given up, come back and found a tremendous enjoyment out of it. Al Oerter is the best example, to such an extent that it inspired him to come back and aim for the Moscow Olympics – which is incredible. You get the club athlete who has never given up, who has always been a good club athlete and here he finds he can be more successful perhaps in veteran athletics. The third group I find in many ways the most interesting; the people who only took up the sport when they were in their thirties or forties or even later, maybe for rehabilitation for health problems or something like that. The three groups mould in beautifully together.'

Kate Hoey, the Minister for Sport from 1999–2001, who used to do high jumping, watched the World Veterans Games in the North East in 1999. 'Just savour the atmosphere for five minutes and you understand how much people are getting out of this. The whole thing is so serious, as well as so enjoyable. I have enjoyed the championships so much. I am just disappointed that so many people in this country have no idea that this has gone on and how wonderful it is.'

It Runs in the Family!

Daniel Caines, 21, who had his breakthrough as a UK international 400m man in Millennium year, continued to be one of the brightest prospects in the UK, with good runs indoors in 2001. He won the 400m in the World Championships in Lisbon. (At the same meeting Mark Lewis Francis ran 6.51 for a World Junior record in the 60m and Christian Malcolm was a close second in the 200m.) Daniel Caines' mother is Blondelle Thompson who ran a 12.1 100m and in 1974 was the UK 100m hurdles record holder with a time of 13:00. Caines' father and coach is **Joe Caines**, who ran for Birchfield and now runs for Royal Sutton. He was credited with a best of 48.2 for 400m in 1971 and as a junior was on the GB relay team with Dave Jenkins, Dave Price, and Peter Beaven. He had listed times of 22.2/48.6 for 200/400. He then left the athletic scene and came back as a world class veteran sprinter in his 40s. In 1993 in Japan he won three gold medals in the sprints. He even won the National Veterans over 40 800m in 1995 and is still a force to be reckoned with in the M45 group. Why did he have such a break from athletics as an early senior to being a veteran then? 'At the time all the sports meetings were on a Saturday and being a Seventh Day Adventist, Sabbath and Church was on a Saturday. It wasn't a sacrifice when you love the Lord and I was so happy I made that decision because sport and success is not all in life.'

Anthony Whiteman, a World University 1500m Champion, with John Mayock, was one of the two leading UK 1500m runners in the late 1990s and ran sub-1:46 for 800m at Crystal Palace in 2000. He talked about his first introduction to running, when I interviewed him for the *BMC News*:

'I used to be kicked out in the morning before school to run. I would go round the corner and wait five minutes and sprint the last 20 metres. Unfortunately as it was supposed to be round the block. My mum Anne Whiteman noticed that I came in the same way that I went out and so realised that I had not been running. After that she came with me and I eventually went along to a local club. She helped start up the Maidstone Harriers, became British veteran Marathon Champion and 2nd in the World Veterans Championships. She ran a 2:59:54 marathon. Obviously that is where my natural endurance comes from. In fact until the middle 1990s she was more famous than I was.'

Runners who walk

Steve Kemp is one who has changed his event from running to walking and then back again to running, as a veteran. At Birmingham University he was on the table tennis team, then he became a sub-1:57 800m man, ran 2:29 in the London, became a good club walker for Southend AC and at 40, took up road running again in 2000. He came second in the Insurance 10 miles Championship at Battersea followed by second veteran in an Italian marathon.

In 1999 **Steve Allen**, won the Essex League and Veterans AC road walk at Eastway and a short time after, on the same day, was placed third overall in the Vets AC 5k road race championship, behind Richard Holland of Woodford Green and Stuart Littlewood of Hercules, who was first over 45. Shortly after that event Steve Allen ran 2:41 in the New York Marathon. Postman Allen, who works for the GPO, does his training around the roads near Mount Pleasant, at 2 o'clock in the morning. He sees the last people spilling out of the night clubs. He also has been learning the routes for a future additional job as a black cab taxi driver.

Roger Mills, the European bronze medallist of 1974, over the 20k walk, managed to blend being a 54 minute 10 miler on the road in the spring with international race walking in the summer. (I remember him clearly overtaking me after a mile in the Romford half-marathon one year.)

A Dramatic Change of Events

Peter Barber, who achieved a British over 65 record for the hammer was previously an international two lap runner. His best 880 yards time was 1:51.8 and he ran a 4.12 mile on the cinders at Motspur Park. Before that he was second to Brian Hewson in the Southern and National Junior Championships.

A Driving Force

Derek Wood is an ex-bank manager and an officer with the HAC. Besides winning veteran titles and being the first over 50 runner in the New York and London Marathons in the same season, he had been a county runner as a young man and ran in the big National Championships at the White City. He was responsible for taking Barnet and District over 60 teams to National titles on the road and country. **Laurie Forster** the M70 winner in the National Veterans cross country of 2000 and ran 2:34 for a marathon in the London when he was 55 years old points out: 'Derek was the driving force literally in our Barnet 60 squad. A few years back he used to take us all around the country. He really pointed the way to higher things for me. Whereas up to then I had been a bit of a fitness man and just a fun runner. He took me under his wing and said, "Right we have got a good squad here and we can do things in the 60 category".'

Mixing it with club competition

At the sharp end of the age groups for major veterans' Championships it appears, in many cases, to be essential to compete against non-veterans. **Roger Honey**, won the high hurdles for Ilford AC in the Southern League Division One at

Hendon prior to winning both M45 hurdles at the BVAF National Championships during the summer of 2000. 'You need to run in senior club competition for as long as you can as it helps you keep going.'

Another exponent of this theory is **Tony Wells**, World Vets 400 hurdles Champion in 2001 and also as an M50, was the winner of both hurdles titles in the European Veterans Championships in Finland who, like Honey, ran some quality high hurdles races against the likes of Alan Pascoe when they were younger. Wells, who also played semi-professional football until he was 40, is now a headmaster at Farnborough School in Nottingham and echoes Honey's sentiments. 'I run for Corby in the Premier Midland League which helps me to keep going – the veteran events are a bonus. It is important to put your neck on the line for a club at meetings of a higher standard. It gives you the confidence to lock horns with the veterans.'

Phillip Delbaugh, a 40-year-old from the RAF, is coached with his sprinting by Madeline Cobb (a Selsonia AC sprinter AAA's Champion 1958 and a European and Commonwealth medallist) but does his own weight programme. A former brake-man for the British bobsleigh team in the 1996 and 1997 World Championships, he said, 'I run "A" string for Hillingdon in the Southern League and regularly come up against guys who are running between 10.8 and 11 seconds so I'm getting the competition there.' Delbaugh added, 'Coming into veteran competition I have the edge. Also I'm training with a 10.5 man, that helps as well.'

John Emmett Farrell was born 4th of June, 1909, won gold medals in his over 90 age group, beating the outstanding 91-year-old Alipio A. Santos of Portugal in the 5000m in the World Veterans Games at Gateshead. Farrell's time was 36:13.91 which slashed the listed World Best of the time by American Paul Spangler (37:39.8). He had stayed for the previous weekend at the house of fellow Scott David Morrison, who holds the World Best for the over 75s, and they did some vital jogging build up work for John Farrell's heroic attempt on the world record.

Looking back through the many years of John Emmett

Farrell's life. He won the Scottish National cross-country Championships in 1938 and 1948. 'The first time was the best because after that it's never the same. My wife had never seen a race till that first one and not only did I beat 300 people but it's a sentimental thing as she stood by me.' He cited the best International 'World' cross country as to when he came seventh and second UK runner behind the winner Jack Holden.

Why then did John continue running and racing at 92? 'So I don't get depressed. It keeps me active, keeps you going and you meet such nice people.'

Earl Fee, a true 'Athletics Enigma'

To me the most exciting race of those World Veteran Games in the North East was the M40 400 metres hurdles where Howard Moscrop of Swindon AC pulled away from class American Peter Grimes 'Hemery style' to win the race in a Championships Best of 53.20. Second was Grimes 53:75, Mike Coker third in 54:84 and Tony Mitchell fourth in 54:96 but, at those Games, perhaps the most astonishing performance of all was when Earl Fee from Toronto, Canada, ran an over 70 world record of 2:21.95, for 800m, shattering the age best of 2:27.57; itself a highly considered record set by Californian James Lytjen back in 1991.

At that time Fee had set thirty world marks but one in particular satisfied him: 'The M65 800m at Buffalo in the WAVA Championships. It was a windy day, I was 66 and ran 2:14.33 and it was age rated 101%. I think that was best.'

Other notable runs he points at: 'I ran 2:17 indoors in 1998 at age 68 which was rated 102%. Mind you, it was on a beautiful bouncy track at Boston. [In 1999] I ran 61.3 for 400 at Boston which was memorable because the blocks slipped, I got cramp and they called us back. I started cautiously after that because of the cramp and came home very strongly. I learnt something from that!'

As a young man, Earl Fee was on the University of Toronto team that equalled the Canadian 4×400 relay record and he had a best flat time of 51 seconds. He then obtained a scholarship to England where he injured himself.

'My testicles swelled up and I had to have an operation. I thought, I don't want this to come back, so I did not run for 33 years. [Eventually] my doctor said it would be OK to take up jogging. When I was 57 – after a year back – I started breaking veteran world records and ran 56.9 for a world indoor best.'

As a vet he has run 100m, 300 hurdles, 1500/mile and cross country but now specialises in the 400 and 800. What are the secrets behind this truly phenomenal runner?

'When I am fit I feel like a 20-year-old,' he remarked. Fee worked as a nuclear scientist for the Atomic Energy of Canada before retiring. He promptly started to train twice a day. In the morning. 'I did things like running in water, stretching and weights and in the evening intervals or other running workouts.

'I do running in front of a mirror with fast arms. I learned that trick when I was at university. When you are standing still you can move the arms much faster. It trains and relaxes you. I work a lot on form.'

Jean Hulls

Jean Hulls, Bromley Vets AC Founder member and Ashford's Jenny Brown, were the two outstanding women all round competitors in world veteran competition in 1999. Jenny Brown's crowning achievement that year was to set a W40 heptathlon world record of 5747 points at Gateshead, followed by a world over 40 record of 4189 points in the European Indoor Championships in Bordeaux in March 2001. Hulls won the W60 heptathlon with 5870 points in 1999 and, like Brown, won gold medals in some individual events and in relays as well.

Jean Hulls, like Sean Power, Gordon Hickey, Chris Melluish, Joe Phillips, Dave Bayes, Jim Day, Dave Burton, Barry Ferguson, Dave Barrington, Colin Shaftoe, Wilf Morgan, Doug Fotheringham, Bob Care, Dave Stevens, Mary Worth, Peter Cassidy, George Phipps, Pat Gallagher, Val Parsons, Zena Marchant, Betty Norrish, Colin Simpson, Arthur Kimber, Ron

Bell, the Dunsfords, the Nicholls, the Greens, the Oakes, Brian & Una Gore, Ian & Betty Steedman, Elaine & Mick Statham, Brian & Phil Owen, Chris White, Bridgette Cushen, Jean Coker, Barbara Terry, Ted Butcher, Mary Wixey, Keith Whitaker, Maureen Lewington, Gordon Porteous (M85 World Champion 1500/500/10,000 in 1999), Maurice Morrell, Arthur Walsham, Jack Selby, Ken Hall, Derek Howarth, Bill Marshall, Les Brown, Rex Bale, Noel Noble, Tom Wood, Eric Horwell, Peter Duhig, Winstone Thomas and Norman Ashcroft (who started the Northern Vets – Dave Lord formed the South West Vets) are just some of the main people who have been tremendous veteran competitors or helpers over a very long period of time and, with their exemplary attitude have made a great contribution towards veteran athletics over the years.

I interviewed Jean Hulls for Martin Duff's 'Veterans Voice' page in *Athletics Weekly*, 9th of June 1999. Hulls was an international in 1959, when she was coached by Ron Murray, the UK high jump coach. 'Ron made me work very hard,' she recalls. 'He coached me to being an international pentathlete against Belgium and the Netherlands. I came second to Mary Rand – and Mary Peters [1972 Olympic Champion] was third.'

John Robinson was her conditioning coach, from Blackheath Harriers. He first began to help Hulls with her 800 metres running when the multi-discipline changed to the heptathlon. He started to be more specific with her training in 2000, calling in specialist coaches for her other events, to help her quest for success at the World Championships. (One of the sprinters in the group she trained with down at Norman Park, at that time, was Helen Godsell a National veteran sprint Champion in 2000 and 2001, who is sister of European Vets M59 indoor and outdoor Champion Bob Minting.)

'Jean was World Champion when she was 50,' said Robinson. 'But an ear infection completely unbalanced her at 55. We think she might have won it that year, but she couldn't. Now she is in the 60 group and flying. Her biggest problem is overtraining. I have to keep her fresh, and from not doing too much.

'The way I can help her most is to say, "You've done enough tonight, you're looking good, you have no injuries, go home".'

Jean Hulls' early career did not last very long and she was 47 when she started competing again, after years of playing hockey. 'I came out and fell over because I was not used to the synthetic tracks,' she recalls with self-effacing candour. 'I had been used to cinders filtering through the spikes. I tripped up three or four times. I could not run on the new surface. But eventually I got used to it.'

It is amazing that Hulls ever got into athletics in the first place, as she contracted polio as a child. 'I had leg irons on for four years,' she adds. 'They said that if I did not wear them my legs would not be straight and would not grow – it was horrible at school because they took the mickey out of me. Once they took them off, I went hell for leather at it. The orthopaedic surgeon said, "I would like you to do lots of exercises". I just found I could run.'

Looking Back with the World Vets over 40 Javelin Champion of 1999, Tom Petranoff

Tom's start in athletics was in the States and he set two world records as an American but got banned for competing in South Africa, which meant he could not compete in his second Olympics. He became a citizen in South Africa in 1991 then competed for South Africa in 1992–93 but got tired of the politics and returned home. There have been so many impressive performances he has achieved over the years, like being Grand Prix Champion in 1985. He traded three victories with Jan Zelezny in 1987 and was second in the World Championships of 1983 and 1992.

The performance that stood out for him was at Westwood on the 15th of May, 1983 when he hurled the javelin 99.72 at the Pepsi Meet.

'I went from a 90 metre thrower to almost a 100 metre javelin thrower in one toss. I sort of lifted the event up to a new level, which created a wind tunnel effect for a lot of throwers in the US and worldwide. I was on a streak there in 83–84 except for the Olympics.'

128

Tom Petranoff has some astonishing stories of other competitions round the world that include the time he was close to the world record with a throw of 89.16 in March 1991, creating a new South African record in Pretoria, in front of the President of the IAAF Primo Nebiolo and Edwin Moses, head of the US. It was a time they were helping decide whether South Africa was fit to come back into the international arena and in front of a 30,000 crowd.

'In Turku, Finland, I was throwing in 1983. It was my second longest throw of 99.72. It was 8 to 9 o'clock at night. It was mid summer and the sun does not set. I had got Phil Knight in the stands. The whole Nike brass. That was the last meet before the World Championships. The stadium was only 100 metres long – they had these nets built up because of my javelin. On my warm-up throw I hit about 94 to 95 metres and that was when I knew I was on because usually with warm-ups I do not try too hard, but the javelin comes down, takes off and sticks in the high jump pit at the other end, while Dwight Stones was jumping. He was there doing his little dance with his Mickey Mouse shirt. Here comes this javelin – wooooh Booom!

'Every time I came up they had to stop the high jump. I threw over 96 and some change. That was three metres from my world record. When a javelin is flying that far and you are coming in – the crowd went Oooooooh! The stadium only held about ten to twelve thousand. People were climbing up on the light posts and up in the trees to watch me. It was magic. There was a bonus schedule and my bonuses started 90 metres and my appearance fee was three or four thousand dollars to go to the meet. I had that bonus that started at 90 and for every metre it went up. After the meet I went into the cash room for the meet and the guy is counting out Finnish marks. I took a grocery bag full of cash. It got down to four or five Finn marks and that was how it drained the meet promoter. They gave the regular appearance money in cash, but the bonus money they had to take out of the tills from the meet. I never forgot the walk up to get the money changed before leaving the country with the bag. I said this is bonus for competition. The lady said what? She goes and gets the supervisor. The supervisor comes out and says, "Tom

Petranoff – no problem". She was sitting there and it took twenty minutes to count the money out.'

Petranoff's training for the javelin

'For the javelin you need flexibility, a lot of swimming, a lot of short stroke medicine ball work. It is shoulder movement, it's not arm movement. You don't use the elbow when you are throwing medicine balls. You use your shoulders.'

Although he considers Jan Zelezny (Sydney Olympic gold medallist) the greatest javelin thrower of all time with more throws over 90 metres than anyone, he would not endorse his style of throwing because, although his torque version is twice as fast as any other top thrower, he considers there is a risk he takes, with his reckless abandonment that could end up with Zelezny not having a javelin afterlife with paralysing effects on his body. The style of throwers he endorses include Steve Backley, Arki Parviainen, Boris Henry and Kostas Gatsioudis.

Had Tom Petranoff learnt techniques that have helped him get a little better over the years? 'I have learnt a lot more about the event myself as far as leverage and the centre of gravity. If I would have known these things that I know now, back when I was a top thrower, I think I would have thrown a lot further. I learnt a lot by working with kids who had never been exposed to the javelin before so therefore did not have bad habits. Kids in the townships of South Africa. It was the kids throwing my training javelin. They are very easy to teach because they do not have the habits. The only thing they threw were rocks at police vehicles. They did not throw baseballs, footballs or cricket balls.'

Petranoff's special Turbo Javelin

'That is my invention to teach kids how to throw the javelin without risk of an injury. It was mainly meant for kids, all beginners, but I found that it is very good for athletes like veterans who are trying to figure out the fundamentals of throwing the javelin. The key in throwing the javelin is, the least the

130

javelin that's slowing down the least is flying the furthest. The only way you can get it to slow down the least is to get it through the point, throw it clean so that there is no wind resistance to it. You don't have to throw it as hard as you think.'

Petranoff's advice to the aspiring javelin thrower

'It does not matter what you want to do in life, if you want it bad enough you must be willing to work hard for it. You are going to have to want it so bad you can taste it, smell it, touch it and feel it and dream it. If you can't do those then you can't do it. If you can't dream it and smell the grass and feel the goose bumps on the back of your neck and turn that sort of fantasy into reality, then you are not looking in the right area for whatever your sport is. I think throwing the javelin is one of the harder events. I think you have to be an all round athlete in order to handle the javelin, for the punishment the javelin does to your body. Zelezny described it as running into a brick wall, but you are trying to run all your energy and transfer into that one specific spot of leverage that you have got to hit and, if you miss...!

Pete Browne

Pete Browne (born 3/2/49) has the remarkable distinction of having been able to compete against the best in the world as a teenager, a senior international and for over ten years as a World Class Veteran Championship competitor. When he started veteran athletics he said, 'Frankly, regardless of whether there were veteran competitions or not I would be running now because I enjoy it and love the sport.'

Having been a good international runner, then racing at the highest club level for Thames Valley Harriers in the British League, did he at first have any problems reconciling himself to veteran competition? 'None at all. As far as I am concerned, I was racing then and I am racing now. There is little difference apart from the number of people in the stands. I have always raced because I have wanted to race, rather than for the money, glory or whatever. It is just a matter of getting the most from yourself and competing against others.'

In the World Veteran Championships at Gateshead Peter Browne ran in the 800m M50 final. He went into the lead at the 600 metres mark and held his form right to the tape and won in 2:05.04 but he stressed immediately afterwards, that it had not been an easy ride for him to win.

'I was absolutely amazed to win that! I had been running a month after doing gym work. As a chief accountant I had been working twelve hours a day and when I got down the track at 8.45 in the evening to train, I only had quarter of an hour before closing time. I also had niggles and scares leading up to the race.

'I had just one 800m race before Gateshead BVAF National M50 final at Edinburgh two weeks before. [1. Pete Browne 2:04.02 (CBP); 2. Walter Wilkinson (NV) 2:04.36.] At Gateshead I thought I had a chance but I did not really think I would win.'

It has often been noted by other United Kingdom veterans that when Pete Browne is on the team he is a great motivator for the rest. (He was a Queens Park Harrier to begin with but for many years he has been a loyal TVH man.) He has vast experience of UK team management and, with the help of his wife Jean (Highgate then Parkside), who has won a National veteran 100m sprint title herself, is extremely popular on the various veteran tours abroad.

Pete Browne's record is impressive. He ran 48:00 for 400m as a nineteen-year-old (he trained with John Wilson who was coached by Charlie Elliott). He won the AAA's Senior 800m in 1971 in 1:47.5 and that year came fifth in the European Championships in Helsinki. (First six: Yevgeniy Arzhanov (SU) 1:45.6; 2. Dieter Fromm (EG) 1:46.0; 3. Andy Carter (GB) 1:46.2; 4. Hans-Henning Ohlert (EG) 1:46.9; 5. Peter Browne (GB) 1:47.0, 6. Jozef Plachý (CZE) 1:47.3.) AAA's Indoor Champion in 1975. In Ovett's career as a junior and early senior he came up against Pete Browne and they traded victories over 800m quite often. Pete admired Steve Ovett more than any other runner.

Pete Browne then points out, 'Besides the AAA's Championship there was one race in Ireland where I beat Noel Carroll for the very first time, my whole family were there. That gave me satisfaction.'

Pete Browne, who won no less than twelve Middlesex 800m titles, went on to say, 'My father Peter lived and breathed sport, and not just athletics. He was born in Ireland and was a good sprinter although he never did it seriously so, my most satisfying veteran win was over 800 metres in the over 40 final in Eugene, Oregon, in 1989 because it was a crusade for me. My father had died in January of that year so I did it for him.' (1. Pete Browne 1:55.20; 2. Ron Bell 1:55.80; 3. Les Duffy 1:56:02. Pete had two listed world best times over the distance M40 1:51.25 outdoors and M45 indoors 1:57.32.

On the 2nd of March, 2001 Johnny Grey (40), who first ran in the Olympics in the 800m final of 1984, ran 1.48:81 at Atlanta, for clearly the fastest 800m ever recorded by a veteran indoors or outdoors to that date, according to athletic statistical authorities Peter Mathews and Mel Watman.

How did it all begin for Pete Browne? 'As far back as I can remember that was all I ever wanted to do. I had that wish to be referred to as "an athlete". At the age of seven I regarded that as one of the highest compliments you could be paid. I remember when I was about nine going on a Sunday afternoon walk with my family to the Welsh Harp. We saw a track 300m or so marked out ahead of us, and I immediately stopped the family, saying, "I am going to run around this track and you have got to time me." They had to drag me away in the end as they really didn't want to spend the rest of the afternoon watching me thundering round!

'I enjoy it so much and I get grumpy if I get a niggling injury that prevents me competing or indeed training for any period. I wonder if there are genuine withdrawal symptoms from lack of training? It certainly feels that way. It is very important for me to be able to train and compete. It is a way of life for me...'

133

What Might Have Been

Eric Smart, was a professional sprinter before athletics went 'Open' and he had won the famous Powderhall Sprint in 1988, was a professional from 1980–94, then 6 years for Wallsend AC.

In 2001 Smart won the National Vets M45 100m at Eaton, after powering his way past John Browne, who had earlier in the summer equalled the world M45 100m record, hand-timed of 11.00. The man who was third was David Elderfield, another excellent veteran sprinter like Steven Peters and Viv Oliver in the 45 group. Eric Smart's time against a headwind at Eton was 11.6.

North-eastern veteran Smart was inspired by Allan Wells of Scotland, who won the 100m in the Olympics of 1980. 'I have done well in athletics but the only burning question would be, if someone had got hold of me at 18 what could I have done at Olympic level! I did 10.45 at the age of 36. What would I have done at 18?'

Vets Diversifying

Jenny Gray juggles motherhood with being a producer with a national television network, as well as doing athletics. She was second over 40 overall, but first over 40 in the UK in the London Marathon of 2001 with a time of 2:57.06. It was her first attempt at the marathon and she did it 'only' on track training. In the summer she won the National Veterans over 40 title for 1500m with a time of 4:43.4. Another to change her events within a few months was **Judy Oakely**, coached by ex-international Gerry North. She ran her first marathon in the London of 2001 in 2:51.28 and like Jenny Gray ran that summer in the National Vets Championships at Eaton. She won the over 35 titles for 5 and 10k. She remarked just before the London, 'As I am getting older doing things like the marathon is the way I have to go. I am never going to be really fast. I have got to go for the longer distance. My endurance will help reap the rewards really.'

Clare Pauzers' husband Valdis enjoys competing in veteran races. In the National Veterans Championships in Bedford in 2000 Clare Pauzers won the W35 1500m in 4:36.29 and has run a 2:43.27 marathon. Her opinion on athletics is common to most: 'Running is a large part of my life and a pleasure to do. We spent four years in Italy at one time and joined an Italian club. It really opened up a network of friendships for us.'

I am sure for the mature athlete, there is more to life than athletics. Something that would be backed up by Clare, as she has a very young child to look after, apart from anything else.

Vince Hancock (57) won the over 55 title in the BVAF 10 miles road Championship in 2000 and in 2001, was third in the M55 National Vets championship 10,000 on the track behind Gareth Jones and Martyn Rouse. After both those last two races Vince and I had avid discussions about various wines together, and only touched on athletics once!

8

Some Pointers on Coaching

Andy Todd was the European bronze medallist in the 400m hurdles in Athens in 1969 in a time of 50.3, coming in behind Vyacheslav Skomorokhov (49.7) of the USSR and John Sherwood (50.1) of GB. Todd had been an English schools and AAA's Junior Champion. 'John Le Masurier helped me with changing my stride pattern, which is one of the greatest things he has done for me.'

Colin Campbell and Martin Winbolt Lewis were two of the UK's best 400m runners in the late 1960s. Colin ran 45.9 for 400m and went on to be AAA's 800m champion indoors in 1970. He ran 1:46.1 in 1972 for a UK outdoor record. He also points to the coaching help of fellow Channel Islander John Le Masurier. 'He is just right for me, more adviser than coach, we work out training and racing together, planning 2 or 3 weeks in advance. For example two weeks before the GB v Poland match this year (1968) plans were made for the Olympic preparation. Not a day-to-day schedule but a flexible plan of sessions to include 2 or 3 times each week. My bank generously allowed me to train twice daily.'

Tommie Smith might be considered as the greatest natural and most fluent 200/400 runner ever while others may plump for Michael Johnson. Back in 1968 in Mexico City, Smith won the Olympic final in 19.8 from Australian Peter Norman (20.00) and John Carlos (20.00). The latter like Smith, gave a Black Power salute on the rostrum at the medal ceremony. Although, at the time it was frowned on and they were thrown out of the Games, history may very well dictate that their bravery was a *very* important move forward, to raise the profile of Black people in the United States.

Smith, who is 6ft 3ins tall, weighed 185lb, was a student teacher at San Jose College when he won his Olympic title. One must not forget that the great Lee Evans who won the Olympic 400m in 43.8 and the 1962 Commonwealth Champion Wendell Mottley of Trinidad, who was a close second in the 1964 one lap event in Tokyo, were well beaten by Smith in 400m races.

'My coach Bud Winter is very good but, as any other coach, he can only tell you what to do; correct your faults; plan your training. He can't do the work for you. A coach is someone who is trying to help you, not tear you down. Bud tells me what to do, and then leaves me to get on with it. He will just quietly watch, and comment from time to time. With the feeling of someone like him watching I think anybody will have the incentive to train.

'For my own part, I am never satisfied until I have pleased myself. Yes, I may well have pleased the crowd but unless I feel self-pleasure, I never feel satisfied. The incentive to please himself is born within a person, whatever his ultimate calling in life, and it is thus important that the teacher or the coach endeavours to bring this out in the individual at an early stage.'

Ian Morris from Trinidad was fourth in the Olympic 400m in 44.25 in Barcelona in 1992 behind Quincy Watts (USA) 43:50; Steve Lewis (USA) 44.21; and Samson Kitur (Kenya) 44.24. 'My coach Oswald Joseph is a very quiet guy, with no diplomas of being a coach but he was an athlete himself so, with that experience he had, he was able to impart that knowledge to me. That was helped by Oswald having been a teacher too. When I was not with him, and on my own, I did the programme he gave me. For my knowledge on training, it is a combination of what he has taught me and what I have heard from other people that has been useful.'

Nouria Merah-Benida of Algeria won the 1500m at the Sydney Olympics in 4:05.10 from Romanians Violeta Szekely (4:05.15) and Gabriela Szabo (who won in 2001 4:05.27). She explains about her coach and husband Amor Benida, 'It helps to run with him in training. He did 3:43 for 1500m in 1993.'

Gael Pencreach (23) from Limoges who runs for St Etienne in France, made the 2001 Olympic Steeplechase final. And had a best time to that date of 8:13.16, which he achieved in 1999 and 8:14.94 in 2000. 'My coach Pascal Denogent is a Professor in sport. He is very practical and listens to other coaches in the world. He believes in changing the training year by year.'

Benita Willis from Australia improved her 5000m personal best time from 15:23 to 15:04 at the Bislett Games in 2001. 'Dick Telford at Canberra AIS is an exercise physiotherapist who coached Lisa Ondieki, who was married to ex-middle distance world record holder Yobes Ondieki. Dick is laid back and does not put pressure on his athletes. He is good on exercise physiology for the training sessions.'

Michelle Collins coached by Trevor Graham, the man who coached Sydney Olympic 100 and 200m Champion Marion Jones and sprinter Tim Montgomery. 'Under the coaching of Trevor Graham and at the age of 29 this year (2000), I have improved on all my pbs: 100, 11.9; 200, 22.57; and 400m, 50.1 and also made the Olympic team for Sydney.'

Marion Jones who won five medals in the Sydney Olympics and was world sprint Champion in 1997 and 1999 adds: 'Trevor is really quiet. He does not like all the attention. Not only is he quiet and reserved as opposed to some of the other big time coaches. He stays in the background. You rarely see him around. He is very loyal and I think that is why his athletes love him.'

Steve Smith the United Kingdom high jump record holder with 2.38m said in 2001: 'My coach Mike Holmes has a good all round knowledge. He never forced me into being very specific in my training. I long-jumped, sprinted and hurdled to start with. It led to a good all round knowledge of all different aspects of the sport. He was very good helping me with the conditioning background and he was quite tough as well.

'The most satisfying performance for me in my career was winning the World Junior Championships in Seoul in 1992.' 1. Steve Smith (GB) 2.37; 2. Tim Forsyth (Australia) 2.31; 3. Takiro Kimino (Japan) 2.29. 'Having competed in Barcelona, not achieved what I could have achieved, to go on two weeks later and prove to everybody what I should have achieved, albeit in the Juniors. I still finished top of the world junior rankings. That was satisfying. You very rarely get to jump your maximum. I had no regrets as I had achieved the best I was going to achieve that year.' The only person to jump higher in 1992 as a senior was Patrik Sjoberg of Sweden with 2.38m. Sjoberg came second behind Cuban Sotomayor (2.34) in the Olympic Final that year.

Judy Oakes' coach is and was Mike Winch, who gained a Commonwealth silver for the shot in 1974 and 1982. He was AAA's Champion indoors from 1979 to 1981 inclusive and National Champion for the UK outdoors in 1979 and 1980.

'I can't think of any other coach athlete relationship that has lasted so long. He started coaching me in 1974. We are still going strong through thick and thin. We understand each other. I often say something then he says it. We are on the same wave length. We anticipate what each other is going to say during the sessions.

'I used to be the worst competitor in the world and could not do it. Every time I got so nervous I did not know what I was doing. My legs would shake; occasionally it happens even now when I get to a major event but then I think "How stupid" competing with these people which I have done in the year. It is no different but the fact that it is a major championship instead of a Grand Prix or something!

'It is just learning to compete and I have been taught by Mike how to compete and how to approach it and that's why, this year when I was very ill at the Europa Cup and I was on antibiotics the day before, I was pretty grim. I was so grim I had to leave the shot at home because I could not carry it to the station, because it was too heavy as I was so ill. I knew that if I dropped out they would be in real trouble. I knew at that stage, I could do better than Myrtle (Augee) as she was not quite ready to compete. I went out there and I got second place which was tremendous. The distance was nothing to write home about but competitively it was a good performance. [Judy Oakes 10th Europa Cup at St Petersburg. 1. Irina Korzhanenko (RU) 20.65; 2. Judy Oakes 18.38.] All through the year I was getting good

139

competitive performances. It was the first year for a long time that I had been able to do that because Mike and I actually sat down and talked about my approach to competition and where I had been going wrong over the last couple of years, and sometimes, you just have to be reminded how to compete. You need someone who has been there!

'I think there are a lot of coaches, very good and competent coaches but, they get their athlete to a certain level and fall down when it comes to the big meeting. It is because they have not actually competed in a major championship themselves so they can't understand what it feels like. I think that is difficult for the coach and the athlete. Until you have actually experienced what it is like, to sit in a room with all your rivals for forty-five minutes. Just sitting there, nothing to say, just looking at each other, psychologically it is very daunting. Unless you have been like Mike has. He has competed in the European Championships and Commonwealth Games and done very well, he knows what the atmosphere is like and he knows the psychology, and a lot of good coaches just can't quite take their athlete that last little bit to majors because they have never actually been to a major championship. It is a totally different ball game. I think that is why it was desperate when we lost Keith Connor to Australia. [First UK athlete to exceed 17 metres for a triple jump, Commonwealth Champion 1978, world indoor best of 17.31 in 1981.] We should not lose athletes of that calibre to coach athletes of other nations. We should keep those people because they have got a lot to offer and a lot of knowledge.'

Dave Ottley, once an English Schools javelin Champion with 66.18 in 1973, went on to gain a silver medal at the Olympics. [1984, 1. Arto Harkonen (Finland) 86.76; 2. Dave Ottley (GBR) 85.74; 3. Kenth Eldebrink (Sweden) 83.72.]

'I always wanted to be good at something. Up until I took up the javelin I never represented my school in anything at all; that included football, cricket or athletics. It was not till my second year in secondary school that in fact I got into the school team and that was for the javelin. I knew that I had a good arm for throwing the javelin. One day I saw someone throwing the javelin. I knew that I had a good arm on me and I took someone on at the javelin – one of the boys above me in years in the school – and I threw further. It just sort of carried on from there. I improved from 91ft to 173ft in my second year of throwing. I met Margaret Whitbread during that time.' (Margaret Whitbread had been an international thrower and UK National coach. Her adopted daughter Fatima Whitbread won the World Championship javelin in 1987 and threw a world record of 77.74 in 1986.) Dave Ottley continued, 'She likes to keep things reasonably basic first of all. She was always trying to ingrain a simple technique of running hard, keeping the speed up at the end, keeping the arm well back, keeping the head and legs in front of the body. So, in those days I was getting a good basis for what I am doing now' (in 1980).

Mike Turner, who is now a schoolmaster at Queens College in Taunton has been an M50 veteran National Champion and was ranked seventh in the country back in 1969. He had a couple of internationals. I felt it would be interesting to go down memory lane because of some of those people he mentioned.

'Sidlo of Poland and the American Cantello I admired, they were sort of gods to me. You could not imagine they were throwing so far. As far as the ones I competed against, there was John McSorely, John Greasley, Dave Travis and John FitzSimons. A good bunch. It was difficult to get in the team. I used to go down with coach Ken Brookman to train on a Sunday morning with John McSorely and Bob FitzSimons. Ken Brookman was a good man in those days and one of the top coaches and javelin throwers to work with. He was throwing as a vet till six or seven or so years ago and held the M65 javelin record.'

What the Coach Thinks of the Athlete

Renaldo Nehmiah. It would have been almost impossible for Renaldo 'Skeets' Nehmiah not to have won the 1980 high hurdles title in Moscow, if he had been able to run. The boycott destroyed his chances. The previous year at the World Cup, not at his very best, he beat Thomas Munkelt the Olympic Champion of 1980. By the end of 1980 Renaldo had recorded the 12 fastest times of the top 16 of all time and that included the top 4!

His coach **Jean Poquette** said, 'When he came to me at Linden High School, Scotch Plains in New Jersey, he was only 5'6½" tall but he had unusually long legs in proportion to his body. I guess at this stage, as a high school coach, I was impressed with the mere fact that he took three steps between the hurdles at such a young age.

'I say that Greg Foster has great speed and strength. He is not the technical hurdler "Skeets" Nehmiah is so I would say that certainly speed and strength are primary reasons why he is a world class hurdler but I think as a result of his great speed and strength they have really overlooked the technical aspects of his hurdling. I think Renaldo is a fine technical hurdler. We developed a new technique, so to speak, a classical technique. Renaldo does not lay out over the hurdles the way a lot of hurdlers do, that is because we took his speed and strength and we concentrated on developing a very, very fast snap-down lead leg. An awful lot of hurdlers, including Rod Milburn, tend to put emphasis on their trail leg – pulling their trail leg through very quickly and they kind of let their lead leg float. What we did was to concentrate on a very, very fast snap down on the lead leg. The European writer for *Track and Field News*, Roberto Quercetani, did a study, one time, comparing "Skeets" with Harrison Dillard and his conclusion was that "Skeets" tends to spend less time in the air clearing the hurdles and getting back down to the ground than any other hurdler that ever lived. So, in spite of the fact that he has got tremendous speed, he is probably truly the fastest hurdler in a 100m dash that ever lived and he also spends less time in the air technically going over the hurdles, which to some extent is inherent. He has great strength which is acquired and practised and he has, I think, excellent technique. He tends to be more vertical than most hurdlers but that is because of the lead leg. If he was going into the hurdles with a very strong lean that would retard that push-down and then his upper body would retard the movement of his lead leg and his particular technique needs a little bit more

142

clearance for his lead leg to do the type of thing it's doing. Technically he may be more erect but for him it is the proper form.' After his best days as a hurdler he changed to American football as a wide receiver for the San Francisco 49ers, then came back to hurdling again. Despite tremendous difficulties in getting back the technical aspect of hurdling, he still managed to be rated in the top 10 in the world again, although not the force he was as the world's number one.

What was the great hurdler's advice to an aspiring youngster? 'Probably the first thing is to learn the form of hurdling. A lot of people notice that they have got a little bit of speed and they are big and strong. They think they can become a hurdler and I would say over 90% of your hurdlers today [in 1980], even the ones that are running fairly decent, are not technically developed. They don't know the technique of hurdling.'

Carl Lewis, the American gold medallist many times over, has been considered the greatest living Olympian. However, in Seoul in 1988 Canadian Ben Johnson was first past the post in the 100m final with Lewis, Linford Christie and Calvin Smith the next to finish. Johnson was stripped of the Olympic title, for taking a banned substance that showed up in a test in Seoul. The time that Johnson had done was 9.79, which was the same time as Maurice Greene, coached by ex-400m international John Smith of the United States, achieved. Greene did that in Athens in June 1999, which was ratified as a new world record.

Having talked to a couple of leading coaches and some journalists the conclusion is sometimes drawn that it might be difficult to get to the pinnacle of individual sporting achievement without very good medical back-up or an extremely good dietician. Whether Ben Johnson's name should or should not be promoted in this book is subject to conjecture but, looking back, it was interesting to hear what his coach had to say about Ben, after he had won the Commonwealth 100m and was, at that particular time, the top competitor in the world over the short sprint. His coach was **Charlie Francis**, who had won Canadian titles at one time and achieved times of 10.1/20.6, the latter beating Pietro Mennea of Italy.

'Ben Johnson has always been very persistent from the time

he joined my group as a 14-year-old. Even though in the early days he was undersize for his age and finished behind the others, he never stopped trying. Whereas it had been much easier for some of the other "super talents" like Tony Sharpe and Desai Williams, Ben had to really work for it and it was a struggle. If people achieve things easily they can become complacent which Ben never was.' Regarding his training: 'Specificity with Ben's training is the main thing. Not a high volume of speed work, but what he does is at a very high rate.'

Obviously John Smith must be considered one of the greatest coaches of sprinters of all time. He coaches 2000 Olympic Champion Maurice Greene, Ato Boldon and Bernard Williams. What did he feel should be the qualities needed to coach such high-calibre sprinters?

'First of all I think you have to have high expectations for the sport. You have to be able to put them in a position that they are going to do things that have never been run before and therefore, you have to lead by example. So, I study a great deal. The other thing that I do is know when to shut up and listen. I try to find things to say. The way you learn how to do that is, you have got to be quiet, because they will tell you what is needed to be said, but you can't do it. First of all you have an impulse when you are connected with them. You have to let that impulse go by. Right when the impulse goes by the answer is there and it is something that you never speak off the top of the emotion; you let the emotion come down. Then you speak and they listen. Impart wisdom, make sure that they learn from their valleys and they stay humble at their peaks.

'I try to stay constant as much as possible. I am not too emotionally high. I don't try to maintain and manage my emotional lows, so it makes it a more consistent day and makes your career long and prosperous. Prosperous, meaning that you always will be in a constant state of improvement and you are constantly learning.'

John Smith won the AAU Championships as a young man in 45.5 in 1971 as well as being a Pan American Games Champion. His experience of having been a sprinter must be invaluable! 'You never find a music teacher teaching music who has not played music. Trevor Graham is such a good coach because he was a good athlete himself, and so it goes on and on. The fruit does not fall far from the tree. More of us are staying in the sport and we are students of the game. We have a love affair with it and the opportunity to express ourselves.'

Nick Bideau from Melbourne Australia coached and coaches many who have reached national or world class: Craig Mottram improved his mile time at the age of just 21 to 3:53.06 in the Dream Mile in the Bislett Stadium, on the 13th of July, 2001.

'I think you have to have knowledge and an understanding of training. How it feels and athletes respond to it. You have got to have belief. You have got to believe that people can do great things because it rubs off. If you doubt it that feeling rubs off too. If you are convinced they can do something and be calm about it, it affects athletes. That is one of the key things that takes athletes from a moderate level to the best level. I have trained so I know how training feels and what it is like. I can come to Europe and I know what to expect. Look at the tremendous championship form of Nils Schumann (German Olympic 800m Champion in 2000) as opposed to his Grand Prix form; you learn something from that. I talk to John Walker, Brendan Foster, and Jeff Mundle (a good coach Stateside and representative of Maria Mutola). I learn from them and get information from them.'

There are many excellent top rated coaches in the UK and here are just a few of those names. National coach Max Jones, Wilf Paish, Tuder Bidder, John Regis, Ron Roddan, Mike Whittingham, Pete Watson, James Hedley, Tommy Boyle, Geoff Warr, James Bryce, Lindsay Dunne, Peter Coe (coach to Seb) Paul Dickinson (coach, BBC television commentator and, in 2000, ex-international and now a veteran field event champion), Chris Black (ex-international still throwing the hammer), Robert Weir as a performer and coach to many (to Olympian Adam Nelson), Mike Smith (Iwan Thomas and a long history of one-lap men and, several good women sprinters like Donna Murray), Malcolm Arnold (John Akii Bua and Colin Jackson), John Trower (Steve Backley and Mick Hill), John Anderson (Dave Moorcroft), Bruce Longden (Sally Gunnell), Olympic finalist

Mike McFarlane (Tony Jarrett and Dwain Chambers), Jock Anderson (Mark Lewis Francis), Linford Christie advised Olympic medallists Katharine Merry and Darren Campbell, Roger Black (advises Mark Richardson), TV commentator Tim Hutchings, former international (the Graffins), and Dutchman Van Commenee, who coached Sydney Olympic heptathlon gold medallist Denise Lewis. Alan Storey has a host of long and middle distance boys under his wing. Stan Long has always been a well respected coach in the north-east. Kim McDonald, who ran against Seb Coe as a senior, was someone strong on management and advice for top distance runners from many parts of the world. West of England coaches Mike Down and George Blackburn are respected by many as good running coaches, as are Mick Woods and Tony Bush in the south. George Gandy has been special to many aspiring distance men and women for countless years. Bud Baldaro is another who used to run well, gets the Midlanders into shape and Mark Rowland (UK Steeplechase rec: 8:07.96). However, there are coaches all over the land who will never get the recognition they fully deserve and I have chosen five of them.

Ron Allison is married to Joan Allison (1970–74 Commonwealth 1500m silver medallist). Ron started his coaching by helping out at Cambridge Harriers 27 years ago. He now has six sprinters and fourteen middle distance runners in his group that train at Sutcliffe Park, Eltham. Nick Francis, Mat Shone and Joe Mills are three of the names. 'I think the qualities of a coach are to be understanding, sympathetic but be hard sometimes as well.'

Pat Gahagan, from Havering, ran 800/1500 in 1:52.7/3:56.7 and in 1984 was Insurance Champion with times of 1:56/3:56. He coaches 25 youngsters at Maysbrook and has advised 800m man Des English. One of the ones he gets pleasure in coaching is Lesley Felton who came into athletics as a veteran over 35 and consistently improved, to come fourth in the W40 age group in the World Veterans 800m in 1999 with a time of 2:19.15. She finished just ahead of one of the famous Colebrooks, Teena Colebrook.

Pat thought that about 80 to 90% of youngsters tend to leave

146

the sport before they reach senior level. Now for Gahagan's feelings on coaching: 'Commitment, unconditional for the athletes which is tough at times.' He continued, 'I like to keep contact with the athletes and treat an athlete as a person. I feel it is definitely a help to continue to compete and train with my athletes.' Interestingly enough Ron Allison and Pat Gahagan often have lunch together in the City to discuss coaching ideas.

John Robinson, from Blackheath Harriers, is a conditioning coach at Norman Park and Ladywell. 'I treat any athlete with the same respect. It is important not to hold on to people but have the courage to pass them on for their own good. I do that to such specialist coaches as Steve Cluney, Dave Liston and Andy Frankish.'

John Sullivan, Alf Wilkins and Frank Horwill are friends who discuss coaching ideas together. Sullivan has been coaching for 44 years. What then does he consider a good coach's qualities should be? 'Look at the interest of the athletes rather than his own interest which so many do. Some coaches treat athletes as fodder.' He adds, 'I give them 100% and expect 100% back. If you have not got fundamental control over your athletes it is a waste of time.'

John, who has been to Mile End and Finsbury Park to coach over the years does 4 hour sessions of coaching 4 times a week and last year (2000) he did 6 times a week for four hours! 'There were two lads who recently came to me from Ilford, one Asian and one Black. After the sessions they specially came up to me and said "Thank You John", that is what makes coaching worthwhile.'

John Sullivan believes in stretching for his athletes, 'Prevention is better than cure, even when you are watching television.'

Sebastian Coe used to do circuit training in a large group in 1976–77 under coach George Gandy at Loughborough. When I talked to Seb in 1984 he believed in stretching. 'I have got into the habit now, nearly all the time. Even when I'm watching television you'll find me stretching. I find it dreadfully boring – stretching. I find I cannot put aside three quarters of an hour a day when I will constantly stretch. What I tend to do is stretch all day. You can feel, after a training run, that the calves are

147

slightly tight or you are a bit tight in the low back or the shoulders. You consistently work on breaking down the muscle areas.'

I remember when I was a youth runner and Ted Fosbrook of Highgate organising **Jacky Bayliss**, Richard Cox and myself to run in the Epsom Youths race. It was won by Peter Milner, like his brother Tony a very useful runner. It was when Michael Holliday's 'Story of My life' was top of the hit parade! Jack ran 4:33 for a mile as a youth and was second in the Middlesex cross country Championships. Jacky Bayliss coaches so very many people at Parliament Hill Fields, it would be impossible to mention them all. I will just pick a few of the ones who have been with Jacky a long time. Shane Snow, who once won the Snowdonia Marathon and has been inside the first 100 in the National Senior cross country at least eight times. There is Chris Beecham, Charles Addison, Dominic Hall, Ben Pochee, Mat Lawson, Pat Davis, Nicky Martyn, Chris Bailey, Duncan Burbidge, Henry Dodwell, Rudi Von Grot, Ron Higgs (Barnet runner who has won over 50 and 55 National Vets titles), Keith Cullen the Chelmsford International, Andrew Hennesey (TVH), Sharon Cooney, Jo Fenn, the Woodford Green international (recently), Becky Long, Astrid Wingler, Natasha Cendrowicz, Esther Evans, the Welsh international, and ex-Olympian Gowrey Hodge (Jim Alford is her hurdles coach) plus Kate Jenrick, the Surrey cross country champion of 2001.

'I got into coaching by accident in 1966. I was only 25/26. You can blame Bob Slowe for that. I just turned up at the track one evening and we had no young athletes' coaches. Dave Holtby was one of those and he was sixteen and he got third in the Southern Youth cross-country the next year, so I had some success with the youngsters. Mick Gordon came into the group and I had the Holland twins. Mick won the first ever AAA's National 800m and did the UK sixteen-year-old best, and that was not beaten in that age group for about ten years, so it was a really good run by Mick.'

Highgate Harrier Jacky Bayliss coaches men, women and takes a great interest in the youngsters too. 'I actually only coach people from about 17 years upwards now. I have coached

148

youngsters in the junior age groups up to National level. I would be prepared to actually go and do it again if the people were dedicated enough to come and train. We have found in the last few years the dedication levels of the youngsters has not been what it used to be. There are too many distractions in the London area for kids to be as dedicated as they used to be. I tend to concentrate more on the older "younger" women now. I certainly would like to do it again if the dedication was there. The jobs people do sometimes make a lot of difference to the amount of intensity they can put into training or racing, in order to achieve a very high level. I think one of the problems that we have got with runners is that, although they want to run quite successfully, a lot of them hold very qualified jobs like barristers, solicitors, architects, and they are never ever going to be able to run at top level because of the nature of the jobs they do, but at the same time, given enough time you can raise their performances to a reasonable level, but they are never going to be able to run at the top level because of the nature of their jobs.'

Judy Oakes, MBE, and the Ron Pickering Award

'It is funny you should mention those two awards because, as it happens those are the two I feel most pride in. One obviously being honoured by your country and the Queen is the icing on the cake particularly when you are not expecting it, which I wasn't. I thought they only give that sort of thing to Olympic Champions. When I got the letter through I thought someone was messing me about. It took me about a week to say "This is really happening!" That was wonderful.

'The Ron Pickering award; Ron was a wonderful man. He did a tremendous amount for the Cinderella events, although I don't like that terminology, he was very knowledgeable and promoted our events through thick and thin, was not scared to put his neck on the block and that was the sort of man he was. He fought for the underdog and had a lot of respect from all the athletes and sports people throughout the world.'

A Voyage Round Sean Pickering's father Ron Pickering

Sean Pickering was a hammer thrower who had an eight years
break and then trained for the shot in February 1995. He was an
Olympic shot putter who did 20:45m and 68:64 for the hammer.
His father Ron Pickering was a big influence on his son:

'Of course he had a huge influence. First and foremost he
was a great communicator, probably the greatest communicator
in the sport. You have to understand his background; he came
into commentating only because he was in the sport. He was
a teacher then a coach. It all dates back to my mother and
her influence as an athlete.' (Jean Desforges was her maiden
name. She gained a European gold in the long jump in 1954,
and before that an Olympic bronze medal in the 4×100m
relay.)

'He learnt about the sport carrying her bag and following
her around while she was the athlete of the family. That was
his initial influence. Then once he began as a teacher and
having the chance to teach anywhere in the country, he chose to
go back into the area he grew up in which was the East End
of London. That was where he could make the biggest difference. From there he was very heavily influenced by Geoff
Dyson, who was national coach at the time, and then my father
took a coaching position as a national coach at the time for
Wales and the South West of England. I was born in Wales and
I grew up in that environment; where Lynn Davies was living
round the corner from us.' (Lynn was coached by Ron and
Lynn's United Kingdom long jump record of 8.23/27.0 that
he did in June 1968 is still on the books in 2002.) Athletes
on the squad were Mike Lindsay, Martin Lucking and John
Hillier. They were all people my father was training with, and
living at our house so, as a kid that was my influence as I was
growing up and that continued. The Olympic Champion for
the hammer and his coach have been staying at our house
this year. A lot of the influence has been about the athletes who
have stayed at our house and the empathy my mother has with
those athletes (being a European Champion herself). Athletes of
that quality felt very comfortable in her presence. We have

always had an open house policy so, throughout my life I have been surrounded by probably some of the greatest athletes in the world and got to know them on a personal level. It has been quite interesting because also on a business side of things, the people that are now in fairly influential areas in sport throughout the world are the same people that I was growing up with. John Boulter, the Vice President of Reebok was also one of the athletes on my father's squad in Wales. It was all a natural process for me being brought up in that environment. However, I like all sports anyway.'

Are there often difficulties in a father coaching his son?

'One of the big frustrations I believe for him with me was, that I was the one person he could not motivate because I had heard it all my life. I knew how he worked with other athletes. I think it was very frustrating for him dealing with me. He could not coach me as a father–athlete relationship. It would not work because I would not respond the way his other athletes would. However we did have a great relationship and he was someone I could turn to for advice but coach/athlete relationship we could not have had.

'It is somewhat difficult growing up with a parent who is well known in the kind of field you are in. Obviously my father's reputation preceded him so, as I grew up I was known as "Ron Pickering's son". I wanted to make a name for myself rather than going into some of the fields he was in. It was important for me to find my own way in sport. I did that by going into sports marketing as the business that I chose.

'It became very interesting turning point in my life when, there was a moment in about 1989–90 after spending my whole life as being Ron Pickering's son that he called me up one night after he had just come back from a function. He had been one of the special guests, at a fairly high level in sport. There were also a number of sponsors there. For the first time he was introduced as "Sean Pickering's father". That was a turning point in our relationship because I had achieved enough in my chosen field and my reputation was such in that area that, for those he was mixing with that evening related to me before they related

151

to my father. So, for him to be introduced as Sean Pickering's father was quite a special moment for us both!'

In 1996, **Robert Weir** gave his opinion on the great discus men at the time: 'I think for me one of the best discus throwers in the world is Anthony Washington not Lars Riedel and, I say that because Anthony Washington is 6'2" and weighs 16 stone and has thrown 71.14 metres. Now, Lars Riedel is 6'7" to 6'8" and weighs 19 stone and has thrown 71.50. If Anthony Washington is not near his size and is competing at his level then technically, someone like Anthony Washington for me is the right person to watch not Lars Riedel. That is not to say Lars Riedel [five times World Champion] is not an exceptional thrower and has a level of consistency as a performer but Washington has different goals and interested in other things. Still, for me, Washington's ability and his level of competition going that far for his size is exceptional!'

Dave Myerscough, a National veteran Champion over 50 and 55 shot and discus Champion, whose son Karl has been a National junior Champion, and his younger son Grant has competed in the English Schools. All three have been useful competitors for Blackpool & Fylde AC. Dave gives us a little of his philosophy to end the chapter.

'What is progress and what is true? I think you have to look at life and try to understand it through your own eyes. Taking all the experiences of others that you can and to be honest. A lot of people are very intelligent but they are not honest enough to face the truth. I feel you can only develop wisdom through being honest enough to face up to reality. That is something I have always tried to do from an early age. Like in the work situation. It amazes me that we are so advanced technologically yet we are lacking in our treatment of other human beings. I know you should take advantage of situations but not to take advantage of one another only to further yourself. I think those advantages should be shared. Maybe when you study nature and animals they seem to take advantage of other species to their advantage but it is not in a cruel way. I think the way to differentiate between humans and animals is, to have the ability to become less cruel. The ability to show more love and respect and understanding, and the opportunity to make it better for not only ourselves but for others and animals. I would reason that is the course we should take rather than just go all out for ourselves and not care about what we do.'

9

London Marathon and Other Long Distance Experiences

I ran my first marathon at Windsor in 1974 in just over three hours. It was in 81°F/27°C temperature in the blazing sunshine. Even in the early part of the race, as we ran out of Windsor Castle, the heat haze was rising from the tarmac. Because of the rules in those days no drinks were offered in the early stages subsequently, even some 'class athletes' like Bernie Allen of Windsor & Eton, got dehydrated. He was among nearly half the field that dropped out in the course of the event.

I broke 3 hours in my second marathon in 1980 in the Cambridge Veterans race doing 2:55.35. There were just a few small groups of people watching, sporadically placed around the countryside. The next year was 1981 and my first of nineteen consecutive London Marathons organised by Chris Brasher and his team. From being a pure 'scrubber' as part of Highgate's 'B' team, I felt like a 'star' overnight. The reason being the map of the first London course was constantly shown on the television nationally, giving immense exposure to runners with modest abilities. Consequently, I spent a lot of time in the WC as the nerves were firing a great deal earlier than they usually would. Since then, it seems the general public, rather than the ardent athletics fan, appear to be interested in those who do the London Marathon no matter at what level or compete for medals in the Olympic Games but nothing in between!

As Chris Brasher used to say 'Everyone is a Winner' in the London! The London, following on from the New York Marathon, grew to enormous proportions, not only as a commercial venture for some but also as a means of creating a massive influx of money raised for charities.

During those nineteen years I had fractured a heel bone, had a hernia operation and lost the sight in one eye but nothing stopped me from preparing for the London till, three days before my 20th a motorcyclist ran into my back, just before I was going to step on the pavement in the City of London. The result was my Robert Fleming's insurance claims files went up in the air, eight ribs and a collar bone were broken plus a bruised lung, so bang went my ever-present status in the London. End result that the ever-present numbers competing in 2000 were down from 40 to 39! People like Jeff Aston, another 'ever-present' runner sent a conciliatory letter to me. The one that moved me most, when I was often flat out on my back, was from John Bryant, of *The Times*, a fine editor and sports columnist, as well as having been a 'class' county standard runner, before having been in a horrific accident to his legs, when out running. He was told he would have difficulty walking again let alone running. 'Never Say Die' John was back again running for Thames Hare & Hounds and Oxford University old boys. John's letter to me:

Dear Alastair,   19th of May, 2000
I was so sorry to hear of your accident which robbed you of your ever-present place in the marathon.

I do hope you are recovering steadily? It will be a long, hard haul by the sound of it but you are equipped, mentally and physically, to battle back with a determination that non-athletes can only dream of.

A dozen years ago I almost lost a leg while training, so I know what you must be going through. All I can offer is the advice I've given to quite a few athletes / anybody can get knocked over, it's getting up again that sorts out who you are.

I know, Alastair, that you will get up again. It will take time & it will hurt, but persevere and you will be back.

I look forward to seeing you running again soon.
                              Yours ever,
                              John (BRYANT)

155

I got caught out with blood pressure, diagnosed after a couple of short distance races in the summer of 1999. I had two of the worst three races of my life. I felt as though I was hitting a brick wall with my chest after running hard for only half a mile or so. I decided the best thing was to see my doctor, Ian Perry, who incidentally, is world renowned as an aviation expert, keeping the pilots flying around the world. He referred me to Dr Peter Richardson, who is a top medical man at the Cromwell and Kings Hospital. Peter Richardson understood the situation, having been a runner as a young man. I then retired from racing, but I knew that I had trained well enough to do the London at 60 years old in 2000. I feel sure I would have run around the 3.45 mark. However, the accident could have been in a small way Divine Providence, because of the punishment one's body continues to take in the latter stages of the event.

Of course, I remember my 2:47.58 best time in the fine weather of 1982 (869 position which in a time that would have given me 361 in 2001!). That will always be a wonderful memory for me but I was beaten by Roger Bourban the 'Running Waiter' carrying a tray with a bottle of water on it! He finished together with current 'ever-present' doctor Mac Speake in 2:47.21.

After the accident I had in 2000 I thought of John Bryant's comments which motivated me to achieve some sort of fitness again. On a very low '5 to 20 miles' a week, I gingerly ran the undulating Croydon 10k, on the 8th of April 2001. I started with the 'Fun' runners. Amita Charkravorty, who was doing her first 'London' in two weeks time was running in front of me, for the middle part of the race, with the words 'Help the Aged' emblazoned on the back of her tea shirt! I did move past her eventually and finished just behind that Herne Hill character, red haired, Andy Lee Gerrard, in 52 minutes 59 seconds, not stressed. It was one of the most enjoyable experiences to be able to get round and that, at least, proved John right!

I must add though, I miss my annual talk before the start of the London with 'ever-presents' Irishman Pat Dobbs (First over 60 in 2001) and a charming Norwegian called Erik-Falck Therkelsen, the Woking Town City manager. Before each

London the camaraderie among the runners is noteworthy, as there is a subconscious feeling of 'All going into battle together'.

Besides my wife and son, Ron Wheeler, who was a great friend, used to come to every London Marathon and was an invaluable support on Tower Bridge. Ron considered that the first London was the best for spectators, being so close to the runners on Tower Bridge and also, it was such a sporting finish with the winners Dick Beardsley (USA) and Inge Simonsen (Norway) holding hands as they crossed the finish line together in 2:11:48. Ron motored us home afterwards each year for our feast which included plenty of wine. Ron Wheeler died of cancer in January 2000, which of course took something from my powerful enthusiasm for running again in the London. Ron worked for a shipping company that were represented on the Baltic Exchange before becoming a top lecturer at Capel Manor Horticultural College. While he was in Nigeria in the 1980s he got shot in the chest by muggers and was given a blood transfusion, in Nigeria, that included malaria. **John Legge**, who had been a business colleague and friend of Ron's took care of all Ron's hospital arrangements at the time. John Legge was another of the exclusive 'ever-present' London Marathon runners.

It was very sad that John Legge (70), should die while out training for the 2001 London which would have been his 21st. Several people have remarked to me, 'At least he died while doing something he enjoyed!' John ran the first London to Brighton road race in 1951 and ran 22 miles of the 2000 race. It was after that he said to me about being an 'ever-present London man', 'You are trying to carry on because something drives you on.'

John Legge was one of those people who gave a lot of time and effort into helping people in athletics especially with road running. On the 26th of October, 1997, as a favour John Legge specially outlined for me some of his achievements in a letter, which was very informative. I thought, for the first time it could be published here for the readers of *Athletics Enigmas* as my personal tribute to John:

I started running during my RAF National Service and in 1949 joined Woodford Green AC. After demob in 1950 I started road running and my first long distance event was the SLH 30 mile race which I finished in 3 hrs 48 m and was encouraged by this to start training for marathon events. In 1951 the first London to Brighton race took place, sponsored by the *News Chronicle* newspaper. I was the youngest entrant at 21 years of age, none of us had any experience of anything beyond 30 miles but remarkably out of the 47 starters some 32 finished despite torrential wind and a howling gale that caused a shipwreck on the beach at Brighton. I finished in 18th place, just two places ahead of John Jewell and Woodford Green were the second in the team race. Two years later I had improved my race position to 6th in a time of 6 hrs 4 m. I've run the London to Brighton many times, three of us from the same club who had run in 1951 celebrated the 25th event in 1976 by running and finishing – somewhat slower than in earlier years! And again in 1991 I ran and finished to celebrate the 40th event.

The Road Runners Club was formed in 1952 as a direct result of the London to Brighton race in 1951 and the drive and enthusiasm of Ernest Neville, a walker and member of the Centurions, those who completed a 100 miles walk in 24 hours. Ernest had huge energy and a persuasive personality. His hand written letters were famous and I still have the first London to Brighton race result written in his beautiful copper plate handwriting. In the early years of the RRC I was the club's Registrar keeping the membership list up to date and producing the address labels for Newsletter mailings to members.

In 1955 I joined Orion Harriers but by some ten years later family commitments reduced my competitive running considerably. Harold Lee, a member of Orion Harriers who finished third in the first London to Brighton race, became Chairman of the RRC Council. Sadly Harold died in 1984 – to my astonishment I was asked to take his place as Chairman of RRC Council. I am not a good public speaker and I found the job a considerable strain in the beginning. At the end of the eighties the AAA Road Running Advisory Committee was formed and I was asked to represent the RRC on this. Upon the formation of the BAF I became Chairman of the AAA Road Running Committee and the RRC representative on the BAF Road Running Commission. After a year or so the South England circularised all their member clubs to gain support for their nomination of Chairman of the AAA Road Running Committee, an action I could not afford to do myself and thus I lost the position. Ever since the formation of the BAF Road Running Commission, however, I have been looking after GB ultra distance running and been the member of the road race selection committee with responsibility for ultra distance international Championship selection.

This year (1997) I have been on the BAF Road Running Commission sub-committee set up to consider ways of raising money for road running. The sub-committee's proposals that aimed to give road running some financial independence was turned down by the BAF Road Running Commission which now seems somewhat farcical with the BAF having the administrators in and in grave danger of financial disintegration.

Of all the positions I have held in athletics that which has given me the greatest pleasure has been being President of Orion Harriers. I was elected their first President some six years ago and held this office for four years.

London Marathon Comment in 2001: More from the 'ever-presents'

Reg Brown (69), who used to box for the Oxford Bermondsey Club, was an East End docker. He now gives classes for physical fitness and weight training to people with disabilities, even people completely chairbound. He can still do 100 press-ups in front of you at any time so strong is Reggie's upper body, however, as an 'ever-present' London runner he was caught out in his 21st London with excruciating hip pain and had to drop out at half way. So the man, who was introduced to running by South London Harrier ultra distance man Tom Roden (sister Anne Roden a celebrated distance runner), had to call it a day and wait for his pending hip operation. In the early 1990s Reggie Brown was mugged (hit over the head with an iron bar) which triggered off diabetes but that did not stop him running till now. He looks ahead to a more gentle pursuit for fund raising! 'I will do more free fall diving from 10,000 feet for charity,' he quipped.

Last year Brown gained £4000 in sponsorship for doing the London for the Diabetic Centre of Guys Hospital. About that painful run for Reg in 2000 where he did 6:29:51 (he did run a sub-3 hour run in his 40s). 'It was really uncomfortable for me this year – very tough. Time didn't come into it. It was only a question of getting across the line. I wanted to be successful in getting the funds for the centre.' That is only one of many charity efforts by 'Reggie' Brown over the last twenty odd years.

John Hanscombe, a Ranelagh Harrier who is 65, has run 44 Finchley 20 mile road races. About being an 'ever-present' London man: 'To be fit enough to do it is a great achievement in itself.

'In the old days before the London Marathon came about, if you could not beat three hours for a marathon you were not considered of good club standard. Now it's different. It's the camaraderie. It is better to get round and be part of the crowd.'

Mickey Peel (58), who is the President of Blackheath Harriers for 2001 and like John was a friendly rival of mine in the Londons, as well as in things like the insurance races and Blackheath's Mob Matches with South London Harriers, said, 'I enjoy the London Marathon, the atmosphere and everything about it. I am able to run a marathon without much training and so it is not stressful to me as it is with a lot of other people. It helped mentally to have run the London to Brighton in the past. My philosophy in athletics is that it is mental anyway. You need a certain amount of fitness to do certain things but it is the man who has got the mental strength that wins through at the end. You can see that on any training run. You get out with the same group of people on a Wednesday night training run and it's not going to be the same order in a race. Once you pin a number on some people can lift themselves some people can't and fortunately I have been one who has always been able to lift myself.' (He did 2:40.30 in 1981 when 39 years old; and 3:21:14 in 2000.)

'What people forget is in the late 70s marathon runners were exceptionally good or exceptionally silly. Even then the standard was so much higher than now. If you had 100 runners, everyone was packing up and going home after three and a half hours.

'I would miss doing the London. When you think we have still got to have the interest to keep up, still got to be available not away on family holidays or business and injury free enough to struggle round. It is quite a challenge and as the years go on it gets harder and harder. Down to 35 ever-presents now!'

A Poisoned Chalice being an 'ever-present'?

Mike Peel comments on that. 'Pete Shepherd (Blackheath Harriers). He has a bad back and should not do it at all. He was a 2:30 marathon and now taking 5½ hours. Pete Greenwood (Canterbury) is another ever-present; at one time he was regularly a sub 2:30 man who does 5 hours now. However, Mick McGeoch and Chris Finill are running 2:37/2:41, and they were in their early 20s when the London began! They are not getting any younger!'

The Younger ever-presents

Chris Finill, when running for Old Gaytonians (Harrow AC) was 22 when he did his first ever London in 1981 in 2:32:55, and **Mick McGeoch** (Les Croupiers) was 25 in that first London and recorded 2:24.19. Now in their 40s they have time on their side to stay on the list!

Chris Finill, who has won the Barry 40, running in that

because of his friend Mick McGeoch organising the event. (By the way another runner who, in recent years, has won the Barry 40 was Simon Pride who not only ran 2:16 in the London of 2001 but is a world class 100k runner to boot.) Another friend of Chris Finill was John Legge.

'It was sad about John but who knows what's round the corner. My wife and I went abroad for six months in 1987. I was away at a time the London Marathon was not on, something I have had to make sure about for an awful long time now.'

The athletes long or ultra distance that Finill admires: 'Don Ritchie. The way he runs and still churns out mile after mile. He has been absolutely at the top at his best and still runs and enjoys it at 55/56. Wally Hayward is another. Those two as Ultra men. Ron Hill was my inspiration when he was at his best in 1968–69. I was nine years old. Watching the Commonwealth Games in 1970 was the thing that inspired me.' (Ron Hill 2:9.28 European, UK and Games best time; 2. Jim Alder 2:12.4; 3. Don Faircloth 2:12.19.)

'From then on I was into cross country and everything up to the marathon. Jim Peters was also someone I admired. He was competing at a time marathon running was deeply unfashionable. He was running consistently well in a pair of plimsolls.' Flora London 2001, Chris Finill ran 2:41:37.

Mick McGeogh looks back: 'Doing 2:17:58 in 1983 was a big victory for me because it was a personal best time. A very significant year as the conditions were perfect. 85 was a special year for me. It was my other sub-2.20 run. It was special because Steve Jones won it.' 2:8:16 from Charlie Spedding 2:8:33 and Allister Hutton 2:9:16. Jones ran 2:07:13 in 1985. At the time of writing the fastest marathon ever recorded was by Khalid Khannouchi who was born in Morocco. His time 2:05:42 in Chicago, 24th of October 1999. Mike continues, 'Steve Jones is a very close friend of mine and it was the only Welsh victory to date. 88 was a very special year for me because it was the year I was able to meet Ingrid. A great thrill. Not a fast year but a significant year as she was running with me in the race. (Ingrid Kristiansen was the first woman, for the fourth time in 1988 in 2:25:41 with Ann Ford second in 2:30:38. Norwegian

Kristiansen had set a world best of 2:21:06 in 1985 and her compatriot Greta Waitz won it in 1986 in 2:24:54.)

Mick then mused, 'Back in London in 2001 Ingrid was giving Paula Radcliffe some advice which was lovely to see. I would love to have seen Ingrid break 2:20. Wouldn't it be nice to see Paula break 2:20 now, that really would be something special!' (Naoko Takahashi of Japan, the Sydney Olympic Marathon Champion, was the first woman to run inside 2:20 with 2:19:46 in Berlin on 30th September, 2001. Then in Chicago in October Kenyan Catherine Ndereba reduced the world's best time to 2:18:47.)

Flora London 2001, Mick McGeogh ran 2:37:20.

Other London Reflections

Norman Hemming (48) from Croydon AC, once a 2:47 man ran 3:40 for the London in 2001 and although he got cramp in the race, he still has a passion for running throughout the year. He did think that it was a bit difficult to sometimes get away and run through well with the huge fields the London attracts now and **Mark Coxhead** (43), a computer programmer in insurance, found difficulties in that respect in 2000. Coxhead who has run 3:14 for the London did 3:30:15 in 2001. Coxhead was optimistic about the future attraction of the London. 'The London as an event is good for running. It's a big magnet and people can focus a lot.'

Tony Seakins (48), who was with Tiptree then Colchester Harriers, ran a 2:37 in the London of 1989 and 2:41 in the London of 1990. 'I feel with the London to do 2 or 3 is okay but I don't want to keep going back year after year, do something different. When I am 50 I will do the New York.'

Julian Catmull (37), who was introduced to running in 1998 by Springfield Strider Graham Romaine, ran in 3:21; 3:15 and 3:12 for the London during the last few years. 'I love the marathon because it is a triumph for the mind over the body. The race I did a personal best in of 3:08 was the Essex Marathon at Halstead. A more enjoyable course as you go through the countryside.'

Maurice Doogan, who ran for Walton, Omega, now Woking, and ran with ex-international Fred Bell's training group, was team manager for the British Veterans at The World Veteran Championships in Brisbane in 2001. Doogan, now in his 60s ran 3:07 for the London when he was 45 as well as having run 56 minutes for 10 miles. 'The London is superb. The crowd lift you all the way.'

Tim Stobbs, who works for the St Paul Group in the City, ran the first ever marathon in London in 1981 in 2 hrs 40 minutes and ran 2:50 in 1994. 'It is a very well organised event, a lot of fun and exciting being in the vanguard in the first London. It was a particular pleasure because I had never done the distance before.'

Bill Foster (42), who has run eight sub-2:20 marathons, was 2nd in the World Veteran 10k road race in Zaragoza, Spain 2000. His time 31:18. Philippe Monnier of France (31:16) overtook him for the M40 title just before the finish in the town. Foster finished in the same time as Johan Hopfner of Germany. Foster has run five Londons with a 2:17 clocking in 1994.

'The London is excellent. Really well organised. I have run New York, Berlin and Chicago. The advantage of the London is that a lot of people know you as a Blackheath Harrier and know you as a runner so you get a lot of support. London is as good as any of them, if not the best.

'I enjoyed running in the European Championships in Helsinki and I ran in the World Cup in Athens. Those two would probably be the best events for me as I ran pretty well in them and represented my country. Beijing was nice because of seeing a different country and a different culture as well. There are so many different marathons that have good and bad points but in the case of London it is very well organised.'

Now Bill is a veteran would he do 2:20 marathons?

'I am going to struggle doing that. It is a case of adjusting your sights to run 2:25–2:30 which is respectable running.'

His twin brother John runs well and I saw him coming fourth in the world over 40 vets steeplechase in Gateshead.

'I don't think John has ever been dedicated to running as I have,' said Bill, 'but he ran 2:45 in the Florence marathon and

2:50 in the Snowdonia Marathon and he has done that on 30 to 40 miles a week, which is not enough training really. I am sure he could run quicker.'

Seamus Kerr (43) from London Irish AC was 9th in the Southern cross country senior one year and 10th in the Irish Championships the same year. In 2000 he was 12th in the London cross country Championships. He ran 2:26:23 for the London in 1985.

'I enjoyed it till I got cramp in a hamstring at about 20 miles. I was running with Ingrid Kristiansen around 19–20 miles and she went on to run 2:21 and break the world record and in the last few miles I dropped a minute a mile. Overall I have enjoyed cross-country more.

'I enjoyed the very first marathon I did because I did not know what to expect or what it was like. It was the New York in 1983 and I did 2:27. I enjoyed that because the second half of the race I was picking up people all the way through. It was the atmosphere and everything else.

'I did not know the pain and the suffering afterwards. You can hardly walk. I only ran five marathons. Mentally maybe they are tough and I blew out in a couple.'

Richard Nerurkar of Bingley Harriers and Paul Evans of Belgrave, who won the Chicago Marathon in 2:8:52, were two of the top UK marathon runners in the 1990s and Richard Nerurkar won his first two marathons in 1993 which included the Hamburg (2:10:57) and the World Cup (2:10:03). He was fourth in the European and fifth in the Olympics, the same place he came in the London (2:08:36).

'As a British runner it has to be the best race to do. It is the biggest road race in Britain. The best atmosphere. It is the most exciting race to do. The only ones I can compare with was running the Olympics.'

Atlanta 1996, 1. Josiah Thugwane (RSA) 2:12:36; 2. Lee Bong-ju (Kor) 2:12:39; 3. Eric Wainaina (Ken) 2:12:44; 4. Martin Fiz (ESP) 2:13:20; 5. Richard Nerurkar (GBR) 2:13:39; 6. German Silva (Mex) 2:14:29; 7. Steve Monighetti (Aus) 2:14:35; 8. Benjamin Paredes (Mex) 2:14:56.

'Probably the crowds weren't as good when I ran in Atlanta.

There is an enormous amount of pride in representing your country on the world's biggest stage. The Olympics and the London Marathon are two of the most exciting marathon experiences I have had as well as the World Cup win. You always get excited when you win a race.

'When you win a race it's always very pleasing so, from that point of view it was the most satisfying marathon that happened that I did, because you have a few things you look back on where you say "If only".

'The London and the Olympics they were good performances but there were one or two things that did not work out quite right in that I had stomach and bowel problems at a crucial stage of the race which obviously made it very difficult.'

Ray Auerback ran 16 marathons with a best of 2:33 and his wife **Margaret Auerback** (Ranelagh Harriers) now a very good 'W50' veteran runner and has a life time best of 2:48. They talked at the 2001 London Marathon Exhibition about the outstanding runners of the past in their opinion. Ray cited Richard Nerurkar as one for the following reasons:

'The combination of Bruce Tulloh [coach to Richard and 1962 European 5000 Champion] and Richard Nerurkar. Richard did 100 miles a week for about ten years. They managed to find a level just below so Richard would not get injured. Sometimes 140 a week for a couple of weeks then go down again so Richard was injury free. They looked at things very scientifically. Both were highly intelligent and they approached things scientifically. Bruce knew so much about physiology because he was a biology teacher. I think they just got it exactly right.'

Dave Taylor at 19 was second in the South African Junior steeplechase. In 1987 he came to England, joined Blackheath Harriers and helped them win National titles on the road and country. He came fourth in the 2000 senior 'National'. He competes second claim for Herne Hill Harriers from distances 800–10,000 (2nd in the AAA's 10,000 at 34). He came fourth in the 1998 Commonwealth Marathon and he has run 2:13:7 for the distance. Dave Taylor has been a manager of a technical department in a publishers. He talked to me at his flat in Tooting about the use of scientific knowledge for the distance runner:

'I think every runner in the last fifty years has been following scientific principles, whether they are realising it or not (although I am not great on my history), since basically interval work was discovered.

'I find scientific testing of some help, although I don't think it replaces the essential ingredients which is interval work, which is a balance of hard and easy training which includes a certain amount of long running. The basic principles of running well over middle distance are firmly established.

'I am very interested in the scientific discoveries about the body and looking for refinements. I have done the VO_2 tests and things over the last couple of years and established certain things. For example; my VO_2 max was high but my lactic tolerance wasn't. Simply by getting on the treadmill and being able to measure the lactic threshold and what level I reached was fine but how long could I sustain it. My lactic tolerance was shockingly low, so they said "go away and do some 800 metre training" and that enabled me in six months to see a big improvement. That training fitted quite nicely into my training. I worked on things like leg strength and lactic tolerance and managed to improve on that. That is one example where science has benefited. I think generally as long as you recognise the basic scientific principles you don't have to be totally into it but, when it comes into things like the marathon it is a help.'

On distance personalities Margaret Auerback said: 'Hilary Walker is a great character in ultra distance running. Regarding some of the most impressive Joyce Smith must be included as she encouraged a lot of women to run. Liz McColgon as well. Rosa Mota had a purple patch where she won everything for about two years. 4 or 5 big races off the back of each other. When she started training in Portugal it was hard for her as she got a lot of abuse running in shorts in the Portuguese countryside.' (1988 Olympic Champion Rosa Mota won the first ever World and Olympic medals by a Portuguese woman and won three European titles. She won major marathons in London, Chicago, Rotterdam, Boston, and Osaka according to Peter Mathews' edited *ATFS Athletics Annual 1993*. The next two outstanding women distance women from Portugal both gained gold medals in the World Championships at Goteborg – Fernanda Ribeiro in the 10k in 31:04.99 and Manuela Machado in the marathon in 2:25.39.)

Ray Auerback: 'Bill Rodgers was the guy who started a lot of people doing marathons. He was the first hero. He won marathons year after year after year.' (Now for some of the entries in *The Marathon Foot Race* on Bill Rodgers in David Martin PhD and Roger W.H. Gynn's book. Bill Rodgers was a hometown runner who won the Boston Marathon in 1975 in a new course record of 2:09:55; then came his win in the New York Marathon of 1976 in 2:10:09.6; a win at Fukuoka in 1977 with 2:10:53 ahead of Leonid Moisyev (Sov) and Massimo Magnani (Italy). Rodgers won the Boston in 2:10:13 in 1978 from Jeff Wells, also USA, in 2:10.15 with Esa Tikkanen of Finland third in 2:11:15.)

Steve Smythe, a journalist and fixtures and results editor of *Runners World* who ran 2:29 in the first London: 'For longevity Steve Monighetti of Australia [obtained a gold, silver and bronze in Commonwealth Marathons]. He has been at the top since 1986 and he is still in tremendous shape now. He beat virtually all the English runners in the world cross country in 2001. He is around 35/36 and has been going a very long time. To be at the top in 14 years I would certainly place him amongst the All Time Greats. Australian Derek Clayton was way ahead of his time, if you consider his best time would have still won some of the big City Marathons like Boston and that was 30 years ago.' (2:08:33.36 at Antwerp on 30th of May 1969; 2nd was Japan's Akio Usami 2:11:27; 3rd Jim Alder 2:16:34.4; and 4th Ron Grove 2:17:35.6.)

Steve Smythe continues, 'On the women's side Katrin Dorre, she won 25 of 45 marathons. Ingrid Kristiansen was ahead of her time as a marathon runner. As far as Ultra runners Kouros is the most remarkable.'

Katrin Dorre, born in Leipzig, Germany, on 6th of October, 1961, won major city marathons in the 1980s and 1990s including London in 1992, World and European Cup races as well as a world 15k in 1988. One example of Greek runner Yiannis Kouros' amazing performances includes a six-day event in May

1988 in New York, where he covered 1,028.37 km (639 miles). Yannis ran the equivalent of just over four marathons a day for six days.

In 2001 El Mouaziz (32) of Morocco went away from the field in the London at 23 miles to win in 2 hrs 7 min. As David Powell of *The Times* explained, 'El Mouaziz never raced on the track or in the world cross country championships.' El Mouaziz was placed 2, 1, 2 in the previous three Londons.

Derartu Tulu (29) from Ethiopia ran a tactical race to win the Women's London of 2001 and was following up two Olympic 10,000m titles and three world cross country crowns. She also won the World Championships over 10,000 in Edmonton in 2001 (31:48.81).

Two of the most prolific London placers were Portugal's Antonio Pinto, 35 in 2001, who came third in the London Men's race of 2001 but had already been placed in the top three in London six times. Another one with multiple success was Dionicio Ceron of Mexico who in 1996 won his third London in 2:10:00.

Mark Steinle was the first British runner in 6th place in the London of 2001 in 2:10:46, after coming 11th in his debut in the London of 2000 in 2:11:18. 'My inspirations to begin with were Steve Jones and Charlie Spedding (84 London winner) in 1985. It was the first London I ever noticed or marathon I ever noticed. That was the year I started running. From that moment on I was hooked on.'

In 1992 at Newark Mark Steinle won the National Youth cross country Championships. It was the first time a Blackheath Harrier won a 'National' cross country title since Sydney Wooderson won the senior title in 1948.

That was the most significant confidence booster for the future for Mark. 'For me it was the last time that I feel a National had any atmosphere to it. Nowadays with having an Inter-Counties and Trial for the World's on another day it has detracted from the event. I can't see why they don't make the National the World trial and bring it back to where it was. That would be very good.

'After that race in major cross-countries I found I could not run on the mud. I was really struggling with it, perhaps my style of running was changing and I could not win anything for ages. I really went off the boil but then, as a senior I won again in the Southern at Parliament Hill Fields which was pleasing because I thought "I can do it again!"

'I find I can soak up the pounding on the road and cope with that quite well. Regarding long distance running I have always done a lot of mileage in training so I was prepared for marathon running. People were saying to me before my first marathon at London that it was really a special event. I had run up to half marathons well but I realise the marathon to me is a totally a special event.'

How does he compare his two Londons?

'It was about the same as last time. It was *déjà vu* when I was running round. I went off the back of the group at the same point as last year and then caught the same people as last year. The only difference was that I ran the last bit a bit quicker. I had that little bit of extra strength. Just the knowledge of knowing what it felt like.'

Regarding the coaching he has had through the years: 'I started with Mick Hamlin at 8 till 2½ years ago. I kind of coach myself now. I saw Alan Storey a lot, but I am the only person who knows what my body is doing and what it feels like so I think, it is only right I should set the sessions. I set my own sessions and ask Alan for his advice, see if it needs sweeping anywhere or slightly changing. It works pretty well.'

Mark Watling, who has been the Blackheath Harriers Captain on the road and country, and in the supporting team when they have won National titles comes in: 'Mark Steinle has strength of mind as well as body. I used to train with him at Tonbridge with Mike Hamlin's group. I watched him grinding out incredibly fast long reps usually on his own because no one could run with him. He has had some difficulties but there again he comes back. Mentally very strong and clearly physically very talented. In 1999 when he won the Southern I won the Southern veterans cross country championships, that says something for Mike Hamlin!'

Mike Gratton won the London of 1983 in 2:09:43, from

170

Gery Helme (2:10:12) and Henrik Jorgensen of Denmark, who came back in 1988 to win the London in 2:10:52. In 1983 prolific distance runner Grete Weitz from Norway equalled the women's world best at the time of 2:28:20. Mick Gratton was an English Schools 5000m Champion in 1974 and was bronze medallist in the Commonwealth Games in 2:12:06 behind the winner Rob De Castella of Australia. (2:09:18 in Brisbane in 1982. Rob 'Deek' Castella went on to become World Champion in 1983.)

Did Mike think that the London was the best experience he had had?

'It is a difficult question because each one is a stepping stone to the next. Being third the year before and third in the Commonwealth Games, in a sense, was just as exciting. They were big improvements. The London, when I won it; you don't expect to win it but you have an idea that you are going to, so when it happened it was not a great surprise. Going from 2:16 to 2:12 the year before was a big surprise. I expected some improvement but not a huge jump like that.'

Of events he enjoyed, were marathons high on the list?

'Marathons are very difficult. They take a lot out of you in terms of your training and commitment to the sport and everything. There were other things like winning the English Schools 5000m Championships which were so much fun. With a marathon you can only do so many. You can do the AAA's 10 miles or the Great North Run and whatever, quite a few of those. In a sense they are almost more fun than doing a marathon. The marathon takes up so much of your life. It is a very serious thing. Certainly for an athlete at the front of the race it takes over your life.'

Mike was 46 when I talked to him at the 2001 London Marathon Exhibition, so did he feel that you had to adapt to new ways of running to continue to enjoy doing it?

'I think so, because people get hooked into marathons when there is so much more to do as well. Certainly for me; I have not run a marathon since 1991 and I have got no desire to do so either. I run five or six times a week and still enjoy the cross-country races. You just have to adapt your life all the time to

171

account for the changes in your life. As you get older you are going to slow down. You have got to adjust to that and still enjoy running. Get over the disappointment of slowing down. It is a reality, it's not going to change. You can still enjoy running, there is no reason you can't do that!'

Mike, a lot of people cut it off in their 30s and don't want to even run any more?

'A lot of people like Brendan Foster just stopped running. Charlie Spedding is another. For whatever reason, it must leave a void in their life which used to be occupied by running. It's a lifestyle thing. It is something I cannot see myself not doing, unless something serious happens.

'I think you have got to have something outside of the hum-drum paying the mortgage, doing a daily job, and running is it for me, as it is for a lot of other people. Stopping just seems to be completely unreasonable. To be running all your life and then just stop at 35!

'It is not just the running, it's the whole social life that revolves around people that are runners. The whole activity of going to races on coaches and trains with all the runners. The little jokes that go around. You would lose that after a while. You can't talk about the Tuesday night 10 and things like that because you are not part of it any more.

'I ran the Basingstoke 10k in 35 minutes with a girl, which is not slow. I know if I got myself in shape I could run 31:32 still, but I have been there year after year, doing really hard training and the motivation is not there any more to do that level of training. I do enough training just to really enjoy it at a reasonable level.'

Stuart Major's wife Pippa Major is also a county runner, both run for Legal & General's 'Temple Bar' team. Stuart comes in about the London: 'It is the best road event. Being part of the occasion, nothing quite like it. Looking back my best year was in 1998, the year before I ran the London in 2:28, I won the 22 mile "Man versus Horse" race that year and ran solo 5ks in 15 minutes.'

Were the courses always accurate in the past?

Talking with Stuart Major about 10 mile races that were such

172

popular events in the 1970s, like 10ks are now, he did wonder if the 10 mile courses were all accurate! He would like to have been able to compare his times in recent years with say, some of the best South London 10 mile ones of the past. Major did feel, however, that there were more very good road racers competing then.

Pat Collins makes an interesting observation on that topic, just after he had run the Croydon 10k that Major won in 31 minutes. 'To get fast times for 10 miles, runners used to often choose the Three Ws – Walton, Worthing and Woking 10s. They were all noted to be fast courses!'

Collins, who is now 61, originally came from Limerick in Ireland. He has run the Comrades Marathon in 6:48 and a marathon in 2:38. He talked about the runners he thought were great and they were all ultra distance men! 'Don Ritchie fantastic and Kouros. Regarding great characters Cavin Woodward of Leamington really enjoyed his athletics.'

Another Perspective

In the late 1990s and early Millennium years many people dwell more on marathon running, but it should not be forgotten that a vital part of the sport is often found a couple of days a year at Sutton Coldfield. That is where much of the cream of British distance running is found.

Dave Walsh, who has been the Road Running Secretary for Wales for eight years and team manager, has a fair range of times: 31:10 for 10k and 50:51 for 10 miles. He points out with no hesitation at all: 'The National Road relay, that's where it is. When I was first able to make the Cardiff team it was a red letter day. I always trained for that. Come January the 1st I would set my stall out. This was the one I would train for mentally and physically. It was 32 years since I first ran in it and (today) I am running it.' (When Cardiff came 8th in the 12 stage in 1977 Dave ran 15:12 on leg 4.) 'In 1974 Cardiff came third. I was first reserve. For me it was like being fourth in the Olympics!'

173

Jamie Lewis, who runs for Swansea, ran 2:15:07 for the London in 2000 and he was unlucky not to make the Irish Olympic team. Lewis led the first leg in the National 12 Stage at Sutton Coldfield in 2001 and was timed at 25:50. It was on a long stage. He also ran a long stage on leg 9 (25:54) in Swansea's team that won in 1994 (according to Chris Holloway's statistics).

'It was good doing the first leg and a damn sight easier than spending the whole day not enjoying it, just waiting your turn. It is just a straight race on leg one.' He continued, 'I live in the West of Ireland now so I don't run for them as often as I would like but the team spirit is good with the club as it was when I ran for Highgate, many years ago when I stayed in London.' (The Highgate Harriers team were seventh in 1991 – 12 stage with Ian Manners, Snow, Southam and Lewis on the first four legs.)

Michael O'Reilly ran 13:59 for the fastest short stage in 1984 and did a 2:10 marathon. He organised the first 10k through streets of London in 2001. Lewis looked up to him as a hero. 'He amazed me at the time. How this little guy could run. He used to come to *Runners Need* where I worked and sit on the chair and fall asleep. He trained so hard.'

Keith Anderson, born in Barrow in Furness on the 10th of August, 1957, was in Bingley Harriers winning National 12 stage relay team when they won in 1996 and, as a veteran has been an international marathon runner. He won the prestigious Barnsley 10k for two years in 31:05 and 31:42, the latter after doing the Commonwealth Games Marathon. His start in athletics makes interesting reading.

'When I turned 30 I was too fat and 13$\frac{1}{2}$ stone. I did not take any exercise. I enjoyed a drink and the odd cigarette. Now I weigh 10$\frac{1}{2}$ stone and when I am racing it should be 10 stone 2 lbs. I am 5'11" in height.

'When I was 13$\frac{1}{2}$ stone I thought I better do something about it. I just started jogging a mile or so to try to get fit. Where I was living in the Lake District, in between Windermere and Ambleside, I started running on bits of hills and things. In the end it got me into fell running. I eventually came from fell

174

running to road running and cross country, when I moved to the Yorkshire Dales where Mike Hawkins lives. He was with Bingley and his brothers were with Bingley, so it seemed a natural thing for me to join Bingley, and that was what happened.'

Some Amazing Feats of Endurance

Regarding the London a man who should be admired for having done it was Chris Moon, whose leg was blown off by a Russian-made PMN mine in Mozambique. He had to have his hand amputated because it was so shattered by the blast. Moon ran the London with an artificial leg in 5 hours 39 minutes. Moon was the first amputee to complete the Great Sahara Run.

John A. Kelley was reputed to have run 60 Boston Marathons, mostly in very good times.

Allen Hansen of Denmark, according to *Metro*, ran over 88 marathons in the year 2000 and was hoping to do 17 more before that year ended!

Ed Whitlock was just short of being 70 years old when he ran 2:52:50 for the Columbus marathon on the 30th of October, 2000. He was then the oldest man to run under 3 hours for a marathon.

Somebody who captured my imagination in 2001, was outside of athletics, and he was Jim Shekhdor, at 54 years old, a management consultant in the West End of London, who rowed 10,000 miles across the Pacific Ocean in 274 days. He was attacked by sharks on the way, and put off having a hip replacement till he had completed his task. Most people's opinion on his effort that I have spoken to said, 'He's mad!' but what a hell of an achievement!

Husband and wife combination of Sandra and Richard Brown, who mix running and walking, went from Lands End to John O'Groats in record time, and so it goes on with many other feats of endurance that can be recalled.

Ultra running and the London to Brighton

Pat 'Paddy' Farrelly, who was from an Irish family, competed for Canada in the 1976 Olympic Games in the 20 kilometres walk (1:41:36.2 in Montreal). Farrelly also ran several marathons. He commented in Mike Hanley's column in the Canadian paper *Hamilton Spectator* regarding Arthur Newton, who achieved a world 24 hour running record of 152 miles 540 yards on 3rd and 4th of May, 1931 in those old 'non-designer shoes'. It was done at the Old Forum, Barton Street East; 'I've idolised him for years. I've read everything I can about him and I thought of him every time I was in competition. I haven't missed a day of training in 50 years and he's been my inspiration.'

Dave Cooper, 66, has been on the council of the 'Road Runners Club of Britain', was fourth in the RRC 24 hour track race in 1981 and was third in the 24 hour race in the German Championships with 155 miles. In the 24 hour indoor race at Birmingham in 1992 Dave Cooper was first with 128.37 miles. Cooper gives his opinion of who stands out for him as 'Great Ultra Distance Men'.

'Kouros was very good at Mega Marathons and I have regard for James Zarie but it is Don Ritchie for me. Running so well in his 30s and 40s and he is now 55 years old. His longevity and range of distances stand out. He coaches Simon Pride and has advised Ian Anderson. He not only runs well still but puts such a lot back into the sport.'

Regarding one of Zarie's performances, he ran 8 hr 7 min 33 sec in the RRC 100km race on the 3rd of November, 1984 but came second to Bob Emmerson of Rugby & District, a '50–54 group runner', who did 7 hr 47 min 44 secs.

As I write this book I realise Don Ritchie is already a legend in ultra-distance running. He is a lecturer at Moray College. At 55 in 2000 he was 8th in the London to Brighton (6:25:51). Don, a Forres Harrier, won the London to Brighton in 1977 (5:16:05) and 1978 (5:13:02). How does it compare for him, running in the race in 2000 as opposed to 1978 when he won?

'It's much harder now.'

There are so many great achievements by **Don Ritchie**, but which one stands out?

'I think the 100k at Crystal Palace in 1968, where I set a world record of 6 hours 10 minutes and 20 seconds, was an excellent race.'

I asked him what he thought was the attraction of ultra-distance running.

'Something I wanted to try and found I was quite good at so I kept going.'

In 1989 Don Ritchie beat Richard Brown's John O'Groats to Lands End record by 2 hours 56 minutes. He completed the 825 miles in 10 days, 15 hours and 27 minutes.

Dave Cooper continues, 'Don Ritchie was a sub 2:20 marathon man who set so many ultra records in 100 and 200k races.'

Dave Beattie, from that good ultra distance club Crawley AC, won the London to Brighton road race in 1990 in 5:54:32. He talked about some of the greatest ultra men who have won the London to Brighton.

'Bruce Fordyce (Wittersrand University AC, RSA, who won London to Brighton three times 1981–83) stands out in my memory. He was almost ethereal. He would float along the road; he was so light on his feet. It was a strangely moving experience to see him run. He was something special. There was an instance after he had won three London to Brighton and went on to win 9 Comrades. After he had won his third London he came into the Corn Exchange, where the presentation was being held. We were like crippled old runners sitting round our tables. Normally when the guy gets up to get his trophy, people will applaud him. But as he actually entered the room and came down the steps into the Corn Exchange there was a spontaneous shuffling of feet and these runners got to their feet and simply applauded him with a standing ovation. I have never known that before or since. Remarkable!

'Stephen Moore in recent times. A tremendous record. The guy who runs his own race and does not get carried away by anyone else's approach to it. He knew exactly what he was doing. He made very good use of the heart rate monitor. He would not let his pulse go above 150 or whatever he had set himself, even if that meant he was letting somebody get away. He was confident he could come good later on in the race. For a guy to get into his 50s and to still be up there. A fearsome competitor.'

What is the enjoyment of ultra-distance running?

'I think Don Ritchie put it very well, someone I would put up there with the other two guys I have mentioned. It appeals to a certain type of personality. That is, patient, cheerful and likes long term planning.

'My training partner Wally Hill, who does very well on the ultra scene still, is an example. He is very thoughtful. He likes to control his training and what he is doing and he has these long term plans and short term plans and that is one of the appeals of ultra running. It's an honest sport and you get out of it what you put into it. People with relatively little natural ability, like myself, never achieve anything on the track at lower distances but through regular training and focusing on long term goals can go far in ultra running. I think that is why it appeals to lots of guys who have not made it at lower distances and they can see, with training, they can get there. It is also a way of life thing. Wally Hill cycles to and from work. Don Ritchie up in Scotland runs to and from work. It becomes a way of life as much as a training regime. I have seen Wally in London running between meetings. I overtook him in the car on the Buckingham Place road when he was running between meetings and that is the sort of personality that just enjoys to run.

'Mark Pickard (from Epsom & Ewell – won London to Brighton in 1988 in 6:06:25) is held in great regard by the average club runner around the time Mark was running. On his sheer performance of 2:22 in the Isle of Wight Marathon, which is still a record really stands out. Bruce Fordyce said he was one of the hardest competitors he ran against, when Mark came second to Bruce in the London to Brighton. And that was after setting personal best for 10 miles but Mark, by normal standards, was a crazy runner. He would run back to back marathons in the same weekend. We love a guy like that! He was out on the edge on his own destroying his body, running an amazing amount of races. He is a very pleasant and modest guy. When he won the

178

London to Brighton it was a lousy day, the rain was pouring down. He just came through. A very popular win.'

An authority on ultra-distance running is London to Brighton Road race organiser, **Ian Champion**. I asked him, What is the magic about the event that starts early in the morning at Westminster and ends on Brighton sea front?

'It's the whole concept of the race. The history, everything about it and the people involved. The past winners. It's unique in this country. Also, I am for the underdog. This event is a minnow in the big spectrum. It has always appealed to me and I have always followed it since I was a boy. I was in the presence of Ernest Neville. A man who spent a life time of organising walking races on the Brighton road and the organiser of the first London to Brighton in 1951.

'I admired Arthur Newton who at 41 ran ultras solo. He was an inspiration I would love to have met him.'

In 1953 Wally Hayward of Germiston Callies RSA, won the London to Brighton in 5 hrs 29 min 40 sec but not long after, a man to rival his performances, a Thames Valley Harrier, called **Ron Hopcroft** (born 27th of February, 1918), now a very respected athletics official, became an Ultra Star. He won the London to Brighton in 1956 in 5:36:25 with Tom Richards of South London second in 5:42:22. Richards won in 1955 in 5:27:24. If you consider Richards to be someone with a high profile, having come second in the Olympic Marathon of 1948 then, looking at it from that aspect there was one other very high calibre performer that did the London to Brighton and that was Ian Thompson of Luton. Thompson had won the European and Commonwealth Marathons in 1974. He ran the old London to Brighton course in 5:15.15 in 1980, which was truly outstanding.

Ron Hopcroft takes up the story in 2001. 'Were there great long distance runners coming into ultra running lately?

'The top class men are not coming into it now!' Ron thought. 'The first London to Brighton is my biggest memory in 1951. It's got to be, never having trained for it then, to suddenly do the London to Brighton!

'When I saw the clock in Brighton and came down towards the finish, I choked up with emotion and had a job to finish.'

179

Ron Hopcroft, who had the record, running from London to Bath and Bath to London, pointed out, 'I could run 7 minute miles for 70 miles.' His results in those days prove that. Ron never retired from running till he was 76 years old, it was only then that he realised he could not run any more.

'I could not run more than 200 yards up the road because there would be nothing in my legs. However I had a ruddy good innings.'

Peter Sugden, from Reading AC, won in 5:36:59 in 1987. 'I ran the 1984 race, leading till 48 miles and Barry Heath (5:24:15) went by me then Don Ritchie went by me. The London to Brighton was what I aimed for, what I always wanted to do. I managed to hold on and win in 1987.'

Sugden was not in the medals when he did his London to Brighton in 1980 but that introduction to the race always was an abiding memory for him. 'When you come down the hill and you can see the pier and the sea. I think that gave me the best feeling.'

Cavin Woodward of Leamington C and AC was the winner of the 1975 London to Brighton in 5:12:17. In his particular case I thought it would be good to give top RRC statistician **Andy Miloroy**'s opinion:

'Although 1975 was perhaps Cavin's greatest year, nine years later he was still able to defeat a very high class European field in a track 100km. Cavin is a very individualistic runner, both in the way he always sets out to lead from the gun, and in his training.'

In 1991 the London to Brighton route was changed over the final 10 miles and the new route was set to 55 miles. It had been done because of the extensive road works on the A23, the main London Road. This added an extra mile and three quarters to the distance, which became 55 miles precisely and also entailed an extra 300 feet of climbing in crossing the South Downs over Ditchling Beacon.

John Legge, RRC Chairman at the time, the first veteran over 60 to finish said, 'This year it's the toughest ever.' So the new test was on for the future. David Kelly a 40-year-old, from Barrow in Furness, won in that year in 6:13:56. Erik Seadhouse

180

(5:24:48) had won from Greg Dell in 1989 and that prolific Serpentine runner Hilary Walker was the first woman in 6:43:22 (since the start of the women's category was in 1979 Hilary Walker has won four times). Dave Beattie took the men's title in 1990. Hilary Walker from Serpentine AC holds the world's best 200k time of 20:18:07 done in Blackpool in 1988. Among her many records Eleanor Robinson holds the Women's 24 hour record of 24,169/149m 142yds and also was the first woman in the London to Brighton in 1986.

It was 1991 on the new course **Carolyn Hunter-Rowe** of Pudsey & Bramley AC won the women's race in 7:18:09, then in 1993 she smashed the women's record with a time of 6:34:10, which placed her sixth overall in the combined race. She reflected in 2001, 'Probably my best race as it was a course record. It is a good place to get grounded on and it is the largest ultra race in the country. I learnt a lot from it because it is a hilly course. It teaches you about pacing and patience. The race has got such a history. It is sad to see the fields dwindling and people not coming into the sport. When you see the Comrades where there are thousands and thousands of people doing it. The press, the media and the coverage involved. The London to Brighton is a bit different. However, it is special and the people who have run in it are.'

Carolyn Hunter-Rowe has achieved world records for 25, 30, 40 and 50 miles as well as 50km.

Since those days one person has stood out as being the most consistent ultra man who did the London to Brighton, **Stephen Moore**. In 2000 he was 50 years old and came second in the London to Brighton. He was a City of London bank executive and the President of the RRC. Moore, according to Ian Champion, was the world's most consistent, ultra-marathon man in recent years.

Moore had ten international vests, has been British 100k Champion five times, held six world records, won the London to Brighton four times, was clear veteran winner in 2001 and followed up a 2:32 marathon in London at 50! He retired from running ultras at 50 but was going to continue to do shorter distances and enjoy retirement running the fells.

181

Stephen Moore was a wonderful thoughtful runner. Just an extract about his winning the London to Brighton 1997 in 6:05:32 would show that. (His other wins 1992, 6:01:09; 1993, 6:07.22; 1999, 6:02:45.)

'I can honestly say I never gave up hope of winning but it was in other people's hands as much as it was in mine. All I was doing was running my own race and I wanted to get the feed back as to what distance I was behind the leader – I was getting that fairly regularly and I was five minutes down at 35 miles. Then it went to 3½ minutes down at 40 miles. I thought "Stephen, this is anybody's game!" As soon as they were coming back there was a real chance. I overtook two people at the bottom of Ditchling Beacon and Karl Barker at the top – I did push it then. It was such a relief! I looked after my nutrition very carefully and piled things inside me at the bottom of Ditchling. As I came through the 50 mile marker I felt great and I had plenty to eat and drink so my legs were feeling pretty good and, looking over my shoulder, I could not see anyone behind me. As soon as I was told I was 1½ minutes clear I was then able to relax and almost enjoy the last 5 or 6 miles.'

It was also in 1997 that **Rae Bisschoff**, a gold medallist in the Comrades, running for Mr Price RSA, a W40, was 15th of the 90 finishers inside the 10 hour cut off point. Bisschoff's time was 7:5:56. 'I really enjoyed running in what was my first London to Brighton.' Bisschoff was the first veteran in the world 100k in Japan in 1994.

London to Brighton v Comrades Marathon

Bruce Fordyce won 9 Comrades Marathons and 3 London to Brightons and looked back to his breakthrough in the Comrades.

'I came third in 1979. That was one of my favourite races of all time, because in the Comrades you get gold medals for the first ten. If you can finish in the first ten everyone in South Africa knows your name and you really make a splash. So I was actually running the race aiming for 8th, 9th or 10th and to finish third was such a thrill, it was unbelievable. Thinking back on that, I can't even remember being tired in the race. Obviously I was tired or I would have won the thing, but when I look back on it now I can't remember any bad patches and I just remember enjoying myself the whole way.

'I progressively upped my training. I started in 1977 and when I think back on that first race I was grossly under-trained and I did not have enough distance to do well then. By the second year I had built up and by 1979 I had two good solid years of virtually unbroken training and I think that was more the secret behind it.'

It was in 1981 that Bruce Fordyce won his first London to Brighton in 5:21:15 from Mark Pickard 5:24:55 and he also had a clear victory in the Comrades with 5:37:28. It was a record from Durban at sea level to Pietermaritzburg at 2150ft above sea level. Alternate years up and down runs.

Shaun Meiklejohn, a gold medallist in the Comrades, from Collegian Harriers RSA, won the London to Brighton in 6:01:02 in 1994 and mentioned his training for the Comrades: 'For the Comrades and 100k races I would put up my mileage to 190, and hold it there for a couple of weeks. My biggest month was 756 kilometres. Where I train at Pietermaritzburg is made for Comrades running, a lot of hills, a lot of variety.'

Clyde Marwick, a South African from Shettleston Harriers, who has finished second in the London to Brighton, was third in 1997 in 6:10:32 behind Carl Barker of Sydney Striders (6:09.01). The winner Stephen Moore of Hertford and Ware AC did 6:05:32. How would he compare the London to Brighton to the Comrades?

'The route is very similar but I would say it is easier. I think the only difference is that you get spoilt in South Africa. At every 2½ kilometres you have a wide spread of juices, glucose, potatoes; whatever you want is there. You don't have to worry about things, so it was a new experience for me to actually have Steve Wicks as my second today in the London to Brighton, as he was there all the time and to be honest with you it worked better, because I could take bananas, iron drinks when I wanted to, so at the end of the day it did balance out. If I had not had a good second it might have been different.'

183

Sarel Ackerman, from Rentmeeter RC in South Africa, was the only man to beat six hours on the 'new' London to Brighton course, 5:55:49 (1995) and 5:56:50 (2000). Only two weeks after the latter he won the Amsterdam half-marathon in 69:48. After his second win in the London to Brighton he said, 'Since I was at Brighton in 1995 when I won, I have been in the top ten two or three times in the Comrades, once sixteenth and this year eleventh. This year I did not have a bad race but it was a bit disappointing being eleventh, just outside the golds.

'The London to Brighton was harder in 2000 than the last time because in 1995 the Comrades was on 20th of May because that year the World Cup was in South Africa so Comrades was held at any earlier time, whereas this year (2000) it was on 16th of June. You have to recover for about a month, then you are almost at the beginning of August. I had to cram my training in quicker than usual.

'I did 5:45 in the Comrades. I ran more or less the same average pace in the Brighton. This is a bit easier course but very hard because you have to work on your own the whole time, the support next to the road is not always that great, that makes it a very tough race mentally to keep going. At one stage when the guys were not far behind I considered slowing a bit to let them catch me and see how I felt, have someone to run with for a while. But then I thought I am going to relax, see what happens and if they don't close the gap...

'The Comrades has got a lot of prize money, which is good and a motivating factor, but a race like the Brighton has a lot of tradition. I am fond of races like this, but you never know whether you are going to come back. I had my tickets paid otherwise it would have been impossible. A lady helped me come here. She worked for a company called 'Sea Muscle Pills', SEATONE, a natural inflammatory product which helps me during my training period.'

Danielle Sanderson of Watford Harriers was first woman in the 2000 race in 7:07:12 in 7th place overall. It was her first try at ultra running. Danielle Sanderson, is a freelance lecturer and mother of three under the age of 10.

'I think my best race was in 1994 in the European

Championships when I did 2:36 in the Helsinki marathon, the only one in the field to do a PB. I have also done a couple of 73 minute half marathons.

'I lived in Brighton for the first nineteen years of my life and my father died nineteen years ago today. It was a sort of memorial run. I went through Burgess Hill where my father worked.'

James Zarie 'The Spartathlon Man', 56 in 2001

Michel Bréal was the original instigator of the idea to include a race from Marathon to Athens in the inaugural Olympic Games of 1896. In recent years John Foden has been a terrific force to put the 'Spartathlon' on the map for future Olympic competition, as well as being an advocate of trail racing becoming more popular. The first 'official' Olympic Spartathlon will take place in Athens in 2004.

Many people are unaware that the Marathon was introduced for the 1896 Olympic Games in Athens. There was no such foot race before that. I consider the Spartathlon, over 250km/155 miles, has a much more relevant part to play in future Olympics, as a true test of stamina for mankind, as opposed to the marathon, which although quite tough, has now become more of a media event. I hope the reader will enjoy reading about James Zarie's feelings about that. First of all let us check his credentials:

James Zarie's record in the 'Spartathlon': 1986 5th in 27hrs 45min; 1987 3rd in 27:16; 1988 17th in 33:53:34; 1990 8th in 29:49:23; 1991 2nd in 26:48:50; 1994 1st in 26:15; 1995 1st in 29:59:42 and in 1998 3rd in 26:44:04.

'The Spartathlon is a unique race with a very unique history behind it and runners go to do it over and over again! Even though only one third of the runners finish within the time limit of 36 hours, and although many fail to finish they still keep going back. Their dream is to finish for then they are automatically called a Spartan – Messenger of the sport.

'When they arrive at the end they touch the hand of the

185

statue, they get an olive wreath and a bowl of water. The Mayor of Sparta shakes them by the hand and they drink the water.'

'It seems the Greeks show themselves at their best with their hospitality towards you, as you go along the country roads and pathways?'

'Absolutely! Having said that you are not allowed to accept anything during the whole run from outsiders. Everything is set alongside the race by the organisers at so many stations. You are allowed to have your own special food and drinks, to be handed to you at every station you arrive at, with your name and number on everything.

'As you are running through the small villages and towns, all the children come out and greet you. About half a dozen or more children on bicycles who are so excited. They come towards you from the village for about a kilometre, then they cycle behind you. All of the people in that village, it does not matter what hour of the morning, they are still celebrating each runner from the first to the last.

'From the heat of the day and then during the night down to freezing point, running through the mountains. Five mountains you are crossing, different temperatures, the next day the heat comes again!

'We went to a special ceremony that evening and all the crowd from Sparta gathered to honour us.'

In 1991 James Zarie was the first athlete ever to pass 600 miles in a Six Day race held in the United Kingdom. It was the 13th of October, 1990 at Gateshead. He won with 100k 505m/622 miles 525 yards. There were runners from all over the world, which included India, Canada and Australia. The second person Oto Seitl (Czech) covered 517 miles 392 yards. That alone points to Zarie's amazing endurance.

Derek Wood, who was an M50 New York and London Marathon Champion, and a National veteran Champion on the track, was a good county runner when he was young and competed as a senior at the White City Stadium. He is now a driving force with his wife to help organise funds and help for Alzheimer sufferers. Derek Wood is also an Officer in the HAC. In May 2001 he was in Barnet and District AC's winning team

186

in the Over 70 National Veteran road relay Championships at Sutton Coldfield.

When he was a Barclays bank manager, before he retired, he gave some interesting advice to clients. Derek Wood felt that, as a bank manager, you must not just have the skill of serving the customer with money or talking about mortgages, debits and credits but give advice to those with serious worries about life as well as finance.

'Certainly my advice on more than one occasion to distressed people who had lost their way perhaps, partly due to mismanagement of their finances, because of mismanagement of their lives, was to go and find a mountain, perhaps in the Lake District or North Wales and just steadily make their way to the top, so there would be a measure of physical endeavour attached to it. Then when at the summit to look around and reap the rewards of nature and perhaps have a clearer mind to enable them to reflect on the positive things that were in their favour. To realise they had two legs and two arms and that they had been able to walk to the top and two eyes to see a magnificent view (assuming it is not foggy) and then they could better gather their thoughts on how to reconstruct their lives. I actually took one financially troubled customer to the top of Snowdon and he both enjoyed it and said it helped him get to grips with his problems. In any event the doubtful advance granted by a predecessor was ultimately repaid. A bank manager undoubtedly encounters a measure of stress but for me it was almost unnoticeable because of the various safety valves that I had.'

10

Salah Hissou and Aziz Daouda, with Abdul Kader and Khalid Skah

Salah Hissou, who was born on the 16th of January 1972 at Kasba Tadla, is advised by **Abdul Kader**, who has been a coach for twenty years. Kader also advises Hicham El Guerrouj, who set world middle distance records and won the majority of his races from 1996 to 2001. It was from school that Salah Hissou went to the training camp where Kader was situated.

'He believes in good endurance for his athletes and a belief in God.'

Being a devout Moslem you could see Salah Hissou appreciated Kader's attitude to his athletes. Hissou described his start in the sport. 'I was sixteen when I started at school. I had heard about and looked up to the great Moroccan runners like Rhadi, El Ghazi and Jaddour. I admired Steve Cram as a runner who was the biggest star we read about in Morocco.'

He then went on to say, 'The time I felt I could get somewhere in athletics came in 1995 in Durham when I was third in the World Cross Country Championships. I understood then, there was more to come.'

Kenyans filled the first two places. Paul Tergat (34:05); Ismael Kirui (34:13); Salah Hissou (34:14) was next followed by Haile Gebrselassie, Brahim Lahlafi and Paulo Guerra.

The writers in the *International Track & Field ATFS Annual* edited by Peter Mathews however, considered his breakthrough came the year before when he was third in the World Cross Challenge 1994/95. It is noticeable in the *Annual* that Hissou's best 5000m on the track prior to 1994 was 13:37.40 in 1991 yet, in 1994 he ran 13:04.93, a big improvement. An interesting result that year to show the power of Moroccan distance running involved Hissou. It was the IAAF/Ricoh World Road Relay Championships held in Litochoro, Greece, on the 17th of April and under the management of that great Moroccan distance runner Said Aouita.

The Moroccan team looked a Dream Team on paper and had an impressive victory over Ethiopia (1:58.51) and Kenya (2:00.51). Morocco did an overall time of 1:57:56 and contained Brahim Jabbour, Elabri Khattabi, Hicham El Guerrouj, Salah Hissou (the fastest on his leg), Brahim Boutayeb and Khalid Skah.

Out of the 30 countries it was interesting to note that the Great Britain team, who came a good fifth, were the first European country in 2:02.12 (Keith Cullen, Dave Clarke, Paul Taylor, Martin Jones, Colin Moore and Barry Royden).

It was after 1994/95 in 1996 that Salah Hissou came second in the World Cross country to Paul Tergat in Stellanboch. On the 5th of June, 1996 Salah Hissou ran 12:50.80 for 5000m in the Golden Gala in Rome eradicating Said Aouita's Moroccan and previous world record time from the books (12:58.39).

'When I broke the National record and improved it by eight seconds, that was particularly satisfying. I have beaten that time by Aouita about 12 times to make me feel that I am the best in Morocco.' Apparently he was pleased to beat Aouita's time because he thought Aouita was not popular among 'all' the Moroccans.

He pointed to the two races that gave him most satisfaction: 'When I broke the 10,000 world record with 26:38.08 (23rd of August 1996 in Brussels) and the World Championships in Seville in the 5000m in 1999.' First four: Salah Hissou 12:58.13; 2. Benjamin Limo (winner in 2001) 12:58.72, 3. Mohammed Mourhit 12:58.50; 4. Brahim Lahlafi 12:59.09.

'The most important thing for me was that I can remember how I ran tactically. I still have the image in my mind of the race and how I achieved the result. I was mentally very strong that day.' On the fourth lap Hissou went into the lead with a 59.91 lap and then went again at the 3000m point. He eventually got away from Lahlafi, Mourhit and Limo in the closing stages of the last lap. Limo of Kenya finished fast in the home straight to gain second position. One must not forget that although Salah Hissou did not place his Olympic performance in 1998 among his two greatest races, he did achieve third place in the 10,000m in Atlanta and fourth the year before in the World Championships in Goteborg.

In 1997 in the World Championships in Athens he achieved a bronze medal. (First 6: 1. Haile Gebrselassie 27:24.58; 2. Paul Tergat 27:25.62; 3. Salah Hissou 27:28.67; 4. Paul Koech 27:30.39; 5. Assefa Mezegebu 27:32.48; 6. Domingos Castro (Portugal) 27:36.52.) Besides that good performance by Hissou, Morocco had a memorable win in the women's 400m hurdles, with Nezha Bidouane winning in 52:97 ahead of Atlanta Olympic Champion Dion Hemmings of Jamaica (53:09) and Kim Batten of the USA (53:52).

Another famous Moroccan's training

Khalid Skah, world cross country Champion 1990–91, Olympic Champion 10,000 gold medallist in 1992, world half-marathon Champion 1994.

'I love Fes and the area around there, especially the Middle Atlas. I feel very happy when I am training around there. It is a very nice atmosphere and the conditions to train in.

'When I first started to run, it was just in my own way and sometimes running with my club team in Fes. I was training three times a week with them, but had to go to school. I was just training with the group then, but it was nothing very special. It was after 1986 I was starting to coach myself.'

Training with Salah Hissou

'I like running in Ifrane (South of Meknes) and Rabat. Ifrane is good with the weather, the courses are well done to run on and even the track is good. All the conditions are good because it is in a small place in a quiet region.'

He continued, 'Sometimes I run alone, sometimes with a group. It depends on the schedule. I train alone on the track but go out in a group for the long distance runs.'

Aziz Daouda explains how the training has to be geared to the individual not a group philosophy: 'One of the biggest principles in our training theories is that you cannot find two persons with the same qualities in everything; it is impossible to imagine a training programme that suits everybody. Everybody has something special.'

About how serious Aziz considers Morocco should be in doing the world cross country is quite revealing:

'We never prepare specifically for the World cross country Championships. We are quite sure that if we say, at one time, that it is important for us we could win it but we never do it specifically. Never! Never! Never!

'For us it is much more important to be good on the track in the summer. In the winter we build in the high mileage and do four or five months of power training. When we come to the cross country we have already been doing at least three months of specific weight work.'

Aziz said that Salah Hissou had a good mind for racing and has a nice build, very nice pace but he has not got good enough speed (even though he is listed as having run 3:33.95/3:52.4 1500/mile). He acknowledged in the summer of 2000 that after 12 years of running Hissou looks for new horizons and something to motivate him. (He was injured at the time of the 2000 Olympics.) He did decide to road race in the future and hoped to do an exceptional time in the marathon.

How did Salah Hissou feel about the dominance of the Kenyans in distance running?

'The Kenyans have been very strong during the last ten years but it does not mean they are the best in the world or that there is nobody to beat them or improve on what they achieve. For the future there will be many nationalities at the same level so, the competition will be harder and the level will improve.'

When Salah Hissou retires from competition he will look back philosophically to what he has gained from athletics:

'Like everything; everything has an end. When I stop running the best thing I will have as a memory will be that I enjoyed myself with my friends and, as I travelled the world, I had good relationships with people.'

11

Haile Gebrselassie

Haile Gebrselassie is 1.64m, 53kg, and was born in Arssi 18.4.73. On page 141 of the *International Track and Field Annual 2000* it says:

'Haile Gebrselassie, a beautifully smooth runner, whose right to be named as the greatest ever grows steadily. In February 99 he set his 15th World Record.' His brother Tekeye was 13th in the World Cup marathon in London in 1991 with a time of 2:12.05 and ran 2:11.45 in 1994. Gebrselassie's European Manager is Dutchman Jos Hermens, who was a good international 10k runner on the track. (He ran 27:41.25 in Stockholm in 1977.) He also held several ultra distance world records (one hour 20,944m/13m 24y in 1976). Although his father was keen on his son Haile staying on the farm, in the fertile central plateau, he realised the burning desire Haile had to run.

In comes Haile Gebrselassie, a very pleasant man to talk to:

'I ran my first race a long time ago at school. It was a 1500m. I won that race but I had not been doing any hard training or had any experience. It was then pointed out to me that, if I continued like that, I could be a good runner in the future.'

Considering that the 1500 did not become an event that he concentrated on in the future, that embraced his many world record successes, it was amazing that many years later in 1999 he came down distance to win the World Indoor title at 1500m in 3:33.37 after taking the 3000 title in 7:53.57 at Maebashi, Japan.

He continues, 'It was two years after that 1500 at school, that I went to the capital Addis Ababa. I competed in the National

Championships in 1991 and qualified for the World Junior cross country in Belgium. I came eighth in that. That was a good race for me, being my first international.'

The winner of that was Andrew Sambo from Tanzania in 23:59; 2. Mundi Muma (Kenya) 24:04; 3. Fita Bayissa (Ethiopia) 24:04; and 8. Gebrselassie 24:23.

About other great runners that were doing well when he was first following athletics, he especially remembers seeing his countryman Myruts Yifter, the 1980 Olympic 5 and 10,000m Champion in action, a real source of inspiration for him. Wolde Meskei Kostre is currently the chief coach in Ethiopia, but back in 1981, ten years before 'Geb' came on the scene, Nigusie Roba was the National coach for Ethiopia and he talked about Myruts Yifter to me then.

'Myruts Yifter is one of the greatest athletes in the world. I found him and so I have, been coaching him from the beginning,' he told me.

'When his coach gives him a programme he always fulfils it – and that is the first quality. Secondly, Yifter is not worried about any competition or afraid of any athlete. Another quality is that when his friends are running with him in the big competitions he always tells them not to be nervous.'

Roba's special memories of 'Yifter the Shifter' are worth relating:

'His first victory over Keino in Tel Aviv was a memory for me because Keino was the top runner in the world then. Yifter started with 800 and 1500 before he moved up to 5000, so it was really a very big surprise. His second success was the Olympic 10,000 third place in 1972 and then the World Cups.'

Haile felt Mamo Wolde (1968 Olympic marathon Champion) and Abebe Bikila were the greatest influence on Ethiopian athletics, historically speaking.

'Abebe Bikila is our father. He brought us into this world. When he won everyone wanted to be like Abebe Bikila. He did a wonderful job. He did great things for his country besides that, as he brought so many into the sport.'

Bikila's two races of note were the two Olympic Marathon finals. In 1960, when he ran barefoot in the race in Rome, the

194

event finished under Constantine's Arch in Rome, 1. Abebe Bikila (Ethiopia) 2:15:16.2; 2. Rhadi Ben Abdesselem (Morocco) 2:15:41.6; 3. Barry Maghee (New Zealand) 2:17:18.2. In Tokyo 1964, where the race ended in the Olympic Stadium: 1. Abebe Bikila 2:12:11.2; 2. Basil Heatley (GB) 2:16:19.2; 3. Kokichi Tsuburaya (Japan) 2:16:22.8. In fourth place was Brian Kilby (a European and Commonwealth Marathon Champion from GB) in 2:17:02.45 with Jozef Suto, Buddy Edelen, Aurele Vandendriessche, Kenji Kimihara and Ron Clarke (who got the bronze in the 10,000) the next to come home. Kilby said, 'I can remember Bikila passing me at 5k and wondering "What's he going to do?" I was sceptical he would go to the front and stay there.'

In 1992 Gebrselassie followed up the previous year's 8th in the World Junior with second in the same annual event in Boston, seven seconds behind Ismael Kirui of Kenya, who went on eventually, to win two senior World 5k titles on the track. In the summer of that year in Seoul was the World Junior Track & Field Championships and Gebrselassie won the 5 and 10,000m. The 5k had three future greats in the frame. 1. 'Geb' 13:36.06; 2. Ismael Kirui 13:36.11; and 3. Hicham El Guerrouj 13:46.29.

Gebrselassie went on to win four world senior Championship 10,000m races outdoors but the person he felt was the hardest competitor he came across was in 1997.

'It was a world record in Zurich in 1997 running against Daniel Komen. That was a very hard race because we were very close to each other throughout.' 1. Gebrselassie 12:41.6; 2. Daniel Komen (Kenya) 12:44.90; 3. Paul Tergat (Kenya) 12:49.87; and 4. Khalid Boulami (Morocco) 12:53.41.

Having broken so many world records it would be good to know his opinion on breaking them at will as he did.

'It is very difficult to know the time before I come to the competition. The world record is a combination of circumstances. Audience, nice competition, pace making, nice track. The weather is most important. If it is perfect it is possible to break a world record.'

When I interviewed him in the summer of 2000 prior to Sydney he talked about the race which gave him most satisfaction.

'The one in Atlanta. It was a very hard race on a track that was made for sprinters not long distance runners. The reason I was so happy with the race was because it was the Olympics that I had won.'

29th of July – 10,000m: 1. Gebrselassie 27:07.34; 2. Paul Tergat 27:09.17; 3. Salah Hissou 27:24.67.

Who would have thought then that four years later he would again have such a tough race with equally tough opposition to overcome. To add to that he had an achilles injury that troubled him, which eventually he had an operation for on the 17th of November, 2000. He had said to the media he would be unable to break any world records in the summer because of that problem. He took that problem into the Olympic Games, and had to contend with running against the man he had so much trouble in beating four years earlier. Obviously, some of his opposition in the race did know that fact and made the race a tactically hard thing for Haile Gebrselassie to win.

The taller Paul Tergat, that great Kenyan runner, put in a withering burst with 250 metres to go and it looked all over, as he started to go away. In what will go down as one of the most monumental efforts ever made in athletic history by a man carrying an injury, somehow 'Geb' summoned up reserves to claw his way back into the race and then, to actually inch ahead of Tergat over the last few metres. An incredible feat to say the least for someone who had been a doubtful starter in the first place!

Sydney 2000 First 8: 1. Haile Gebrselassie 27:18.20; 2. Paul Tergat 27:18.29; 3. Assefa Mezegebu (Ethiopia) 27:19.75; 4. Patrick Muti (Kenya) 27:20.44; 5. John Korir (Kenya, leading with 600 to go) 27:24.75; 6. Säid Berioui (Morocco) 27:37.83; 7. Toshinari Takaoka (Japan) 27:40.44; 8. Karl Keska (Great Britain) 27:44.09.

Looking back in 2001, although Haile Gebrselassie had been at the top for a long while, he was philosophical about his reign coming to an end one day. He talked in glowing terms of the abilities of Hicham El Guerrouj, 'A fantastic athlete' he thought and, as far as Noureddine Morceli was concerned, 'My favourite athlete. A wonderful guy' also, there was ex-world record holder for the 10,000m Arturo Barrios of Mexico, 'He ran the world record of 27:08.23 back in 1989, also a great athlete.'

'When you talk about sport and talk about athletics you cannot always be at the top for a long time. Always you have to give a chance to the youngsters. It's like a machine. A model 98 car cannot go as well as a model 2000. The model 2000 will be faster. You have to accept these things!'

That comment he made to me in a Croydon hotel in the summer of 2000 has great significance. After an achilles operation, race-rusty, and then having just recovered from a high temperature (earlier in the week) in Edmonton 2001 Haile, far from ducking the opposition, lined up for the World Championships 10,000m. At one stage in the last lap as he made his effort to go clear, it looked as though he was going to add to his tremendous winning sequence of past victories but, despite his acceleration, both the Kenyan Kamathi and his compatriot Mezegebu sprinted past him giving him no chance to retaliate in the home straight. At least Haile came away with a bronze medal. First six: 1. Charles Kamathi (Kenya) 27:53.25; 2. Assefa Mezegebu (Ethiopia) 27:53.97; 3. Haile Gebrselassie (Ethiopia) 27:54.41; 4. Yibetal Asmasu (Ethiopia) 27:55.24; 5. Fabian Roncero (Spain) 27:56.04; 6. Jose Rios (Spain) 27:56.58.

On October 7th 2001 Haile became a World Champion on a new surface. At Bristol he won the World Championship half-marathon in 60:03 from fellow countryman Tesfaye Jifar, also in the winning team. (Paula Radcliffe won the women's championship in 66:47.) The London Marathon organiser Dave Bedford signed up Haile for the London Marathon on 14th of April 2002 for an amazing £350,000. "He is the greatest distance runner who ever lived, I have no doubt of this", he was quoted as saying in the autumn of 2001.

Haile runs 15 to 25 miles a day for training in the winter and summer, so the reader may be prepared for his next comment about cross-country racing: 'At the moment (2000) it is very difficult to compete at cross-country for me because I am still a track runner. Maybe when I move to the marathon I can run cross country.'

The Bonus of International Competition

'The thing I love most about travelling around to the races in the world is that I love the athletes because when I get to the competitions, athletes from different countries and different regions are interesting to meet. They all have different characters. I think that is wonderful.'

His Natural Love of Running

'Away from competition I love to run in my home town in the forest, which is my best method of training. Seeing the flowers, the trees, wild animals. That is what I want to continue to do in the future when I stop competing. Run and hear the noise of the birds, and smell the trees and flowers. Besides that what I love to do is stay at home with my kids and my wife that is most important for me.'

12

Maria de Lourdes Mutola

Maria Mutola was born in Maputo, Mozambique on 27th of October 1972. She is 1.62m, 61kg. Maria Mutola will go down in history as Mozambique's outstanding sporting ambassador, not just for the gold medals she achieved, but for her consuming interest in improving the standard of sport in Mozambique, through her Maria Mutola Foundation.

'It is basically to evolve sport especially track and field in the country. I do as best as I can for them. I hope when I retire one day that I can go back and help them.'

Her early school days were spent at Maputo where she first took an interest in sport. Besides running, she played soccer, handball, and did judo and swimming. She showed such great ability at soccer from 5 to 15, that even now they still ask her to play soccer for the Mozambique's women's team!

'It never fits in with my schedule, but I can remember I grew up with sport and just fell in love with soccer. I saw one of my brothers Carlos growing up and he made the national basketball team. He inspired me to do sport. In all the sports I did, I was trying to find something that just fits me.'

The Olympic Solidarity Committee gave Maria Mutola a grant to do sport abroad.

'My goal was to learn English because I did not speak English at the time and I chose to go to the United States. I wanted to find out what America is all about.'

She went to Springfield High School, Eugene, Oregon, but naturally it was not easy to begin with for her with such a cultural change.

'It was very difficult. I was unhappy and homesick because I spoke no English and had no friends. I was only seventeen so it was tough to begin with.'

She met her present coach Margot Jennings, who had been a college long distance runner and, almost immediately, with her guidance Maria Mutola blossomed out as a future prospect.

In 1988 she had run her fastest 800m of 2:04.66 but did not improve on that till 1991 when she met Margot Jennings and, neither knew at the time, she would become a world class performer. A couple of 800m races that year radically changed things.

In the UK the benchmark for male club athletes who run the two-lap event is to be able to run sub-two minutes. Then they can say they are of a good club standard. In the case of women athletes, if they can do that they are considered of 'international' calibre. With that in mind Maria Mutola takes up the story.

'I had thought, if I break 2 minutes one day I can start to think of being one of the stars. I ran in a mixed race, where I was living in Oregon and, a boy who trained with me said that, if I stayed with him in the race I could break two minutes. He did around 1:58 and I did 1:59. At first I thought they might have stopped the clock before I finished. It was a help to have learnt the pace judgement.

'It was after I broke 2 minutes my coach said to me that, if I dedicate myself a little bit more I could become a World Champion one day and I actually believed her!'

Later that year was another extraordinary day in the athletic life of Maria Mutola. She wanted to go to New York for the New York Games which would be her first Grand Prix.

'A lot of the organisers in New York did not want me in the 800 race because, they thought I was too young and unknown and, how were they going to pay someone from High School, with all her tickets. They wanted me to pay my own way. Eventually we got some sponsorship, through a friend with Nike West as long as I would wear their uniform.'

'I went to New York, won the race in 1.59. I beat a lot of the top Americans – Mary Slaney, Joetta Clark, Meredith Rainey and Celeste Halliday. Nobody expected me to win so, that race for me was remarkable.'

'It was that year she started breaking records which included an African Junior 1500m record with 4:12.72 for 1500m. She ran the fastest ever 800 by an African junior of 1:57.63 That was done when coming close up fourth in the World Championships in Tokyo in September, very nearly gaining a medal.

First six: 1. Lila Nurutdinova (URS) 1:57:50; 2. Ana Quirot (CUB) 1:57.55; 3. Ellas Kovacs (ROM) 1:57.58; 4. Maria Mutola (MOZ) 1:57.63; 5. Letitia Vriesde (SUR) 1:58.25; 6. Christine Wachtel (GER) 1:58.90. 7. Ann Williams (GBR) 2:01.1; 8. Svetlana Masterkova (URS) 2:02.92.

'It was a very good race even though in Tokyo I had a problem with my right leg, and a stress fracture during the race. I can remember how I felt the pain! Pain! But I discarded it because I wanted to hold on till the World Championships were over then I could rest. If I had not had that I would have been second or third.'

She then said modestly, 'The winning time was a little faster than I was capable of doing but it was very close indeed.

'It was then very difficult to run with the pain for a month. I used to sleep with magnet things on my leg. I had electric treatment which really helped but did not do the job, so I had to rest a lot. It had been difficult with the three rounds in those World Championships and I really felt it with 300 to go in the final.'

In 1992 Maria Mutola went to the Toronto World Indoor Championships and won the 800 final in 1:57.18 with Svetlana Masterkova, who later became the double Olympic Champion in Atlanta, second in 1:59.18. Joetta Clark and Ella Kovacs were next in.

'That was a big memory for me because it was the first World Championship win for Mozambique and I won. I started to believe in myself and that I would win even more races. To know you are one of the top runners in the world is a special feeling.'

In 1992 she improved her 1500 time to 4:02.60 and came fifth in the Olympic Games 800m final in Barcelona in a personal

201

best time of 1:57.49 behind Ellen Van Langen of Holland who recorded 1:55.4. In second place was Lilia Nurutdinova of Russia 1:55.99, and third Ana Quirot 1:56.80, with Inna Yevseyeva of the Ukraine fourth in 1:57.2. In 1993 Maria achieved her fifth African record of the season in the World Championships at Stuttgart in August, winning the final of the 800m in 1:55.43 from Lyubov Gurina of Russia (1:57.10) and Ella Kovacs of Romania (1:57.92). Diane Modahl of GB was fourth in 1:59.42.

'Although one has to fear anyone who makes the final, the big thing for me was that I did not think I was actually going to lose if I ran my own race. The time was 1:55 and everybody's best was about 1:56 to 1:57 I knew to be able to win the race comfortably I have to produce a very fast time and I had to run the last 200m the way I always like to run it!'

In 1994 Maria Mutola won the 800m in the Westklasse in Zurich in 1:55.19 which was the fastest in the world that year with Natalya Dukhnova of Bulgaria second in 1:57.87 and incidentally, she ran 51.37 for a PB in the 400m that year in Monaco. In 1995 she ran her fastest ever 1500m in 4:0.16 in Eugene, in a mixed men's and women's race. In the Olympics of 1996 at Atlanta Maria Mutola gained a bronze medal. 1. Svetlana Masterkova (RUS) 1:57.3; 2. Ana Quirot (CUB) 1:58.11; 3. Maria Mutola (MOZ) 1:58.71; 4. Kelly Holmes (GBR) 1:58.81; 5. Yelena Afanasyeva (RUS) 1:59.57; 6. Patricia Djate (FRA) 1:59.61.

Perhaps Maria's time of 1:57.62 in the preliminaries, which was faster than the winner of the final, may have taken a bit out of her.

In the World Championship of 1997 in Athens Maria Mutola gained a bronze to go with her Olympic bronze. Anna Quirot won in 1:57.4 with Yelena Afanasyeva next in 1:57.56.

In the 1998 Commonwealth Games in Kuala Lumpur, Malaysia, Maria won in 1:57.60 from Tina Paulino, also from Mozambique in 1:58.39. In third was Diane Modahl of the UK, who was unable to defend her title in 1994 in 1:59.71. 'That was something special to me,' Maria Mutola said.

In 1999 the year before the Sydney Olympics Maria won the

Grand Prix Final in Munich in September with a time of 1:59.10 beating Formanova who had beaten her in the World Championships in Seville in August (Formanova 1:56.68 to Mutola's second place of 1:56.72 with Masterkova next in 1:56.93).

In Sydney 2000 Maria Mutola became the first person from Mozambique to win an Olympic title. In the final Helena Fuchsova led through the bell in 55:04. Kelly Holmes who had recently come back from injury then took the lead at the 600 metre mark and made her brave attempt to come home first. Maria went past her on the outside in the home straight and then Steffi Graff took her with just 30 metres remaining. Under the circumstances Kelly Holmes was elated to get the bronze as was Maria Mutola with her crowning achievement.

Maria Mutola (MOZ) 1:56.15; 2. Stephanie Graff (AUT) 1:56.64; 3. Kelly Holmes (GBR) 1:56.80; 4. Brigita Langerholc (SLO) 1:58.51; 5. Helena Fuchsova (CZE) 1:58.56; 6. Zulia Calatayud (CUB) 1:58.66; 7. Hazel Clark (USA) 1:58.75; 8. Hasna Benhassi (MAR) the African Champion of 2000 1:59.27.

In 2001 Maria came up against her biggest rival in the world, at the time Stephanie Graff. It was at the World Championships indoors in March at the Lisbon Arena. In a thrilling finish, the result was 1st Maria Mutola 1:59.74; 2nd Stephanie Graff 1:59.78 and 3rd Helena Fuchsova 2.01.18. Then in the same year in the World Championships in Edmonton, outdoors, Maria inched past Stephanie in the last few metres to win, with a time of 1:57.17 to Stephanie's 1:57.20.

'It is thrilling to be representing 17 million people at the World Championships and the Olympics but they depend on you, so there is a lot of pressure sometimes but I have got used to that.

'The 800 is my favourite event as it is very exciting and something I have a lot of experience of and know how to run every single step but, before an Olympics or a World Championship, it is important to be careful how many races you put into your body. It is hard to relax at the Olympic Games as it so concentrated. At smaller Grand Prix meets there is not a lot of pressure and you can relax yourself and, if you are in good shape, try to use a pacemaker so you can run fast times for the fans and the organisers. Sometimes I would push myself to the limit.'

What did athletics give to Maria?

'Diplomat stature and to be able to travel all around the world and represent your country, meet different people, different cultures and learning a lot of geography, a lot of exciting memories.'

Regarding her training and the methods she adopted Maria Mutola comes in to conclude, 'I read about Sebastian Coe as he was an excellent runner for his time. He really impressed me a lot and, even my coach talks a lot about him and all his training. She tried to give me similar type of work. To have the endurance for 1500 and speed for 800. To use the 1500 to train for 800s like Sebastian Coe did.

'I train a lot over distance but not so much cross country as I used to in High School a long time ago. Now I do long runs, fartlek for 3 miles, and speed work in the summer as we get close to racing on the track.'

13

Allen Johnson

Born 1st of March 1971, Washington DC, 1.78m/70kg, Allen Johnson was Olympic Champion 110 hurdles 1996. In that competition he looked smooth, light on his feet and wearing the familiar shades. He was World Champion outdoors and indoors in 1995 and World Champion outdoors in 1997 and 2001. 1. Allen Johnson (USA) 13:04, 2. Anier Garcia (Cuba) 13.07; 3. Dudley Dorival (Haiti) 13:25.

I interviewed Allen Johnson at the Raddison Plaza Hotel, Oslo, on the 12th of July, 2001. It was the evening before he won the Golden League 110m hurdles in 13.21 in the Exxon Mobil Games in the Bislett Stadium.

Allen Johnson took up hurdling as a suggestion from his High School coach.

'In the very beginning I was a long jumper and really more a field events person. Andrew Tisinger looked at me one day and said, "You have long legs, I am going to make you a hurdler." It was that simple! The following week in practice I started hurdling. I did the intermediate hurdles which was over 300m in the State of Virginia where I lived. I did the high and long jump plus the triple jump a bit sparingly.'

As a matter of interest his best performances outside of his speciality the high hurdles were: 400h 52.00, HJ 2.11, LJ 8.14, TJ 14.83. 100/200/400/10.10w/20.26/48.27.

'At the beginning I did not have anyone to really look at. I just did what felt comfortable to me and got instruction from my coach at high school. Once I got to college at the University of North Carolina I started watching tapes of Roger Kingdom,

Tony Dees and Jack Pierce. My coach at that time was Charles Foster. [Fourth in the Olympics of 1976 in 13:14.] He basically showed me a lot of little things from different hurdlers and what they did well. For example, to see how Roger Kingdom approaches the hurdles aggressively, and how Jack Pierce uses his technique over the hurdles and things like that.'

Colin Jackson, at the time of writing, is the world record holder at the event and adds to what Allen said about Roger Kingdom: 'Roger Kingdom's major quality is that he is a good competitor. One of the toughest I have had to race against. He uses his height, weight and his speed to his best advantage.'

The first hurdle race where things started to click for Allen Johnson and make him think he could become world class was in 1993.

'It was in the USA v Great Britain match in Edinburgh, Scotland, and I was running the hurdles. Colin Jackson was to my left. I was 22 years old, and it was the same year that Colin went on to break the world record.' 12.91 in Stuttgart 20/8/93.

'I just remember the gun went off and I was running beside Colin Jackson. I got so caught up with what I was doing then, I crashed the sixth or seventh hurdle or something but, after that race I realised "I can run as fast as anybody else" because I knew I had a mental lapse in the race and the rhythm I was running on wasn't that difficult. I was running hard. I did not feel I was out of myself or anything like that. It was that moment that I knew this is something I do pretty well. He went on to run 13:01.' (Allen ran third in that race on 2/7/93 in 13:34.) 'I was with him for five or six hurdles. To this day I would like to see a tape of it very badly because I have never seen it on tape.'

Building up for the Olympic Gold Medal Win

'My Olympic preparations started in the fall of 94. That was my first full season on the circuit and I took a week and a half off and then went right back into training for the 95 season. Things started clicking for me in 95. I ran a lot of races. A lot of repetitions over the hurdles and basically using the same technique I use today.'

The Rivals for the Final on 27th of July 1996

'I felt it was going to be Mark Crear as my main competition as well as Colin Jackson (2nd to Roger Kingdom in 1992); Schwarthoff was running really, really well and anything was possible. I also had Emilio Valle to my right. He was a tough runner. Going into the final I was thinking mainly of what I had to do and make sure I got out the blocks well and make sure I did not make any mistakes. I felt extremely confident and I felt like I could run however fast to run to win, no matter how fast the next man ran. At that moment I felt I could run a step faster.'

The late **Rod Milburn** (USA), who won the 1972 Olympic final in Munich which was in a world record of 13.24, from Guy Drut of France, the 1976 Olympic Champion gave me a vivid account of his final that is worth mentioning here, to lend a little atmosphere to the occasion:

'When I got in the blocks in the final, I could remember it was a very good evening, the temperature was about 75 degrees, the stands were packed solid. I could just feel the electricity; it was a great feeling sitting out there before 100,000 plus people and the millions that were looking at TV, so that in itself was a great support. I felt almost weightless. Into the starting blocks I went. The only thing I was focusing on was the gun sound, it is all spontaneous. I think I had a very superb start. We were together for the first three hurdles, that was where I started to make some little moves. I think by the sixth hurdle I made a tremendous gap of about two and a half to three metres on the field. To my left I had seen Willie Davenport (1968 Olympic Champion) up until that point. I had seen him and almost heard him. Going down into the seventh and eighth hurdles, I looked to my right and could see Guy Drut vividly, coming through very strongly so at that point the main thing was really to just concentrate and relax, move without clipping the hurdles because if I was to clip anything from the seventh to the tenth hurdle I would have been in serious trouble with Guy Drut for sure because he was the one coming very strongly for second place.'

How was it for Allen Johnson at Atlanta? 'It is like I was one with the hurdles. It is not like they are barriers, it was just like me and the hurdles together are just one. I know every inch of it and everything.'

July 29th 1996 (wind +0.6): 1. Allen Johnson (USA) 12.95 Olympic record; 2. Mark Crear (USA) 13.09; 3. Florian Schwarthoff (Germany) 13.17; 4. Colin Jackson (2nd in 1992; Great Britain) 13.19; 5. Emilio Valle (Cuba) 13.20; 6. Eugene Swift (USA) 13.23; 7. Kyle Vander-Kuyp (Australia) 13.40; 8. Erik Batte (Cuba) 13.43.

Allen Johnson won in the 1997 World Championships in Athens in 12.93 from Colin Jackson who did 13.05. He was then plagued with injuries which hampered his racing time in 1999 and 2000, but still had the belief that he could get back again to his best.

'I know how effortless it feels when my technique is on I don't then have to run hard to run fast. That is why I honestly believe that I will be able to run hurdles for a long time because technique is not something that will leave you like speed or power will.'

What then about the injuries for Allen Johnson?

'What injury does is make you sit down and let your body heal. When we are competing we have little micro tears all in our muscles that we deal with every day so we are used to it; we don't actually realise how good we feel if we took two months off and basically did nothing. In that sense it does help but the flip side of it, is that's downtime and you lose your sharpness in that time. If the injury happens at the wrong time of the year and you come back and you are rushing things, and you don't do your base work like you normally would or you jump into speed too fast, then another injury pops up, so it is almost like a chain reaction and when you get injured your muscles get weak.

'When I am injured that is probably my worst time because

running the hurdles is what I love doing the most and I am just counting down the time to when I can get back.'

Races not to be forgotten in Allen Johnson's memory

'The first time I ran under 13 seconds in Cologne in 1995. That was a great race. I remember talking to my coach before and he had told me, "Make sure you run the first three hurdles." Going into it I was totally relaxed. I said I don't care what happens just make sure. Run hard for the first three hurdles and finish the race. I remember getting out there over those first three hurdles good, and then I eased up a little bit. I was in the lead and then I felt Tony Jarrett coming on my right hand side so I bore back down again and went across the finish line and the clock said 12.97. I said, "Man I could not believe 12.97 was that easy", of course later it was rounded up to 12.98 but at the time I did not know it. I thought well I finally did it, I went under 13.00 seconds. That is when I said to myself, "Well I am 7/100ths of a second off the world record. Maybe that is something I can do." So from that point on, the world record was a very real possibility for me. Everybody who runs an event thinks about the world record. If I do this or that I can do it but it was at that moment that world record was truly a possibility for me in my mind.' (18/8/95 0.2 wind, 1. Allen Johnson 12.98; 2. Tony Jarrett 13.11; Allen Johnson ran 12.92 at the USA Trials in 1996 which was 0.01 outside the world record!)

'Also in 1995 winning my first World Championship outdoors, that was important to me and that was the first time I was winning on the world stage. Once again it was Tony Jarrett. We were running side by side.' World Championships Goteborg, Sweden: 1. Allen Johnson (USA) 13.00; 2. Tony Jarrett (GBR) 13.04; 3. Roger Kingdom (USA) 13.19; 4. Jack Pierce (USA) 13.27. Jarrett had beaten Johnson in the World Cup at Crystal Palace the year before in 1994.

'Winning the World Championships was really good for me. For me it validated everything I had done earlier in the year. Once again, I was a newcomer and people wondered "Is this guy for real?" The Atlanta Olympic Games of course was another memory.

'In 2001 the United States Championships was certainly a memory. I was coming back from injury and I had not been running well up until then. My best legal time was 13.46 going into the Trials. The media and press picked me to finish 4th to 6th place. I felt, with the disappointment of Sydney [withdrew semifinal through injury], that I needed to be on the World Championships team for a shot at trying to win another title, because the next opportunity would be when I was 32 years old! I was not willing to wait for a shot.

'I just remember the weather was bad. There was a head wind but I did not think it was strong as it was but I was so focused on my race, my hurdles. I was one with the hurdles. The gun went off and I was immediately able to go separate from the pack. I ran 13.22 into a 3.2 head wind. I have got to say, if that is not my best race ever it is in the top two or three I believe!' (Eugene: 1. Allen Johnson 13.22; 2. Terrance Trammell 13.46; 3. Dawane Wallace 13.60; 4. Dominique Arnold 13.64.).

Weights

'For the past few years I have done more heavy weights just for strength and power. I will put on a little bit of muscle but not a lot, no matter how hard I lift.'

Regarding his friend Renaldo Nehemiah, who often accompanies him to meets on the circuit, 'I admired him as a hurdler definitely. When I am doing something wrong he can see it and let me know. He does not really try and coach me as I have a coach, Curtis Frye. I think Curtis Frye's strength as a coach is that he is a great motivator. He will make you believe that you can do anything. He is not afraid to try knew things or learn something new. He is never one to say, "Oh well, I know everything so whatever it is you have to say is not good enough because I already know it all." He is always going to listen to anything and take in all information, process it and use what he thinks is the best and incorporate that into the training. If some-

210

thing is not working then he will change it. If it is working he will stay with it.'

The Toughest He Has Run Against?

'I would say Tony Jarrett was the toughest. Colin Jackson was faster but Tony Jarrett would never break. He would fight you all the way to the finish line. There is never a point in the race where you can say, "Well, okay, I have got him" because, just when you think you have got him, he hits another gear or pushes you just a little bit harder. Then I have to say Colin because he is so fast and capable of doing so many things. He was capable of putting you at a deficit immediately. That was always a real threat. Mark Crear is someone I have had so many battles with. He is another one who will never break in a race. I could be on a streak beating him five or six times in a row and he would never let that deter him. Every time he would come back a little bit stronger. Those three people stand out. Anier Garcia of Cuba [Olympic Champion in Sydney in 13.00] was another tough one in 2000 and I am sure we will have a lot of close races in future.

'I would like to hurdle on for a long time. Definitely 2004. I don't know how the body holds up to training. I would like to go to 2008.'

14

Steve Backley

Steve Backley was born 12th of February 1969, in Sidcup, Kent. He is 1.96m/100kg. The *International Athletics Annual 2001* edited by Peter Mathews stated: 'In 2000 Steve Backley became the first Briton in any athletics event to win an Olympic athletic medal in three Games'. The merit in that comment was and is obvious, and added to that he was European Champion three times consecutively and Commonwealth Champion in 1990 and 1994. He also achieved two silver medals in the World Championships. His first International Championships success was when he won the European Junior javelin Championships back in 1987.

In 1989 he was elected as male athlete of the year on the strength of winning the European and World Cup finals, the World Student Games and the IAAF Mobil Grand Prix final. His Olympic Games performances were:

Barcelona 1992: 1. Jan Zelezny (TCH) 89.66; 2. Seppo Räty (FIN) 86.60; 3. Steve Backley 83.38

Atlanta 1996: 1. Jan Zelezny 88.16; 2. Steve Backley 87.44; 3. Seppo Räty (FIN) 86.98

Sydney 2000: 1. Jan Zelezny 90.17; 2. Steve Backley 89.95; 3. Sergey Makarov (RUS) 88.67

Jumping forward in time to 2001 to the 23rd of July and the Norwich Union Grand Prix at Crystal Palace. The consistent Steve Backley threw 81.54, 82.27, 81.95, 85.07, 85.73. Jon Ridgeon the ex-championship medallist over the 110/400 hurdles was the Master of Ceremonies with his microphone

212

blazing out encouraging comments in the infield. The place was alight in the packed stadium as Backley took his final throw. The spear left his hand and up it went, shimmering against the early night sky and, down it came point first into the green turf at 90.81 metres; with added sound effects from the PA system piercing the still atmosphere. He told David Powell of *The Times*, 'This was my best throw ever because when I threw 91.46 (25.1.92) in New Zealand [his third world record] it was with a three to four metres per second tail wind.'

It was just over a week before that in the morning of the 13th of July, at the Raddison SAS Plaza Hotel, Oslo, that I talked to Steve. That was before his evening competition at the Exxon Mobil 'Golden League' Bislett Games. Steve threw 82.51, just ahead of Germany's Raymond Hecht who had a mark of 82.11 but behind Peter Blank (Germany) who had just one throw in the first round of 86.90; Poland's Dariusz Trafas was second with 85.78. Blank's performances created both an interest for Steve as well as for me as a *Veterans Athletics Newspaper* correspondent.

'The guy Peter Blank who was second in Nice is 39 years old and he threw 88.70 metres this year' [2001].

(The World's Veteran record is currently held by Jorma Markus of Finland who threw 78.84 in 1994.) 'If Peter Blank stays healthy he is going to throw a new vets record next year without too much trouble!' thought Steve Backley.

Longevity in the Sport

'Peter Blank, who is 39, started throwing in 1994, seven years ago. He did not start throwing seriously till he was the age I am now. He has only got seven throwing years in his body, so he is actually quite a young thrower. It is a slightly different sort of situation for me. I have been throwing since I was about 15/16. I would like to think I have got another three years through to the next Olympics in Athens, then I will probably call it a day.

'I studied Sports Science at Loughborough. I enjoy the science of sport. I am interested in other things.

'When you look at the javelin throwing, traditionally, it is a very Eastern bloc dominated event. When you look at the Eastern bloc throwers, that is all they do. They don't appear to do anything else but throw javelins. You go to a training camp with Jan Zelezny. He wakes up, trains, he eats, sleeps, trains, eats and sleeps and that is all he has in life apart from fishing. That is his little release valve. I am not exaggerating when I say there is nothing else going on. He is married and got kids from when he was a lot younger. They are grown up kids. He does spend some time with his kids which is great. I am not saying he has the need for stimulation or he has a need for having a Western attitude. His interaction with other people is very low. The Eastern bloc attitude of just a very simple life, which is what he has.'

I pointed out that there are a massive amount of things to sidetrack someone in the UK, so many hobbies, sports, computers and a vast amount of television and radio stations etc.

'I think a lot of people try and spread themselves real thin and do so many things. I think that is where it becomes difficult. The other thing I think that is difficult for a full time professional athlete is expectation. You become a successful runner or successful javelin thrower, you are then expected to go along to television and appear on TV and be interviewed and have all the charm and charisma of an international athlete which has nothing to do with performing and that is a difficult skill to learn. It is not something that necessarily goes hand in hand. It might do!

'I always respect people who are themselves and really show themselves. Then you are expected to stand up in front of people and coach, which is totally different from being an athlete. There are all these different things pulling at you. I think the closer you get to finishing your career the more they are pulling on you. Maybe you have got a mortgage. The normal things everyone has to deal with.

'I am aware also of the fact you need to do something solely and not spread yourself too thin. The pulls into other life are

214

quite strong with me at the moment because I have allowed that to be the case. I am into golf and I am developing connections and interests in that world and they have a sort of gravitational pull and that is where your interests go. You have to specialise and if you try and do two things at once you only give half of yourself.'

His love of being a member of Cambridge Harriers has been there from the start. He was on the team at one time with sprinter Karl Ferguson who is the son of veteran Cambridge Harriers hurdler Barry Ferguson.

'I have got fantastic memories of the club. As a kid, my Dad John was a great motivator. He ran 1:50 for a half mile and at 47 ran 2:47 for a marathon. He had me running cross countries when I was six years old. I was in the under 12s Bexley cross country Championships when I was 6, running against kids who were two foot taller than me. My Dad said "Just try and beat one person." There were 200 kids running along, and there was some kid who kept walking at the back and I ran along and ran past him at the end. I think he instilled that competitive instinct in me then and that led into colt/boy/youth athletics. I think my best day was in the Kent Championships when I was about 11 or 12 and I was second in the 400m. That was about as good as I got. I did make the final of the South of England in the top 8.

'Having said that I did get knocked down by a car when I was 8 years old and then tried to get back into running and did that but, by the time I was 13 or 14, I was starting to grow. A tall skinny lad and struggled really to run.

'I was at Hoo, Deangate, one day and it was a club meeting and there was a guy throwing this particular day. I was asked to fill in for the javelin, just to get a point. I was told "You only have to throw 10 metres to get a point." I said "Great I'll do that!"

'I went down to the track. There was this guy warming up and I could not believe how well this guy was throwing. A young guy called Gary Jenson [2nd in the European Juniors eventually]. He was about 16 at the time and he was throwing this day. I had never met him before. He was warming up and throwing 45 metres and when you are a kid and you have never

215

seen something thrown that far, that was amazing to me. He was of good stature. Looking at him I thought, that is a real good athlete. I could see his physical qualities with his power, speed and agility. He ended up throwing 62 metres this day for a new 16-year-old age best. It looked the other end of the field to me from where I was standing, it just looked amazing. There was another guy who threw 40 metres for second place and I threw 25 metres.

'I just remember thinking, "I think I can throw 40 metres and I would love to try to do that."

' "Don't talk about it, just get on with it and find out if you can do it," I thought. That is what I did. I took a javelin home. My Dad used to take me out to a local field and what we did was put a twig in as a marker and try to throw 30 metres and my Dad just had me throwing and seeing if I could reach the stick and, when I had reached it, he would move it up two or three metres. We found a way of either throwing a bit higher or a bit lower or run a bit faster.'

Janis Lusis who competed for the USSR

In 1965 I spoke to Janis Lusis the man who was born on 19th of May 1939 in Latvia and went on to win an Olympic gold (1968), silver (1972) and bronze (1964) and won four European titles (1962–71 inclusive). He was married to Elvira Ozolina the Olympic javelin champion of 1960. I interviewed Janis in a Lancaster Gate hotel, London, in 1965 and it was interesting to compare his start in the sport with that of great thrower Steve Backley!

'As far as I can remember it was in 1957 when at the age of 18, I first took a serious interest in track and field athletics. At the time I was a pupil at a secondary school in Kandava, Latvia. Until 1957 then, although I tackled most sports, and the three jumps on the athletic side, long jump best 5.70/18'8½"; triple jump and high jump, I held no great interest in anything in particular, and certainly not the javelin as I had never thrown it!

'After winning a javelin competition in Riga, I met and talked with the Latvian javelin champion – his best was just over 67.90m/223ft and he said that I would "never make a good javelin thrower". This was probably the turning point as far as my performances were concerned. Then and there I made up my mind to prove him wrong and, within two years, I was throwing further than him.

'He did, I must admit, give me plenty of advice in the technique of throwing the javelin, but I started with the man who then coached me, Valentin Mezzalitis. It was he who, after a long discourse on track and field athletics, suggested that I concentrate on the javelin at the expense of the long jumping, which was probably the event that took more of my interest at that time.'

Memories at Bislett

On the 28th of July, 2000, Trine Hattestad threw 69.48m for a new women's javelin world record in the Golden League meeting at Bislett. Being Norwegian she had the crowd spellbound! Hattestad [born 8/4/66] went on to win the Olympic title in Sydney with 68.91. It was her fifth Olympic Games. The Games at the Bislett Stadium is a big memory for Steve Backley too:

'Back in 1990 I threw a world record in Stockholm of 89.58m. A week later on the tour we came to Oslo and stayed at the Raddison. Zelezny went out and threw 87.88 and then in the third round, I kind of knew it was on, and he picked up the Nemeth javelin and threw 89.66 which was 8 centimetres further than my world record. He did his lap of honour with his flowers. The crowd went crazy. I just remember it being a real electric atmosphere. I tried and tried so hard that night to throw further and it did not come off. Then another week later we went to London to Crystal Palace for the next leg of the Grand Prix circuit and I had two throws at 86–85 and then picked up the Nemeth javelin that Jan had used to throw the world record with the previous week and threw 90.98, and so the world record was broken in three consecutive weeks running which was unheard of.'

Jumping ahead to 2000 Steve Backley became the first Britain in any athletics event to obtain an Olympic medal in three Games, but let us look at some of his results with him through the years. Olympics 1992, 3rd; 'That was my first Olympics.' 1996, 2nd; 2000, 2nd; 'Three Olympic medals I can't be disappointed with that.'

However he did point out about the sequence, 'Third 1992, 2nd 1996 and it had to be 1st written all over it for 2000 to finish the sequence kind of thing. World Championships 1991 BNQ 15th. That was the biggest disappointment because I was in good shape that year. 1993, 4th because I was injured, that was a horrible year. And then two seconds, 1995 and 1997. It was tough because Zelezny beat me in one of them. He had a fantastic day.' 1995 Gothenburg: 1. Zelezny 89.58; 2. Backley 86.30; 3. Boris Henry (Germany) 86.08. 'In 1997 a guy popped up from South Africa, out of absolutely nowhere to win.' 1997 Athens: 1. Marius Corbett (RSA) 88.40; 2. Steve Backley 86.80; 3. Kostas Gatsioudis (GRE) 88.64; 4. Mick Hill (GB) 86.54. 'Never having won a world championship that was slightly disappointing that it did not come off in one of those then, there was the European Championships. I was 1st, 1st, 1st (1990, 1994, 1998). I would not change that for anything.'

Since Tessa Sanderson, Fatima Whitbread and Steve Backley came on the scene, the javelin was promoted more in the United Kingdom. Certainly with the International Athletes Club, Andy Norman and later ex-world class hurdler Alan Pascoe, things have become a lot better and the javelin has become a fascinating event to watch, with a much wider audience than before.

One of the great times for javelin throwing was at Crystal Palace on the 20th of July, 1990 in the Parcel Force Games when Steve Backley threw a world record of 90.98 which was the best throw in the world that year.

'It did create interest,' Steve admitted. 'It is not every year we get a world record at Crystal Palace or in Britain. The event was taking on a new phase, a new front. Partly because it was this new javelin and it had been around for a few years.'

The specification of the javelin has changed a lot in recent years!

'It has probably changed for me and my era of throwers more than it has for anyone else in the history of throwing because, when I started it was the old spec pre [April] 1986 when we had the old floating javelins, thrown 104.80 metres by Uwe Hohn (GDR). I was only 17 but I did throw the thing, then there was the big change, the big shift in the centre of gravity, which turned the javelin over and the world record was reduced considerably, by about 20 metres or so, and javelins actually stuck into the ground. I think that was the biggest change in the actual structure of the event.'

Would Steve like to have been able to throw the 'old style' javelin as a senior?

'It was the same weight, but the thing to bear in mind is therefore the principles of making the javelin go a long way were exactly the same. It was all about the speed of release. So, with that in mind the differences are purely after the javelin has left your hand, where you have no control over what it is going to do. It feels slightly different as the nose feels slightly heavier on the new specification javelin. The world record dropped down to 84m by the end of 1986. That developed as a record through the rest of the 1980s and into the 1990s. Then in 1991 there was a javelin made by Nemeth with the roughened tail section which flew further, and I was the first to throw over 90 metres with that javelin at Crystal Palace.'

(As a matter of interest Miklos Nemeth from Hungary won the 1976 Olympic javelin title with 94.58 in Montreal, which was a world record at the time and his father Imre Nemeth won the Olympic hammer gold medal in London in 1948 with 56.07.)

Were the Old Champions as good as the ones now?

'I think you will find that if you took the world's top 10 throwers of today they would be 10 of the best 12 ever, of all time, in terms of their ability to throw. That obviously does not take into account of their ability to compete, where Janis Lusis became one of the greatest ever.

'The developments now going on with the carbon javelin – The first time I actually threw it was at the Olympics. I thought I would have a go with that.'

It very nearly came off?

'I still just can't quite believe it didn't.'

A great philosopher once said that 'Man is the sum total of his whole existence' which certainly puts Steve Backley high on the list, as far as the history of the javelin is concerned. That must give him satisfaction, despite the fact that he did not take the Olympic title?

'The only reason I would have wanted to win and do want to win the Olympic title before I retire, is purely for PR, personal contentment and personal gratification. I am very, very satisfied with my performance in 2000. I felt as though I did myself justice; I performed as well as I could have hoped for, and really the journey is really what it is about in terms of contentment anyway. I think and feel that the only reason is for PR and that is the least important factor if you actually think about it from a philosophical point of view. I could also say the same for the 1996 Olympics. I was leading with 87 metres with the first throw of the first round, and it was only when Jan Zelezny – 2000 was almost a carbon copy of 1996 anyway so, from both Olympics – 1992 is a slightly different story but, at two Olympics I can say where I would not ask for it to be any different.

'I threw a world record in 1990 and won the European Championships, that was my first real break onto the scene. I think in terms of success, three European titles. In terms of athletics PR, three European titles over the span of 8 years. That is probably the thing I am most proud of.'

Did Steve feel that Jan Zelezny had special qualities?

'Without a doubt. I think anyone who comes in to an event, especially a technical event and they change the perception of what it is about. I think that is always a remarkable person with remarkable qualities. Jan has certainly done that. He has come into an event, did not only do it differently but beating people differently. That was a real eye opener in terms of how you prepare, and how you actually apply yourself.

'Where people have expectations of how you perform and how you do it. If you don't conform to those parameters you are not quite doing it right. Here was Jan Zelezny doing it differently.'

220

All or Nothing At All

'I am very consistent and that is possibly why I have a good Championship record but Jan is an "all or nothing" thrower. He goes for it!

'I am a very keen golfer. An example in golf would be; if you are hitting your driver. I would be the guy who stands very steady over the ball, swings, turns slowly aggressively through the ball. Jan would be the guy who stands five metres away, takes a run up, takes a full swing and lashes at the ball and, if it comes off, it is going to go miles; if it doesn't and used to be unlikely to, then it's not going to.'

Finland has a tradition of having outstanding javelin throwers and can always be usually relied on to have some world class throwers at the Olympics. In the *IAAF Olympics Finals Review 1896–1996* (editor Nick Davies) it was pointed out, for all the Olympics up to and including Atlanta, for gold, silver and bronze on a points basis, the order was Finland 1st with 232pts; 2nd URS/EUN, 76; and 3rd Germany, 73.

'That is true and no different in 2001. Finland's medal tally for major championships is phenomenal. The Czech Republic has got a great tally from one person, Jan Zelezny – three golds and a silver, but Finland has had a phenomenal record with different people like Pauli Nevala (64); Jorma Kinnunen (68); Hannu Siitonen (76); Arto Härkönen (84); and Tapio Korjus (88).'

Technical Coach to Steve Backley and Mick Hill

'John Thrower helps us both with the technical preparation. I have other people who help with the physical preparation. John Thrower's help is a very specialised help. He is a unique person in that respect. He simplifies the coaching process. He formats and presents it in a way that is very understandable and does not cloud the issue. A lot of coaches love the idea that it is complicated and try to make it more complicated to confuse the issue, to make it seem more important than it is. John is the opposite. He would work on maybe three or four basic points. Basic principles that have a big impact and leave the rest as idiosyncrasies of the person. I think that is by far the better way to be, as long as the four things are the real good fundamental points that are necessary to throw far.'

Qualities needed to be a good javelin thrower

'The three technical things for me I have simplified and defined in my own mind. I actually think it is the same across the board and they are:

'Good rhythm on the run up, therefore good rhythm through physically and all the sort of general physical attributes that go along with that as well. The ability to have a rhythm to create power into something. Power has a rhythm by definition, also the time. Time being an important element; there is a rhythm to it, so that is the first point.

'Second point is range. Again anything that has power in any physical bio-mechanical facet where the leavers are involved, where turning moments are involved and the basic physics. The longer the leaver the greater the speed at the end of the arc. Turning moment of the leaver determines how fast you can create power. Range for a big man is an important thing. What comes along with that is strength. For example in my passion for golf the word they would use would be "width". If you don't have width in a golf swing you can't have power. You see people try to throw and everything comes in short, it looks fast but it does not go very far. The best analogy I can think of is the ice dancer, spinning very quickly on the spot and they put their arms out and slow down, bring them in and speed up. The same amount of energy is being dispelled with those two movements. People look at me and say, "You did not seem as though you actually threw very fast", but the javelin still flies because I had width and range in my throw. A very important point.

'The third one is the last one, "contact". You have contact with the floor at one end of your body and the contact with the

222

javelin at the other. A great amount of force comes back up through your legs, when you run. Even when you are jogging three times your body weight comes back up through your knees. For Jonathan Edwards in the triple jump it is something around eleven times your weight so, for a 70 kilo man you don't need a great mathematician to say that is a great deal of strength and power to hold your limbs, fixate your limbs when you land in the triple jump. In the same way as when you throw, that contact with your spikes into the tartan, and your hand on the javelin, to actually maintain that contact – if you let one of them go, if say you slip on the floor – it is an obvious example that the javelin is not going to go very far. It is to do with the point control – if you don't control the point of the javelin it's not going to go very far.

'Rhythm, range, contact are the three mechanical physical things that somebody needs to throw far. Whether they are tall, short or thin, they need those qualities.'

What about injury back-up?

'Two people play the biggest part. Marcus Zambarda, masseur/soft tissue therapist. He also works on balance in your body, energy flows, rhythms in your body when you are running. He can watch you running, as he has a good eye for seeing how people move. He has been a great influence. The other guy, Kevin Lidlow, who is a chartered physiotherapist, and Doctor of Chinese medicine. He has a great mine of medical knowledge across the board. He is just over the water in Essex from where I live in Kent. Whenever I had surgery, which I have had a number of times now, he has actually been in the surgery room working on me while I am out under general anaesthetic. They are both geniuses.

'In terms of training I learnt a lot off Jan and his coach Jan Pospisil from the Czech Republic. They have a kind of unique way of training towards the javelin. How they prepare cleverly. I learnt a lot off them. The move to go and train with Jan was a bit of a gamble but I did that in 1997 when I was world number two. It was a good year for me but I still felt I wanted to find out what Jan was doing and whether it was something nobody else was doing. I went to the training camp with them and learnt how they talk with each other, how they train and what they do. I still do training camps with them.'

It has always appeared to me that there is a wonderful camaraderie between most field events competitors and so it was interesting to hear what Steve felt about his toughest rival Jan Zelezny.

'Yes we do have that friendship. There are others I would say are more true friends in the real sense of the word. I think though Jan and I, even though we compete against each other, do still have a unique friendship. We talk to and support each other. In terms of life-long friends, it's Mick Hill. Whether we are at different ends of the country we are there to help each other out, and that is something great to take away from the sport.'

In 1998 Steve Backley won his third European Championship gold medal in Budapest with his friend Mick Hill second. 1. Steve Backley 89.72; 2. Mick Hill 86.92; 3. Raymond Hecht 86.63; 4. Sergey Makarov 86.45; 5. Juha Laukkanen (Fin) 84.78; and 6. Mark Roberson (GBR) 84.15. That one meant a lot to Steve Backley.

'1998 was the best but the only disappointment was it was not the world or Olympics. I think I would have retired there and then if it had been, as it would not get any better. That was possibly one of the great highlights of my career, standing on the rostrum with Mick Hill. I thought that was absolutely brilliant, better than world records, better than Olympic silver.

'I have got a bit of memorabilia and photos on my wall. Photographs of Lasse Viren, Seppo Räti, Pauli Nevala, some signed and some not. I have got my Olympic vests. I have got a picture of Mick and with Mick and I straight after that European Championship final. The Union Jack round our shoulders, giving it whatever, and that picture just captures the moment. Great memories, very good.'